DESPERATE HOUSEWIVES, NEUROSES AND
THE DOMESTIC ENVIRONMENT, 1945–1970

STUDIES FOR THE SOCIETY FOR THE SOCIAL HISTORY OF MEDICINE

Series Editors: David Cantor
Keir Waddington

TITLES IN THIS SERIES

1 Meat, Medicine and Human Health in the Twentieth Century
David Cantor, Christian Bonah and Matthias Dörries (eds)

2 Locating Health: Historical and Anthropological Investigations
of Place and Health
Erika Dyck and Christopher Fletcher (eds)

3 Medicine in the Remote and Rural North, 1800–2000
J. T. H. Connor and Stephan Curtis (eds)

4 A Modern History of the Stomach: Gastric Illness, Medicine and British
Society, 1800–1950
Ian Miller

5 War and the Militarization of British Army Medicine, 1793–1830
Catherine Kelly

6 Nervous Disease in Late Eighteenth-Century Britain: The Reality of
a Fashionable Disorder
Heather R. Beatty

DESPERATE HOUSEWIVES, NEUROSES AND THE DOMESTIC ENVIRONMENT, 1945–1970

BY

Ali Haggett

First published 2012 by Pickering & Chatto (Publishers) Limited

Published 2016 by Routledge
2 Park Square, Milton Park, Abingdon, Oxfordshire OX14 4RN
711 Third Avenue, New York, NY 10017, USA

First issued in paperback 2015

Routledge is an imprint of the Taylor & Francis Group, an informa business

© Taylor & Francis 2012
© Ali Haggett 2012

To the best of the Publisher's knowledge every effort has been made to contact
relevant copyright holders and to clear any relevant copyright issues.
Any omissions that come to their attention will be remedied in future editions.

All rights reserved, including those of translation into foreign languages. No part of this book
may be reprinted or reproduced or utilised in any form or by any electronic, mechanical, or
other means, now known or hereafter invented, including photocopying and recording, or in
any information storage or retrieval system, without permission in writing from the publishers.

Notice:
Product or corporate names may be trademarks or registered tradem arks , and
are used only for identification and explanation without intent to infringe.

BRITISH LIBRARY CATALOGUING IN PUBLICATION DATA

Haggett, Ali.
Desperate housewives, neuroses and the domestic environment, 1945–1970. –
(Studies for the Society for the Social History of Medicine)
1. Housewives – Mental health – History – 20th century. 2. Housewives –
Social conditions – 20th century. 3. Depression in women – Social aspects. 4.
Sex role – Health aspects – History – 20th century.
I. Title II. Series
306.4'61–dc23

ISBN-13: 978-1-138-66195-0 (pbk)
ISBN-13: 978-1-8489-3310-1 (hbk)

Typeset by Pickering & Chatto (Publishers) Limited

CONTENTS

Acknowledgements	vii
List of Figures	ix
Introduction	1
1 Reflections on the Desperate Housewife	11
2 The Art of Marriage: Marriage and Mothering during the Post-War Period	29
3 The Housewife's Day: Personal Accounts of Housewifery and Mothering	49
4 Lightening Troubled Minds: Mid-Twentieth Century Medical Understandings of Affective Disorders	75
5 Not Something You Talk About: Personal Accounts of Anxiety and Depression	105
6 For Ladies in Distress: Representations of Anxiety and Depression in the Medical and Popular Press	129
Conclusion	171
Appendix	181
Notes	183
Works Cited	213
Index	231

Say not 'I have found the truth', but rather, 'I have found a truth'.

Kahlil Gibran, *The Prophet*

ACKNOWLEDGEMENTS

The research for this project was funded by the Wellcome Trust and I would like to thank them sincerely for their continued support. Many archivists and librarians have assisted me along the way, and I would like to express my appreciation to the staff at the British Library, Euston; the British Newspaper Library, Colindale; the Trustees of the Mass Observation Archive, University of Sussex; the Women's Library at London Metropolitan University; and the Exeter Health Library at the Peninsula Medical School. In the crafting of this book I have also been expertly guided by Keir Waddington, Mark Pollard, Ruth Ireland, Nick Ascroft and Eleanor Hooker at Pickering and Chatto.

I am indebted to the thirty-five women who came forward to offer me their recollections of post-war domesticity, without which the oral history component of this book would not have been possible. Without exception, these women received me with warmth and generosity, and for this I am extremely grateful. I hope that in this work I have been able to do justice to their contributions. I am also grateful to Kate Fisher for sharing with me her expertise on the practice of oral history. Some of the oral history material has been reproduced in an article entitled 'Desperate Housewives and the Domestic Environment in Post-War Britain: Individual Perspectives', *Oral History*, 37:1; and in a chapter entitled 'Housewives, Neuroses and the Domestic Environment in Britain 1945–1970', in M. Jackson (ed.), *Health and the Modern Home* (New York: Routledge, 2007). I am grateful to the editors of both publications for their kind permission to reproduce the relevant sections of material.

Every effort has been made to contact the copyright holders of the images reproduced in this book. Individual accreditations are cited with each illustration; however, particular thanks go to The Wellcome Library, London; The British Library, London; and the *BMJ* for their kind permission to reproduce the images. Thanks are also due to Lee Snook, the University of Exeter, for advice on obtaining copyright permissions and to Alasdair McCartney at Wellcome Images for the efficient way in which he dealt with my requests.

I would like to thank the Centre for Medical History, the University of Exeter, for providing a vibrant intellectual environment and for supporting this research. Sarah Hayes and Deborah Palmer have generously contributed their friendship and intellectual enthusiasm and Claire Keyte has provided exceptional administrative assistance. I am grateful also to Hilary Marland for her advice on various aspects of authoring this book and for raising stimulating questions about my research.

Finally, there are three people who deserve special thanks and without whom this book would not have been possible. My greatest debt will always be to Mark Jackson whose kindness, generosity and intellectual expertise has been instrumental, not only to this book, but to my academic achievements more broadly. Phil Hobbs opened the door to academia for me many years ago and without his inspiration this book would never have come to fruition. And finally, sincere thanks go to my husband David for his love and understanding, and for the faith he has shown in me throughout this process.

I dedicate this book to my parents Peter and Margaret, and my sons Thomas and Connor.

LIST OF FIGURES

Figure 6.1: Largactil, *BMJ*, 1 April 1961 — 135
Figure 6.2: Largactil, *BMJ*, 27 July 1963 — 137
Figure 6.3: Largactil, *BMJ*, 24 April 1965 — 138
Figure 6.4: Aventyl, *BMJ*, 26 September 1964 — 140
Figure 6.5: Stelazine, *BMJ*, 11 September 1965 — 142
Figure 6.6: Advertisement, *BMJ*, 2 September 1961 — 144
Figure 6.7: Advertisement, *BMJ*, 12 March 1966 — 145
Figure 6.8: Nactisol, *BMJ*, 4 December 1965 — 149
Figure 6.9: Durophet, *BMJ*, 16 April 1966 — 150
Figure 6.10: Lucozade, *Woman's Own*, 25 June 1960 — 159
Figure 6.11: Horlicks, *Woman's Weekly*, 30 September 1961 — 160
Figure 6.12: Sanatogen, *Woman's Realm*, 24 September 1966 — 163
Figure 6.13: Sanatogen, *Woman*, 18 February 1967 — 164
Figure 6.14: Complan, *Woman*, 11 February 1967 — 166

INTRODUCTION

The roots of this book lie in my enduring fascination with the generation of women who were married and raised families in the decades following the Second World War. These women, many of whom had childhood memories of the war, began their married lives in a rapidly changing world. On the one hand, historians have described the period as 'the golden age'. Rising incomes and the new educational opportunities afforded to many by the Eleven Plus exam resulted in a blurring of class distinctions. The shift in trend towards home-ownership and the new 'consumer durables' that flooded the market during the late 1950s, resulted in a renewed emphasis on the importance of 'home'. The introduction of the contraceptive pill during the 1960s finally offered women the prospect of real choice in family planning. All these changes were duly energized by the expanding media: women's publishing, cinema, radio and the television.

On the other hand, the post-war period was marked by darker undercurrents. The development of nuclear weapons and the ideological tensions between the liberal democratic West and the communist Soviet Union resulted in the growing fear of atomic warfare and mass annihilation. On a more personal level, feminist authors and commentators in Britain and the United States were indicating that, for women, the new suburban housing estates were causing psychological and psychosomatic disorders. Betty Friedan proposed in *The Feminine Mystique* (1963) that housewives were beginning to experience illness as a result of domestic boredom and stultification. Family life, it seemed, did not bring with it all-encompassing fulfilment, particularly for those who were academically and intellectually able. Such claims were in fact a continuation of a much longer, and now well-documented, history of the alleged association between domesticity and mental illness. The image of the 'desperate housewife' indeed continues to resonate in our culture, and the banality of domestic life is invariably portrayed as pathogenic.

Women's lives during wartime and the immediate post-war years have provided fertile ground for feminist academics. However, more recently, historians such as Judy Giles, Joanne Meyerowitz, Lesley Johnson and Justine Lloyd have provided a reappraisal of women's experiences, and they cumulatively suggest a reassessment of feminist ideas.[1] Women's voices, nonetheless, remain largely silent in this narrative, and there has not been any organized synthesis of medical discourse about neurotic illness and individual experience. At the heart of this book is an exploration of the tensions between the rhetoric put forward by feminist commentators and the experiences of ordinary middle-class housewives. It focuses specifically on the popular perception that such women developed symptoms of neurosis as a result of the banality inherent in the domestic role. It also addresses the widely held belief that, as a consequence, pharmaceutical companies deliberately targeted women and 'mothers', in the advertising of psychotropic medications.

The book traces mid-twentieth century discourse about the 'desperate housewife' as it emerged in intellectual circles and was duly interpreted in popular culture. Fundamentally, it also places these debates within the context of the psychiatric landscape, where, on both sides of the Atlantic, biological psychiatry, psychology, psychoanalysis and psychosomatic medicine were variously vying for authority in the sphere of mental health. The somewhat serendipitous developments within psychopharmacology during the 1950s and beyond were of course to have a significant impact on these debates and are also central to this story.

Although the focus of the research is primarily on Great Britain, the analysis necessarily draws widely on literature from key figures in the United States, where ideas about suburbia and its inhabitants became so influential. The project explores the period from the end of the Second World War until the early 1970s. However, the book begins in Chapter 1 by tracing the emergence of popular representations of the mad housewife during the 1960s and 1970s. These materialized during the height of the women's liberation movement as a critical parody of traditional 1950s housewifery. As the book will argue, these ideas were largely formulated in the United States by women who were highly educated and often politically motivated. The notion that the tedium associated with housewifery and mothering literally made women 'ill', provided much-needed substance to feminist campaigns for equality with men on a range of valid economic, social and political issues. Although Stephanie Coontz has shown that a sizeable number of American women welcomed Friedan's ideas,[2] the notion that a homemaker's role was unrewarding and undervalued was received less favourably among ordinary suburban housewives in Britain.

From a medical perspective, it is true that women undoubtedly appeared to feature as 'neurotic' patients more regularly than men. However, as Joan Busfield has rightly noted, there are complex reasons for this, and once patient data is disaggregated, female predominance is far from monolithic.[3] What certainly emerges from this project is that there was little in the language of biological and psychological medicine to suggest that the housewife's role made women ill. Indeed, a range of alternative theoretical and professional considerations played centre stage in their debates.

Structure and Sources

At the core of this book are the oral testimonies of a group of women who were wives and mothers during the post-war period. The respondents were drawn from the National Women's Register (NWR), an organization formerly known as the National Housewives' Register. This group, still active today, originated in 1960, when a housewife named Maureen Nicol wrote to the *Guardian* suggesting that 'housebound housewives with liberal interests' should form a national register in order that groups could explore interests outside the domestic arena.[4] Nicol had moved with her husband to a new neighbourhood and soon found herself isolated from friends and family. She received what she described as 'an avalanche' of letters from other readers, and began to compile a national register from which local groups were organized. The National Housewives' Register was not a pressure group for any particular cause. Its primary objective was to put people in touch with one another in order that they could meet to discuss intellectually stimulating topics. Although many women left fulfilling careers in order to raise a family, the objective was not to spurn domesticity. Instead, women sought to fill an intellectual vacuum with useful discussion.

Members of this organization were approached for this project primarily because of the ethos of the group, which implied that its members felt a need to participate in discussion about intellectual topics outside the home. The sense of 'isolation' often described by them would thus suggest that in many ways these women closely resembled those that were repeatedly described by social commentators such as Betty Friedan. Indeed, many of them had excelled at grammar school, and, prior to raising children, it was common for them to have undertaken employment they found enjoyable and challenging – albeit usually within roles deemed acceptable for women, such as clerical work or teaching. Women who described themselves as having originated from a working-class background recounted the ways in which they too aspired to middle-class ideals through the opportunities afforded to them following the Butler Education Act (1944) and the implementation of the Eleven Plus exam.

Exploration of the NWR archives at the Women's Library led me to advertise for respondents at the organization's national conference. Women with experience of post-war domestic and family life were invited to contact me, and in total, twenty-nine women were interviewed. A further six women who were unable to meet for an interview sent written testimonies and a number of those I met began by contacting me with written accounts of their lives. All the women were married and their details can be found in the Appendix.[5] The women were all members of the NWR at the time of interview; however, a number of them had joined in retirement and were not members during the 1960s. In recruiting from this group of women, the primary intention was to find interviewees in

Britain for whom parallels could reasonably be drawn with Friedan's women. Although girls in Britain were less likely to receive a university education, these women were without doubt intellectually able and were educated to a high level within the British system. During their young married lives, they were also well-informed about current affairs and the social, political and economic developments of the period. If the 'problem with no name' was likely to emerge anywhere, it seems reasonable to suggest that it might have been among women like these. The interview style was semi-structured with open-ended questions, the aim of which was to provide a relaxed environment in which the women felt comfortable talking about their personal lives. All the interviews took place in the respondents' homes and lasted a minimum of one and a half hours, with some taking much longer. Several women invited me to stay for a meal, and such occasions allowed me not only to listen to the narrative provided, but also to interact with other members of the family and take an interest in photographs and other memorabilia.

Much has been written about the emergence of oral history during the 1970s and its mission to 'challenge and contest what were perceived to be dominant discourses framed by gender and class'.[6] Similarly, within the history of medicine, historians have shown that one clear objective was to uncover the patient's perspective and provide a reappraisal of existing work on great figures and major medical discoveries. These histories sought collectively to expose previously hidden voices, recollections and experiences.[7] However, since the 1990s oral historians have become less concerned with validity and authenticity in oral testimony, and more interested in the ways in which people 'construct' memories of their past and attempt to make sense of them.[8] Penny Summerfield, for example, drawing upon post-structuralist theory and the work of the American historian Joan Scott, argues that 'women "speaking for themselves" through personal testimony are using language and so deploying cultural constructions'. Thus, 'no one's personal testimony represents a "truth" which is independent of discourse'.[9] This focus upon the processes that occur in the construction of narrative has provided an important framework within which to analyse oral histories. It has certainly enabled historians to acknowledge the breadth of experience so often missing from feminist accounts of women's lives. Recent oral histories provided by both Penny Summerfield and Judy Giles have begun to reflect the variety and complexity of attitudes revealed by women during and after the Second World War. However, Anna Green is right to point out that this focus upon cultural discourses has led historians to minimize or even discard the value of individual memory.[10] She is critical of the way in which Summerfield, in her oral history of wartime women, for example, 'establish[es] public, cultural scripts within which individual narratives must fit',[11] arguing that there is little room in such analysis for the 'self-reflective individual'.[12]

In analysing the oral histories for this project, I accept that when making sense of their lives, women were drawing upon a range of cultural discourses that were available to them. However, I fully support Green in her contention that individuals maintain the capacity 'to engage critically and constructively with inherited ideas and beliefs'.[13] Among the women interviewed, there was a marked consensus of opinion about the positive values of mothering and homemaking. Although the women were arguably drawing upon the 1950s 'discourse of domesticity' that strongly favoured the housewife's role, this does not mean that the significance they attached to their experiences was not valid or 'real' for them.

The oral history is supported by evidence from Mass Observation reports and surveys. This research enterprise was founded in 1937 by three young intellectuals: Tom Harrisson, Charles Madge and Humphrey Jennings. Their objective was to observe and record people's behaviour by employing sample surveys and interviews.[14] A regular panel of volunteer writers were also recruited to answer monthly questionnaires and over 300 of these kept full personal diaries during the war.[15] As Summerfield notes, 'Mass Observation's mission was to liberate "facts" about what people did and said in order to "add to the social consciousness of the time"'.[16] The scope of the material extends from the coronation of George VI in 1937 to the years following the war, when the focus shifted to market-research style surveys driven by the post-war boom in commodity culture.[17] Aspects of the material that relate to demobilization and home-life following the war are of particular relevance to this research, primarily because they focus upon the moods and feelings of ordinary people. Moreover, the volunteers who came forward tended to have originated from a middle-class background. Many had won scholarships to secondary school and the vast majority of women classified themselves as housewives.[18] In order to reconstruct the cultural climate of the post-war era, the book also draws upon evidence from contemporary texts on marriage and parenting. Specifically in relation to the newly inaugurated welfare state and the recent trauma of war, it examines the rationale behind the 'breadwinner' model of the family. Centrally, it questions the notion that traditional gender roles featured primarily as a conspiracy to ensure that women remained at home as unpaid workers. It is suggested instead that partners embarking upon marriage accepted a range of rights and responsibilities that were specific to the post-war period. Husbands and wives thus viewed their roles as equal but different.

The sentiments expressed by women about the importance of home are also closely related to the developments in housing and material circumstances of post-war families. During the two decades after the Second World War, the combined forces of low unemployment, low inflation and rising incomes resulted in a new period of consumer culture in which the housewife played centre stage.[19] The Conservative government, that won the election in 1951, promoted consumer spending by relaxing credit and lowering taxes.[20] The Conservatives deliberately devised an election campaign that targeted the 'woman voter', with topics such as food shortages, fuel supply and house-building. They pledged that the strengthening of family life would continue to be of paramount concern to the Conservative Party.[21] The period was marked particularly by the shift in trend towards home-ownership. Owner occupation accounted for only 10 per cent of housing stock in 1914, but this rose to 35 per cent by 1939, and to 59 per cent by 1981.[22] Throughout the 1950s and 1960s, spending on consumer goods such as televisions, motor cars and holidays also grew steadily. The arrival of the radio in the 1920s had already transformed the housewife's day as 'listening to the radio could be combined with domestic labour'.[23] Throughout the 1930s, as reception improved, the radio became a new focus for family entertainment. Programmes such as 'Woman's Hour', first broadcast in 1946, attracted female listeners with its range of topical issues, fashion and cooking. Watching television was a family-centred activity, since very few homes possessed more than one set.[24]

Indeed, Mark Abrams noted in the *Listener* in 1959 that both middle-class and working-class families were spending greater sums of money on household goods. He observed that rising standards of living had resulted in a blurring of class distinctions. Although people with high incomes still came at the top of ranking surveys, he showed that manual workers were increasingly prepared to describe themselves as middle-class because they owned a car and other domestic consumable items. The implication was that greater efforts were expended in making the home a place that was warm and comfortable and 'a pleasant place to live'.[25] Husbands that 'once sought to escape the crowded shabbiness of their homes' now spent their evenings and weekends with their families enjoying 'common fireside relaxations'.[26] Abrams suggested that this new emphasis on the importance of home had resulted in wives gaining greater status and control: 'If the home has now become [the husband's] centre of activity, and if most of his earnings are spent on his home or in his home, his wife becomes the chooser and the spender ... her taste forms his life'.[27] These changes, he argued were increasingly reflected in the popular press:

> Publications dominated by fiction, astrology and romantic or simple-minded 'human interest' news stories are beginning to lose ground to those which appeal to the housewife as consumer – those which provide women readers with a substantial quota of guidance on how to set about putting together 'ideal homes'.[28]

Given the favourable economic circumstances, women's publishing became a highly profitable commercial enterprise during the 1950s, drawing huge profits from both sales and advertising. Peacetime sales were at first artificially restricted, but in a few years, as the privations of war receded, circulations soared to record levels.[29] The Conservative governments of the 1950s enjoyed an important ally in the magazine industry which was keen to generate profits from advertising

Introduction 7

revenue following post-war austerity. The government, in turn, saw the magazines as an important vehicle for generating consumer demand.[30] Mary Grieve,
editor of *Woman* magazine during the period, remembered:

> After years of strictures, rations and restraints, a whole new world of commodities
> flowed in on the flood-tide of the nineteen fifties ... women's magazines with their
> sympathy with the situation and their printing techniques, carried this new life
> straight into the homes and hearts of millions.[31]

Woman's Own and *Woman*, first published in the 1930s, proved to be the
most popular periodicals among the middle-class readership.[32] The former was
intended for 'the up-to-date wife' and the latter, as the first to be published in
colour, was described as 'a real event in publishing'.[33] Other magazines such as
Woman's Weekly, *Home Chat* and *Woman and Home* focused on knitting and
fiction, entertainment and relaxation, whereas *Woman's Own* and *Woman* aimed
to be 'more dynamic and modern – colourful, with higher literary and artistic
qualities'.[34] The weeklies *Peg's Paper* and *Red Star* were directed at working-class
women, offering 'fictional escapism – romance, glamour and mystery'.[35] Cynthia
White argued in her history of women's magazines that 'the vast majority of
women's periodicals are, by tradition, trend-followers ... the status quo is their
frame of reference'.[36] Although they may not accurately reflect 'real life', women's
magazines certainly provided a medium within which normative codes of gender were reflected, renegotiated and reinforced. As Janice Winship has observed,
'letters pages are full of memories intertwining the personal and the social'.[37] In
order to explore the ways in which women expressed themselves through magazine culture, the letters, articles and problem pages of *Woman's Own* and *Woman*
have thus been examined alongside the oral history testimonies.

Following the introduction of the National Health Service (NHS), magazines increasingly included 'doctor's diaries' and articles about medical matters
and disease prevention. These items usefully indicate contemporary health
concerns as women increasingly 'wrote in with appreciation about articles that
gave information, saving them a trip to the "overworked doctor"'.[38] Indeed, the
popular press provided an important space within which ideas about anxiety
and depression were conceptualized and understood. As Katherine Ott has
observed, people acquire information about symptoms in a variety of ways: by
talking with friends and health practitioners, and reading magazines and books.
What we eventually come to regard as illness is therefore filtered through a mesh
of cultural influences.[39]

In addition to the contributions from individual women, the project draws
upon evidence from medical debates to examine the ways in which minor mental
symptoms presented in primary care and in psychiatric outpatient departments.
As Callahan and Berrios have noted, the post-war period in Britain was rife

with intra-professional rivalries between psychiatrists, psychologists and psycho-analysts.[40] In Britain, organic theories of mental illness and physical treatments predominated, augmented by the therapeutic optimism of new psycho-pharma-ceuticals, beginning with the antipsychotic drug chlorpromazine during the early 1950s. Historians have nevertheless argued recently that the influence of psychological thought was not insignificant.[41] Clinical psychology, as professional practice, did not get underway in Britain until the Second World War, largely as a result of psychological testing that was developed to screen the selection of servicemen.[42] However, it increasingly expanded from the realms of aptitude testing into therapeutic activity. The development of behaviour therapy during the late 1950s and early 1960s offered the first major form of treatment for psychological disorders.[43] At the same time, and in a variety of ways, psychosomatic theorists were increasingly interested in the individual's response to their environment and the role of the emotions in disease. Such debates were considered at length in the pages of professional journals and in academic monographs. This literature consisted of clinical research papers and reports, clinical trials for psychotropic drugs, editorial articles and patient case-studies. Collectively, although they reflect the diversity of opinion about the causes and treatment of psychological illness, there is a discernible lack of evidence to suggest that monotonous housewifery was causing neurotic illness in middle-class suburban wives.

As Mark Micale has recently noted, defining the subject matter in relation to psychological illness is problematic.[44] Psychiatric symptoms have been conceptualized and understood in myriad ways throughout history and it is indeed 'impossible to re-diagnose retrospectively with any reasonable degree of accuracy'.[45] From the early classification system put forward by Emil Kraeplin in the late 1800s, mental symptoms have been interpreted as evidence of 'madness' under classification schemes that have shifted and changed through time. Following the Second World War and during the immediate post-war period there was considerable professional debate about the diagnosis of symptoms and the categorizing of disorders. However, the purpose of this study is not to make clinical judgements about specific cases; rather, it aims to explore the ways in which patients and physicians understood the causes of illness during the period. The symptoms that interest me are those that were described by commentators such as Friedan and are now described in the International Statistical Classification of Diseases and Related Health Problems (ICD) 10 as 'mood' or 'affective disorders' – the depressive states and anxiety disorders that are not caused by cerebral disease or brain injury. These are the categories of mental illness that featured most commonly in this project. However, the more severe psychiatric conditions such as personality disorders and chronic obsessive states that warranted inpatient care are included in discussion where they illustrate a point of reference in relation to the overall classification, cause and treatment of psychological illness.

Introduction

9

The next chapter of this book traces the emergence of the 'desperate housewife' as she was constructed in American intellectual circles and duly reflected in classic literature and film. Although much of this has been well-covered, I offer original readings of classic works and suggest that they were in fact part of a broader movement that included not only feminists, but other social commentators who variously put forward a critique of the uniformity and conformity of the post-war western world. I also argue that many of the protagonists in film and fiction were in fact able to find contentment in domesticity when they were in fulfilling relationships. In this chapter, I also revisit the experience of mental illness among contemporary poets and novelists in Britain and the United States, for whom domestic life appeared to be so damaging. Sadly, these gifted individuals are remembered, not only for their work, but for their all too often tragic encounters with serious psychiatric disorders. I propose that, although these women did not settle well into the domestic role, there were a range of additional social factors that might plausibly have affected their mental health. Chapter 2 attempts to reconstruct the values that underpinned the institution of marriage and the family unit in Britain. It examines a wide range of texts on marriage and mothering from contemporary 'experts' such as Mary Macaulay and John Bowlby and advice literature from the National Marriage Guidance Council (NMGC). It suggests that, although post-war ideologies of marriage and mother-love undoubtedly bolstered the traditional domestic role for women, they must be seen within the context of uncertain times, following a world conflict that had caused great suffering and loss. Under these circumstances, a renewed significance was assigned to the importance of 'family' in which men and women worked collaboratively for the good of the future generation.

Chapter 3 examines the 'meaning' of home and the experience of domesticity and mothering among the women interviewed and those that contributed to discussion in the popular press and for Mass Observation. I suggest that, although there were arguably a number of inherent challenges, many women settled with ease into family life and domesticity. The testimonies certainly do not reflect the powerful descriptions of emptiness and despair put forward in the United States by Friedan and her contemporaries. The women's responses are set within the value system that existed during this specific historical period, where husbands and wives largely viewed their relationships and responsibilities to one another as 'complementary'; as equal but different. Chapter 4 places housewives and neurosis within contemporary medical, psychiatric and psychological debates. It does not seek in any way to undermine many of the valid critiques of psychiatry and its treatment of women.[46] However, it suggests that gender was not central to debates about causation and treatment of psychological illness. Discussions centred largely on professional tensions between biological and social/environmental practitioners. Where the social context of disease was emphasized, physicians suggested that disordered personal relationships were an important precursor to mental disorders. Serious traumas such as bereavement and childhood abuse were also noted as environmental stressors that might impact negatively on mental health. However, mothering and homemaking did not feature significantly as causes of depression and anxiety. Thus, although greater numbers of women than men appeared to report symptoms, the 'monotony' that was alleged to be inherent in the domestic role did not appear to be spreading a pathology among middle-class wives in suburban Britain.

Chapter 5 focuses on the experience of those interviewees who endured symptoms of anxiety and depression. It also draws upon contemporary articles on nervous disease from published texts and the women's periodical press. The women interviewed articulated a range of adverse circumstances that had affected them, and some indicated a familial tendency to depressive disorders. However, none of them directly attributed the onset of symptoms to their role as mothers and homemakers. Many of them identified the origins of illness in emotional difficulties connected to their relationships with family members; to marital difficulties in particular. The women interviewed also recounted their experiences of treatment for psychiatric disorders. Although psychological talking therapies were virtually non-existent on the NHS, many of the women were aided by unofficial 'counselling' sessions with supportive family doctors. Although some women were prescribed psychotropic medication, this was not uniformly viewed in a negative light by those receiving treatment. In some cases, women argued that antidepressants gave them clarity of mind and the courage to make positive and necessary life-changes which led to their recovery. Chapter 6 examines the claim that women were prescribed psychotropic drugs more frequently than men and that, as a consequence, they were over-represented in promotional material from pharmaceutical companies. This chapter draws upon evidence from the pharmaceutical industry to suggest that in fact, drugs for anxiety and depression were not primarily marketed towards mothers and housewives, but increasingly to a wide range of individuals of both sexes and all ages. Finally, the concluding chapter not only examines contemporary debates about gender roles and mental illness, but it revisits popular representations of suburbia in recent films such as *American Beauty, Far from Heaven* and *Little Children* in which it is often now the suburban father who is stifled by conventionality and conformity.

1 REFLECTIONS ON
THE DESPERATE HOUSEWIFE

Mother needs something today to calm her down
And although she's not really ill
There's a little yellow pill
She goes running for the shelter of a mother's little helper
And it helps her on her way, gets her through her busy day

Rolling Stones, *Mother's Little Helper* (1966)

The genesis of the so-called 'second wave' of feminism is well known. Although multifaceted and fragmented, feminist groups in Britain and the United States sought collectively to gain equal rights and privileges with men and to draw attention to myriad ways in which women continued to be oppressed by a patriarchal society. Betty Friedan's seminal text *The Feminist Mystique*, first published in 1963, is widely held as the inspiration that revitalized the feminist movement. At the centre of Friedan's thesis was a critique of the popular notion that truly 'feminine' women could gain complete fulfilment from the domestic role. Friedan noted that 'millions of women lived their lives in the image of those pretty pictures of the American suburban housewife, kissing their husbands good-bye in front of the picture window'.[1] Friedan of course, was by no means the first to confront the stifling confinement of marriage and motherhood. Charlotte Perkins Gilman, for example, described her descent into despair in her autobiographical journal *The Yellow Wallpaper*, published in 1892. In this narrative, she wrote about her experience of nervous depression and the way in which she was prescribed enforced passivity and 'forbidden to work' until she was well again.[2] During the 1950s, Anne Sexton began writing poetry following a psychiatric breakdown. Her therapist was later to note that although Sexton 'was trying her best to live up to the 1950s image of the good wife and mother, she found the task completely beyond her'.[3] Just a few years later in 1963, inspired by Sexton, Sylvia Plath published her semi-autobiographical novel *The Bell Jar* in which she described the experience of mental illness and psychiatric treatment. Her collection of poems, *Ariel*, published posthumously in 1965, echoed many of the sentiments put forward by Friedan about motherhood, sexuality and marriage.

12   *Desperate Housewives, Neuroses and the Domestic Environment, 1945–1970*

There are many excellent texts that examine the key figures and developments within the feminist movement during this period and the remit of this book is not to duplicate such work. Rather, my intention is to explore the various aspects of the domestic role in more depth, in order to provide a more nuanced appraisal of women's experience. In contrast to the views of Friedan and others, many of the women interviewed for this project found their role as mothers and home-makers enjoyable and rewarding. Those who endured symptoms of anxiety and depression did not locate the cause of their problems in their role as homemak-ers. Instead, they recounted memories of distressing childhood events, unhappy marital relationships and occasionally a familial predisposition to mental illness. These testimonies were widely supported by case studies published in the con-temporary medical press of women who received treatment in primary care or psychiatric outpatient clinics. Such reports often detailed harrowing accounts of spousal abuse or dysfunctional family circumstances, sometimes dating back to childhood. This book, therefore, should be placed within the genre of recent scholarship about post-war women that suggests 'not all housewives experi-enced their role simply as exhausting or stultifying'.[4] Why the views expressed by women in this study were at variance with those put forward by feminist commentators is the other central question explored in this book. As other historians have begun to suggest,[5] I will argue that Friedan and other highly educated second-wave feminists were politically motivated. Their experiences of suburban housewifery were thus shaped by factors that were perhaps unrepre-sentative of ordinary middle-class housewives. As Judy Giles has rightly pointed out, 'those who wrote or spoke about suburbia in Britain or America did so from positions outside the phenomenon they so roundly condemned'.[6] However, the objective of this book is in no way to challenge the many important initiatives of the women's liberation movement from the 1960s. Instead, it aims to refine feminist critiques of domesticity that have linked the roles of mothering and homemaking unproblematically with mental illness.

The Housewife, the Home and Feminism

For Friedan, writing in 1963, to women born after 1920, feminism was 'dead history'.[7] It ended, she argued, 'with the winning of that final right: the vote'.[8] Although women were still actively concerned with the rights of other oppressed groups, 'no one was much concerned with rights for women: they had all been won'.[9] In Britain too, the feminist movement went into decline after the passing of the Equal Franchise Act in 1928. Feminist societies were often portrayed as radical, even revolutionary groups of women who wished to transform society and break up the family.[10] Nevertheless, as historians have pointed out, main-stream women's societies and political organizations continued to expand;

however, they broadly represented the interests of wives and mothers working within the home.[11] The agenda shifted to give prominence to matters which did not affect the two sexes equally such as family allowances, birth control and housing.[12] Thus, as Judy Giles has noted, interwar feminism did little to challenge the 'assumptions upon which the sexual division of labour, both within the home and as an organizing feature of society, were founded'.[13] The challenge for Freidan and her contemporaries who formed the Women's Liberation Movement of the 1960s and 1970s, was thus to define and articulate an altogether different kind of oppression that was subtly 'exercised and reinforced through "personal" institutions such as marriage, child-rearing and sexual practices'.[14] Central to this objective was the notion of 'consciousness-raising', whereby activists sought to transform the 'personal' into the 'political'.[15]

Friedan's contribution to this was important because she claimed that her views had been shaped by her experience as an 'ordinary housewife'.[16] She was able to draw convincingly upon emerging critiques of the mass migration from the city to the suburbs in her description of suburban housing estates as 'ugly, endless sprawls' that encouraged millions of women to 'seek fulfilment in the home'.[17] As Mark Clapson has argued, during the twentieth century, the United States and England evolved into societies that were dominated by the suburbs.[18] Although the move from urban centres was inspired at different times and by different factors, there were many important similarities between the two countries. As the century progressed, the image and appeal of a suburban home became culturally pervasive in both England and the United States.[19] However, Friedan argued that the cities provided more opportunities in education and employment for women; whereas women in the suburbs were vulnerable to the 'new mystique' – the notion that they must keep on having babies in order to justify their very existence. Such women, she argued, were increasingly seeking medical help for fatigue, alcohol abuse and boredom.[20] In extreme circumstances, she noted, doctors were seeing cases of a strange new medical disorder, 'housewife's blight'. This condition had been described to Friedan by a doctor in Pennsylvania who reported that women 'who bury themselves in their dishpans' were presenting with 'great bleeding blisters' on their hands and arms. He added that the condition was not caused by detergent and could not be cured by cortisone.[21] The Australian-born academic, Germaine Greer, included a chapter on 'misery' in her best-selling book, *The Female Eunuch*, published in 1970. She argued that women everywhere were lapsing into the apathy and irritability of the housewives' syndrome: 'Nagging, overweight and premature ageing are the outward signs of misery, and they are so diffuse among women in our society that they do not excite remark'.[22] Both Friedan and Greer reached the best-selling list with their books. However, Greer was criticized for the commercial packaging and promotion of *The Female Eunuch* which later attracted accusations of 'hype'.[23] Stephanie Coontz has recently published a study of women's reactions to *The Feminine Mystique* in the United States and argues convincingly that the book struck a chord with many women there. However, she also acknowledges that the book was extremely divisive and some claimed that prior to Friedan, middle-class women were 'living in peace in what they considered to be a normal, traditional, worthwhile lifestyle'.[24] As this book will illustrate, women's lives there differed greatly, and there are a range of social, political and educational factors that account for Friedan's reception in the United States.

By conflating the housewife's experience *in* the suburban home with broader social concerns about new ways of living, Friedan and Greer were able to vitalize their moves to make publicly visible the ways in which women were defined and controlled by existing social structures. Their critique of 'home' also drew upon a longer tradition in which homes have often been seen as ambiguous social spaces; at times extolled for the ways in which they fostered mental and physical health and happiness, and at other times, indicted as sites of depression, neurosis and decay.[25] During the interwar period, for example, a 'new' class of female neurosis was described in 1938 by Stephen Taylor, Senior Resident Medical Officer at the Royal Free Hospital.[26] He argued that the 'mind-numbing' banality of the new housing estates built across England after the First World War was the cause of much psychological distress in young housewives.[27] Although Taylor proposed that the roots of this condition probably lay psycho-dynamically 'buried in a heap of infantile and adolescent manure',[28] he argued that the stimulus was undoubtedly a failure of environment. Taylor described the disappointment and isolation inherent in suburban living: 'The small labour-saving home, the small family and the few friends have left women of the suburbs relatively idle. They have nothing to look forward to, nothing to look up to and little to live for'.[29] Although Taylor appeared to be discussing a new class of neurotic patient, 'Mrs Everyman', he was in fact using a medical case-study as a platform from which to express a number of broader fears about changes affecting interwar British society. Later to become a Labour MP, it is not surprising that Taylor was critical of what he saw as the false values promoted by a materialistic consumer society and the 'jerrybuilt' houses constructed by speculative builders. He also articulated more serious concerns about the increasing secularization of society and the loss of traditional values and kinship ties. Published in the *Lancet,* which had a reputation for controversy, Taylor's intention was arguably to communicate his concerns to a wide audience, in accordance with the *Lancet*'s objective which was to 'inform and reform'.[30] Taylor's 'Mrs Everyman' can be seen thus as a rich metaphor for emerging mid-twentieth social, economic and political concerns.

Evidence from research undertaken twenty years later contradicted Taylor's original thesis. Alongside a colleague, Sidney Chave, who had previously investigated rates of illness on a London County Council estate, Taylor undertook research into levels of psychiatric morbidity in Harlow, one of the eight new towns constructed following the New Towns Act, 1946.[31] These new neighbourhoods presented an alternative to the growing congestion in London and residents were promised employment and quality housing in a green environment. In addition, each town included a church, a primary school and a community centre. It was hoped that the design would encourage social cohesion and help prevent isolation. However, Taylor and Chave were surprised to find that rates of primary-care consultations for the minor neuroses did not differ significantly from those recorded previously by Chave on a London County Council estate. As Hayward observes, 'the distribution of these symptoms did not correlate with the image of the anxious young housewife produced in Taylor's original work'.[32] The two researchers concluded that subclinical neurosis was a disease entity 'with its roots deep in the physical or emotional background of the individual'.[33]

The results of a further study undertaken by two physicians from the Maudsley Hospital, E. H. Hare and G. K. Shaw, were published in 1965.[34] This research also indicated that rates of minor mental illness did not differ substantially between the older communities and new towns. The authors analysed the responses to 2,000 questionnaires and argued that, although residents commented on the lack of amenities in the new town, this did not affect their overall levels of satisfaction with their environment. On the contrary, many commented that they 'liked the clean air'. Although the distribution of illness by gender was not the primary focus of the study, Hare and Shaw noted that women between the ages of twenty-five and forty-four years who lived in the new district had higher rates of neurosis and fatigue. However, they also noted that more women from this group were caring for three or more small children. They therefore decided that this factor might account for the more general rise in levels of fatigue. Significantly, the authors concluded that 'there was no evidence that housewives who went out to work either full-time or part-time differed from those who did not go out to work, in health, social attitudes or in social factors'. Indeed, they observed that housewives who also went out to work consulted their general practitioners more regularly than those who stayed at home.[35]

Despite these findings, within feminist circles, the association between the middle-class housewife, domestic life and neurosis endured. Friedan proposed that women were longing for opportunities outside the domestic arena and that educated wives experienced symptoms of desperation, tiredness and despondency. She was also increasingly critical of the stereotypical images of women disseminated by the media. She maintained that they were largely devoid of 'any mention of the world beyond the home', and that 'the only goal a woman is permitted is the pursuit of a man'.[36] She advised women to marry later, and, wherever possible, to gain a university education. Educators, she argued, should 'see to it that women make a lifetime commitment to a field of thought, to work of serious importance to society'.[37] In Britain, commentators also indicated that many middle-class housewives felt isolated in their role.[38] Nevertheless, they were inclined to evaluate the circumstances facing women from within a more conventional set of ideals. The social researcher Judith Hubback, for example, argued that 'reasonable modern feminism builds on the diversity of the sexes – it is not crudely egalitarian'.[39] While agreeing broadly with Friedan that women should educate themselves, she considered that this was important in order that they may lead a professional life after rearing children.[40] Hubback accepted that a woman would eventually marry and that the husband's job would 'inevitably colour all her life'.[41] She recommended that university courses should therefore be 'specialised to suit careers applicable to women'.[42] The academic Viola Klein, who moved to England from Czechoslovakia before the Second World War, also investigated the 'woman question' and, in 1963, published *Britain's Married Women Workers*. She analysed a Mass Observation survey undertaken in 1957 and noted that the numbers of married women working outside the home were rising. This was accounted for by various social factors that included a fall in the age of marriage, fewer children, improvements in domestic technology and the expansion of suitable employment in the administrative and welfare sectors.[43] Although Klein endorsed the idea of married women's employment and proposed that it was beneficial not only to the individual but also to the economy, she remarked that the majority of women surveyed envisaged that their role as mothers would take priority. In the early 1960s, most women anticipated working only until they started a family.[44]

The conclusions put forward by Friedan and her contemporaries on both sides of the Atlantic provided the impetus for more detailed feminist investigation into the economic, political and social status of women. During the 1970s and 1980s, the sociologist Ann Oakley, daughter of the social policy theorist Richard Titmuss, undertook a number of research projects into motherhood and housework. Her work was important, not least because it highlighted the dearth of research on housewives in the home, but primarily because it drew attention to the material undervaluation of domestic labour. Building on the idea put forward much earlier by Simone de Beauvoir in *The Second Sex* (1949), Oakley was one of a growing number of academics to suggest that attitudes towards parenting, and more specifically 'mothering', were socially constructed. She argued that the division of labour need not be determined by gender and that the biological theory of 'mothering' was a myth that had been used to validate the social order.[45]

Such works promoted a greater understanding and acceptance of women's experiences of mothering and homemaking. However, the discontent and frustration evident in the interviews undertaken by Oakley were expressed by housewives who were beginning to encounter expanding opportunities in both educational and professional arenas – opportunities that were largely unavailable to those of the immediate post-war period. Increasingly, women of the 1970s were faced with new and conflicting choices against a backdrop of increasing expectations of emotional fulfilment promoted by film, television, radio and popular print. It is therefore perhaps understandable that Oakley's housewives understood their role to be unattractive and undervalued. Centrally, social commentators and historians have tended to underplay the complexities of individual experience and portray women as a homogenous group. Indeed, Judy Giles has argued that the emphasis upon the liberation of women from the home has meant that the 'feminine desires for home as safety, connectedness and continuity have received little attention in academic scholarship'.[46] In her discussion of *The Feminine Mystique*, she suggests that Friedan's tendency to homogenize suburbia and the women who lived there, followed precisely those tendencies that Friedan herself so passionately deplored in the modern world – denying identity and individuality to the women she described.[47]

The 'Mad' Housewife in Popular Culture

Lesley Johnson and Justine Lloyd have argued that the antagonism meted out to the figure of the housewife by second-wave feminists has been problematic. They suggest that the image of the unhappy housewife was in fact conjured up by feminism in the attempt to construct a narrative that would make sense of, and dispel, the sense of contradiction and tension women felt between public achievement and femininity.[48] Certainly, by the 1970s, the discontents described by early second-wave feminists had inspired a new generation of novelists, filmmakers, poets and songwriters who began to depict the suburban housewife in all her misery. The British rock band The Rolling Stones proclaimed in their 1966 hit *Mother's Little Helper* that mothers were disillusioned and exhausted looking after husbands and children, to the extent that they were relying on tranquillizing drugs to 'get them through their busy day'.[49] More broadly, in popular culture, the image of the stifling domestic environment soon became inextricably linked to mental symptoms such as anxiety neurosis and depression, and in extreme cases, to severe depression and suicide.

Susan Faludi has noted that housewives in fiction appeared 'frequently befuddled, a little dopey and a lot doped; a state generally induced by a combined overdose of Valium and vacuuming'.[50] The American author Marilyn French is well remembered for her bestselling novel *The Women's Room* (1977), which was made into a television movie in 1980 starring Lee Remick. The book was initially 'massacred by the critics', but soon reached the best-selling list.[51] By 1980 it had sold 3 million copies;[52] however, it is unclear how many of these were sold in Britain. The central theme was the stark choice facing women: a loving sexual relationship that would inevitably lead to children – or a career. French's dark novel traces the life of protagonist, Mira, through her overwhelmingly unhappy 'conventional' marriage, post-divorce to her journey of 'liberation'.

There is indeed much in *The Women's Room* that would have resonated with women during the 1970s. Mira and her contemporaries faced the difficulties associated with avoiding pregnancy and the consequent barriers to academic and professional opportunities. Mira recalled the words of her mother: 'Sex led to pregnancy ... and pregnancy led to marriage, to a marriage enforced on both, which meant poverty, resentment an immediate baby and "a life like mine"'.[53] Women also faced certain economic hardship and social stigma following marital breakdown. *The Women's Room* is described as a classic feminist text not only because of its discussion of the political and cultural oppression of women, but also because of its representation of the day-to-day life of a suburban housewife which was seen as typically 'painful, oppressive and deadly dull'.[54] However, a closer look at the novel reveals that, despite her focus on feminist issues, even Mira was, at various stages in her life, able to find joy in domesticity. Her first marriage is portrayed as loveless and empty. She is sexually unfulfilled and prefers the domestic space when her obdurate and insensitive husband is at work. However, the narrator notes that 'There were joys in Mira's life: the children themselves. They were a deep pleasure ... the tedious days were filled with miracles'.[55] Later, following the break-up of her marriage, Mira gains a place at Harvard and eventually falls in love with Ben, a younger man. It is during this period, when she experiences true ardour and appreciation from him, that the domestic role takes on new meaning. The narrator describes the scene one evening while Mira prepares a meal for Ben and her sons:

> She danced into the kitchen, unloaded her purchases, put beef bones in the great pot to simmer and began to wash and chop vegetables ... Outside, she heard small children playing ... peace cupped her heart and held it gently. Smiling, she stood at the kitchen sink, holding a bunch of string beans ... her home was humming, happy and bright.[56]

Mira admits later to a friend that she is 'shocked' to have reverted to buying into the 'American Dream', observing with some discomfort that 'nothing is ever simple. What do you do when you discover you *like* parts of the role you are trying to escape?'[57] Mira thus illustrates perfectly women's ambiguous relationship with domesticity. On the one hand, the domestic environment has been seen as a key site of female oppression; on the other hand, the nurturing role in the home provided a real sense of peace and contentment. For Mira and other key figures in fiction and film, it was often not domesticity that made women ill, but instead, unsupportive and unfulfilling relationships with spouses or other family members.

The English author Penelope Mortimer's novel *The Pumpkin Eater* (1962) was inspired by her own turbulent relationships with men. Mortimer was twice divorced, and during her marriage to the barrister and writer John Mortimer,

Reflections on the Desperate Housewife 19

both parties were said to be serial adulterers. *The Pumpkin Eater*'s central themes are infidelity and domesticity. The unnamed narrator is on her fourth marriage, with children from each husband, and she suffers an emotional breakdown following the discovery of her husband's repeated affairs. She alludes to a troubled past, describing her repeated attempts at marriage as a means of 'escaping from [her] childhood'.[58] This novel was also released as a thought-provoking drama in 1964, adapted by Harold Pinter, starring Anne Bancroft and Peter Finch. In this dramatization, the protagonist, named Jo, is tormented by her husband's affairs. Jo's symptoms of anxiety and depression are evident in the opening scene where she appears wandering aimlessly around her loveless home. She later experiences a complete 'breakdown' while shopping in Harrods. On one level, the film problematizes Jo's compulsion for repeated pregnancies, insinuating that her need for more children is a substitute for emotional security. However, although the film is indeed a bleak portrayal of marriage and family life, on a more subtle level, it is in fact more broadly a critique of the 'middle-class dream', so widely endorsed on both sides of the Atlantic. This is manifest in the director's use of 'flashback' to Jo's previous marriage, in which she is pictured in their modest, yet chaotic and happy home, with children playing noisily all around. Later, married to Jake who is an increasingly successful screenwriter, Jo benefits from all the material advantages of middle-class suburban wealth. The home is immaculate and filled with expensive possessions. However, its sterility is symbolic of the emotional emptiness of the marital relationship. Although he has willingly taken on her children, Jake becomes resentful of what he describes as 'that bloody great army of kids'.[59] Discussing his wife later with her psychiatrist, he notes disapprovingly: 'She's a beautiful woman and all she wants to do is sit in a corner and give birth'.[60] Although pregnancy might well be filling an emotional vacuum for Jo, she in fact appears happy in her domestic role and, like Mira, experiences loneliness and despondency because of the deficiencies in other interpersonal relationships.

Although there is a clear feminist message in these films, they must be seen as part of a broader critique of the conformity and emptiness of the post-war world. Their creators were building on ideas put forward earlier, by authors such as George Orwell, William H. Whyte, David Riesman and Herbert Marcuse who all variously disapproved of the social and cultural changes that took place in mid-century Britain and the United States. The views of these individuals notably came from different intellectual circles. Marcuse and Reisman were influenced by the Frankfurt School which, during the interwar years, had reacted against the perceived failure of Marxism in the Western world. Frankfurt school theorists proposed a new 'applied' or 'cultural' Marxism, which incorporated Freudian psychoanalytic theory to explain, and in turn to modify, the so-called impulses or drives that had resulted in the 'workers of the world' failing to unite. Orwell's views, in contrast, were founded upon his disdain for the growing

20 *Desperate Housewives, Neuroses and the Domestic Environment, 1945–1970*

salaried middle-class. Orwell's family originated from what he described as exactly this kind of 'genteel poverty' and he began to distance himself from its culture and values during his twenties.[61] He argued that they were 'simply the working class on better wages, smothered under a different class of drudgery, but smothered just the same'.[62] Whyte, an urbanologist, formulated his view of post-war America as a result of many years observing human behaviour in the urban environment. As editor of the global business magazine *Fortune*, he was well-qualified to comment on American corporate culture and the suburban middle class. Collectively, despite their disparate influences, each of these authors in their own way denounced the cultural changes of the post-war Western world.

Orwell, in his novel *Coming up for Air*, written in 1939 before the new housing estates were built following the New Towns Act in 1946, famously described existing suburban housing estates as 'semi-detached torture chambers'.[63] Notably, his disapproval extended to the more generalized mass production, evident not only in housing, but in industry and food manufacturing. The protagonist in *Coming up for Air*, George Bowling, eating a frankfurter that he describes as 'a kind of funeral snack' at a local London food outlet, conveys his feelings thus:

> It gave me the feeling that I'd bitten into the modern world and discovered what it was really made of ... everything's made of something else ... everything comes out of a carton or a tin, or it's hauled out of a refrigerator or squirted out of a tap... nothing matters except slickness and shininess and streamlining.[64]

William H. Whyte in his memorable book *The Organization Man*, published in 1956, was critical of the growing layers of middle-management within large American corporations, and the ways in which 'mass organization' fostered conformity and stifled creativity. Americans, he argued, were increasingly buying into the 'myth' of the well-balanced, well-rounded life: 'Listen to them talk to each other over the front lawns of their suburbia and you cannot help but be struck by how well they grasp the common denominators which bind them'.[65] Herbert Marcuse and David Riesman also provided what are now viewed as groundbreaking critiques of modern Western society. The German philosopher Marcuse argued in his left-wing text *The One-Dimensional Man* (1964) that the capitalist economy had not in fact 'liberated' society. Instead, he proposed, the manipulation of artificial needs, driven by consumption, technology and the media had resulted in the artificial manufacture of 'happiness'. In mid-century society, he noted 'people recognize themselves in their commodities; they find their soul in their automobile, hi-fi set, split-level home, kitchen equipment ... social control is anchored in the new needs which it has produced'.[66] Riesman, an American sociologist, put forward a specific character type to describe this category of the modern Western individual: the 'other-directed' person. He or she was 'driven' by their desire to define themselves by their peers and by the 'way' others lived.

Riesman argued that this had been a result of society's shift from production to consumption.[67] As a result, American society resembled 'a lonely crowd' – the title of his book, written with Nathan Glazer and Reuel Denney in 1950.

Suburbanization was thus just one aspect of the developments that affected society in post-war America and Britain. The new communities that were constructed on the outskirts of large cities were part of broader social changes that many found alarming because of their tendency towards dreary functionality and uniformity. As Malvina Reynolds expounded in her popular song about suburban California, *Little Boxes*, released in 1962:

> Little Boxes on the hillside
> Little boxes made of ticky-tacky
> Little boxes, little boxes
> Little boxes all the same ...
> And they all play on the golf-course
> And drink their Martini dry
> And they all have pretty children ...
> And they all get put in boxes
> And they all come out the same.

Mark Clapson has rightly pointed out that, despite the broad similarities the histories of suburbanization on both sides of the Atlantic possess profound differences.[68] He further suggests that the negative conclusions that have been uncritically deployed about suburbia are misleading.[69] Nevertheless, 'pathogenic' suburbia firmly took its place in popular imagination and framed the discourse of novels such as *The Man in the Gray Flannel Suit* (1955), written by Sloan Wilson, and *The Stepford Wives* (1972), written by Ira Levin. Both of these were adapted as films, in 1956 and 1975 respectively, and the latter became an iconic characterization of the frustrated housewife. The phrase 'gray flannel suit' from the former, became synonymous with the American commuter-businessman, increasingly forced to put work before his family in the pursuit of the American Dream: the suburban family home with the picket fence and picture window. However, the central character, Tom Rath and his wife Betsy are increasingly discontented in their suburban home, Betsy remarking one evening, 'I don't know what's the matter with us... your job is plenty good enough. We've got three nice kids, and lots of people would be glad to have a house like this. We shouldn't be so *discontented* all the time.'[70] Ultimately, in this plot, it is the husband who struggles with the conformity and material culture of the post-war world. As the concluding chapter of this book will illustrate, this theme was to re-emerge in cinema productions much later in the twentieth-century.

Following the 1974 release of *The Stepford Wives*, which became something of a cult movie, the phrase 'Stepford wife' entered common language as a way of describing women who conform subserviently to the domestic role. The darkly satirical film was released at the height of the women's liberation movement in the United States. It was not well received among active feminists who claimed it was 'anti-women'; however, the English Director Bryan Forbes and the cast were in no doubt that it was in fact 'anti-men'. On an obvious level, the housewives of Stepford are notably fixated with domestic chores and behave in a servile, slavish manner towards their husbands. The central character Joanna Eberhart, is duly concerned that, one by one, all the wives in 'Ajax country' are becoming disinterested with the world outside the home. The film builds to a curiously outlandish conclusion, as all the women are found to have been replaced by identical robot-like figures that have been programmed to be 'perfect' wives, both physically, emotionally and performatively – a plot devised by the sinister local 'men's association'.

The film has one obvious message: that life in Stepford, despite its 'good schools, low taxes and clean air', is harmful to women. However, collectively the film also works on a number of other more subtle levels. There is underlying marital discontent among all the female characters, who only seem truly content in their 'post-robot' existence. Joanna has a difficult relationship with her controlling husband Walter, declaring at one point, 'you pretend we make decisions together, but it's always you – what you want. Why bother to ask me at all?'[71] The film also provides a critical social commentary about the advance of science and technology. There are frequent visual and spoken references to the biochemical and electronics industries, and an underlying fear about the consequences of unchecked scientific 'progress'. Indeed, the film reaches its disturbing climax as Joanna uncovers the robot-like model of herself. Asking the character Dale Coba, who has been central to the conspiracy, why husbands should want to do this to their wives, he responds, 'Why? Because we can. We found a way of doing it and it's just perfect. Perfect for us, and perfect for you.'[72]

As with many of the films and novels produced during this period, it is the feminist message in *The Stepford Wives* that has remained firmly embedded in popular consciousness. However, they in fact reflect a much broader critique of post-war middle-class values. These concerns were not only pertinent during the 1960s and 1970s. As will be shown in the concluding chapter of this book, anxieties about suburbia, gender roles and middle-class family values were manifest in myriad ways throughout the late twentieth century in films such as *American Beauty, Far From Heaven, Safe* and *Revolutionary Road*.

Suburban Madness, Poets and Novelists

As the biographies of women such as Charlotte Perkins Gilman and Virginia Woolf suggest, female writers of the mid-twentieth century were by no means unique in their experiences of mental illness. Nevertheless, the link between stifling domesticity and madness became all the more salient during the 1950s

Reflections on the Desperate Housewife   23

and beyond as second-wave feminist commentators began to draw upon the notion of the 'desperate housewife' to support their campaigns for equality. The American confessional poets Anne Sexton and Sylvia Plath both chronicled their experiences of suburbia, family life and mental illness in poetry and novels. Their biographers are unequivocal about the links between domesticity and madness.[73] Diane Wood Middlebrook, writing of Sexton, noted that she 'wrote about the social confusions of growing up in a female body and of living as a woman in post-war American society'.[74] Elaine Showalter in her book *The Female Malady* (1987) described Plath's semi-autobiographical novel, *The Bell Jar* (1963) as 'a protest against the feminine mystique of the 1950s'.[75] Showalter argues explicitly that women's mental breakdowns were a result of the 'limited and oppressive roles offered to women in modern society'.[76]

However, the biographies of both women illustrate that they experienced a host of difficulties that could plausibly have been detrimental to their mental health. Recounted in Sexton's biography, for example, are numerous traumatic circumstances that affected her deeply, long before she encountered suburban housewifery for herself. In the first instance, her father was an alcoholic and Sexton retained distressing memories of his drinking binges. She remembered that he singled her out for verbal abuse when he was drinking, complaining that her acne disgusted him and that he could not eat at the same table as her.[77] Indeed, Middlebrook noted that 'his drinking permanently destroyed her trust in his love'. He drank heavily for ten years before entering a private hospital for treatment. Sexton recounted the family's disturbing relationship with alcohol and remembered that her mother drank two drinks every noon, and three drinks every night 'come hell or high water'. Once her father stopped drinking, her mother would 'stand at the sink and slosh – pour the whisky right down'. Her father continued to drink 'on the sly'.[78]

Sexton and her siblings also felt neglected emotionally. Her parents were of the generation of the roaring twenties, 'good-looking, party-going and self-indulgent ... the children vied with each other for praise, particularly from their elusive mother'.[79] As a consequence, Sexton developed a close relationship with her great aunt, whom she named affectionately 'Nana'. However, the security gained from this alliance was shattered when Anne was fifteen. Nana became prone to periods of mental illness, as did other members of the family. During a particularly difficult period, her paternal grandfather also suffered his second mental breakdown and was hospitalized. She recalled: 'My father was drinking every minute, Nana was going crazy – my grandfather was crazy and [my sister] was having a baby'.[80] It has been suggested that Anne was a victim of sexual abuse at the hands of her father. Although this claim has never been confirmed, Middlebrook maintains that 'it is clear from many sources that Sexton's physical boundaries were repeatedly trespassed by the adults in her family, in ways that disturbed her emotional life from girlhood onwards'.[81]

Certainly, Sexton went on to lead a highly unconventional married life herself. She embarked upon repeated extramarital affairs and experienced great difficulty adjusting to motherhood. While there is little doubt that she loved her daughters, she also admitted that at times she was neglectful and suffered from the fear of harming them.[82] That Sexton was unable to function in the domestic role is arguably true; and so it was that she 'began to release her terrible energy, not only in symptoms, but in writing'.[83] However, we cannot claim with certainty that Sexton was typical of ordinary suburban housewives. It is at least possible that her experience was affected by the events in her past and her unique talent that compelled her to escape the confines of family life.

Middlebrook does acknowledge that, among Sexton's social peers, emotional problems were widespread.[84] Indeed, Sexton recalled that, during her acquaintance with Sylvia Plath, they regularly discussed their psychological problems: 'Very often, Sylvia and I would talk at length about our first suicides; at length, in detail, in depth ... We talked death with burned up intensity, both of us drawn to it like moths to an electric light bulb.'[85] Plath was also emblematic of the stereotype of caged creativity. However, she was clearly predisposed to mental illness long before her own marriage and motherhood. Indeed, she made her initial suicide attempt during her first year of college. It is widely accepted that she experienced a difficult childhood, losing her father suddenly at the age of eight. It is clear from her biography that she was disturbed by the events that followed his death; her mother worked long hours to provide for the family and Plath was required to move schools frequently. Linda Wagner Martin, Plath's biographer, noted that 'Sylvia wrote often and consistently about her sudden fall from happiness into despair'.[86] Plath was also greatly affected by her grandmother's illness and was said to have dwelled 'on the deaths of beloved people'.[87] Wagner Martin argues that 'her despair was not her suffering, but the impossibility of communicating her suffering to another person'.[88] Central to Plath's experience was undoubtedly her fall into depression and the electroshock therapy that terrified her and caused memory loss.[89]

The British novelist Penelope Mortimer's experiences during childhood and marriage were analogous to those of Sexton and Plath. Her clergyman father had lost faith in God and her mother was distant. She described their marriage as loveless; they never shared a bedroom and her father was 'boiling with frustration and envy' due to his wife's abhorrence of sex.[90] Mortimer 'survived' seven different schools, and occasional attempts by her father to assault her sexually. By the time she entered into marriage herself, she had little by way of a positive example upon which to formulate her own ideas about romantic love. She recalled that she had no constructive ideas about marriage at all, but thought

Reflections on the Desperate Housewife 25

it 'preferable to depending on people who wanted to use me for obscure and unpleasant purposes'.[91] Like the protagonist in her novel *The Pumpkin Eater*, Mortimer entered into a string of sexual relationships, resulting in six children from four men. In the second volume of her autobiography she notes that her novels were all, in part, based upon her life. Fiction was for her otherwise impossible to write since she 'didn't know the characters'.[92] She wrote movingly in both fiction and memoir about her own extra-marital affairs and her husband John's flirtations, attractions and infidelities, recalling how she 'furiously resented the hints, confessions, implausible excuses and furtive muttering on the phone'.[93] Mortimer finally ended up having what she described as a breakdown following the termination of her eighth pregnancy.[94] Having been persuaded by her husband that she should abort the child, she also decided to undergo a sterilization. While still in the clinic, 'all sewn up like a mailbag', she discovered John was having an affair.[95] The grim entry to her diary on 9 May 1961 read, 'Being pregnant, aborted, sterilized, wounded – it's not surprising, I know, that nothing heals'.[96]

Mortimer was treated periodically with electroconvulsive therapy (ECT), and long-term with a cocktail of what she described as 'uppers' and 'downers'. Much later, in 1977, she noted that her addiction was 'by no means cured, though symptoms were disguised under a thin layer of what I call reason'.[97] Her divorce from second husband John Mortimer was traumatic. She recalled that straightforward agreements made between them were 'later qualified and elaborated by solicitors until they were unrecognizable, then hostilities would begin again: painful, wasteful, pointless'.[98] Looking back upon her life in 1978, Mortimer poignantly noted that she had never really established her true identity: 'Layer upon layer of images – daughter, woman, wife, mother, writer, lover, teacher – had formed an impenetrable crust over whoever I was in the first place'.[99] Being a wife and mother was perhaps not quite enough for Penelope Mortimer; and being an accomplished writer was always important to her. However, her own fertility and love of babies was clearly manifest and she endured many distressing experiences during her life that undoubtedly contributed to her psychiatric breakdown.

If Penelope Mortimer's childhood was difficult, the novelist Anna Kavan's was desperate. Born in France to British parents in 1901, Kavan's early years were spent with a nurse; a ten minute visit each evening before bed being the only contact with her mother. At the age of six, Kavan was sent to boarding school and her world collapsed at the age of fourteen when, it is alleged, her father jumped to his death overboard on a ship bound for South America.[100] She recalled that, by dying, her father had condemned her to lifelong loneliness, 'I felt myself alone in the world, more than I'd ever been ... I couldn't forgive my father for abandoning me'.[101] Kavan went on to lead a decidedly unconventional life. Born Helen Woods, Kavan published novels initially under her married name Helen Ferguson, but adopted the name Anna Kavan in 1939. Her life was dominated by her addiction to heroin which was reflected in the hallucinatory nature of much of her writing. In her novel *Sleep Has His House* (1948), for example, she combined semi-autobiographical memories of her unhappy childhood with fragments from her subconscious.

Kavan was divorced twice and made repeated suicide attempts throughout her life. She felt that she had inherited a sombre constitution and, as a young woman, wrote in her diary; 'I have an unhappy nature and there is something dark and incomprehensible about me which invites misfortune'.[102] Although there was said to be a trace of melancholia and morbidity in her father's family, her life was more than once, touched by tragedy. In addition to the loss of her father, her baby daughter died in infancy and her son Bryan was killed in action during a bombing raid over Germany in 1942.[103] Kavan was not suited to mothering and was distant to her son in much the same way as her mother had been to her. However, his death affected her deeply and she made one of many suicide attempts shortly afterwards. Jeremy Reed has pointed out in his biography of Kavan that her psychiatric history remains speculative as she destroyed most of her diaries and the majority of her correspondence before her death. Nevertheless, it is evident that she 'lived with an oppressive sense of dysphoria and that her negative mood was constant'.[104] In the end, her drug use resulted in almost total withdrawal from normal human intercourse and she wrote in letter to a friend in 1965 that 'Life is just a nightmare, the universe has no meaning. Depression is as good an introduction to oblivion as any other.'[105] Since most of her personal papers were destroyed and her domestic life could by no means be considered conventional, it is hard to construct a sense of how Kavan felt about her role as a woman. Her writing most certainly reflects a lifetime of rejection and dysfunctional relationships; however, it is her struggle with mental illness that is articulated most strongly in her work.

Raymond Marriott, Kavan's friend, once said that difficult childhoods were commonplace among children of her class: 'some survive them and some don't. Anna didn't.'[106] Why this might be so is unclear. The Anglo-Irish author Elizabeth Bowen (1899–1973), for example, endured her father's mental illness and the death of her mother at the age of thirteen. Both she and her husband had repeated extra-marital affairs. With the exception of a stammer, Bowen survived her difficulties remarkably unscathed, and, as her biographer Victoria Glendinning notes, 'She did not come out of all this as a "nervous child" ... Elizabeth was tough ... serious illness apart, this was so for her whole life.'[107] Nevertheless, based upon the experiences of these women, the link between domesticity and mental illness becomes somewhat tenuous. Indeed, a number of male poets, who presumably did not fulfil a domestic role, also experienced psychological illness during the period. Their biographies reflect similarly disruptive family lives. The American poet John Berryman, for example, encountered his father's suicide as a young child. He went on to suffer from repeated bouts of alcoholism and nervous exhaustion and participated in recurrent infidelities, finally committing suicide in 1972. Randall Jarrell too, born in 1914, experienced traumatic parental divorce and went on to attempt suicide in 1965. Robert Lowell, another of Sexton's 'confessional' contemporaries, also suffered bouts of depression and repeated breakdowns during the 1950s. Arnold Ludwig has suggested that, although as yet unexplained, there appears to be a link between creative genius and madness.[108] Indeed, he argues, the question of whether creativity and madness are related has been posed since antiquity. In his discussion of Delmore Schwartz, another of Sexton's peers, he notes that, during his thirties, Schwartz had serious and persistent bouts of depression that evolved into full-blown manic episodes. This was exacerbated by the consumption of massive amounts of alcohol and his dependence on barbiturates and amphetamines.[109] Jeremy Reed, one of Anna Kavan's biographers also argued that 'normal people do not create imaginative art. The feeling of uniqueness that is part of the creative experience, and the need to continuously re-vision reality, are not the psychological quotient required by most people to get by.'[110]

Conclusion

To suggest that experiences of the past might have influenced the health of these individuals is not to conclude that creative women of the period were necessarily contented with domestic life. Their work is indeed often imbued with the spirit of weariness and dismay. However, given the consistent disruption and chaos in their lives, it is perhaps not surprising that they had difficulty functioning in their roles as wives and mothers. It is also true that these women were influenced by new ideas that emerged from intellectual and political circles during the period, and thus, cannot be compared to the average suburban housewife. Sexton, for example, was aroused by the intellectual debates she participated in at The Radcliffe Institute, in particular those with her longstanding friend Maxine Kumin. Kumin had achieved a college degree and masters before settling down to raise a family and as a graduate 'had ventured into the heady intellectual terrain of post-war existentialism'.[111] Middlebrook notes that Kumin was stirred by Betty Friedan's *Feminine Mystique*, and that a bracing criticism of the women's situation was circulating at the Radcliffe Institute. As a consequence:

> [Sexton's] years at the Institute introduced her to feminist ideas, and, in her daily dialogues with Maxine Kumin, they could tailor feminist insights to the particularities of their own situation as writers who were women, as women who were much alike and as women raising daughters to have high expectations of life.[112]

Born some time earlier, Kavan and Mortimer seemed less overtly influenced by early second-wave feminist ideas that had begun to circulate in the United

States. However, Kavan's work does indeed echo the dystopia of the post-war garden suburbs and class hegemony. As Geoff Ward has shown, whereas the literary 1930s had been all about borders: 'political, psychosexual, traitorous, or more usually a fusion of these things'; in the 1940s the paradigm changed to 'homecoming and return', reflecting the complexities of a world recently at war.[113] Collectively, the work of both literary authors and social commentators reflected many things, including the experience of being a woman. Nevertheless, these women were far from 'ordinary' and broadly unrepresentative of the average, middle-class suburban wife. Viola Klein, for example, born in 1908, attended the Sorbonne; and Alva Myrdal was engaged with the women's movement and worked as Secretary to the Swedish Government Commission on Paid Work. Similarly, Judith Hubback was educated at Cambridge and married the son of Eva Hubback – the joint founder of the Townswomen's Guild. Betty Friedan claimed that her feminism had its roots in suburban captivity; however, Daniel Horowitz has recently argued that, to the contrary, her experiences as a labour journalist and her involvement with the Popular Front played a significant role in fostering her feminism.[114] Ann Oakley too maintains that her interest in feminism was motivated by her experience as 'a conventional suburban housewife'.[115] Conversely, however, she has also admitted that 'feminism has never been a mainstream or a fashionable political belief. You have to be a bit of an outsider to be a feminist. That describes me exactly.'[116]

The following chapter draws on evidence from contemporary texts on marriage and parenting to reconstruct the cultural climate of the post-war period in Britain. Specifically in relation to the newly inaugurated welfare state and the recent trauma of war, it examines the rationale behind the 'breadwinner' model of the family, questioning the extent to which traditional gender roles were promoted as a conspiracy to ensure that women remained at home as unpaid workers. It is suggested instead that partners embarking upon marriage accepted a range of rights and responsibilities that were specific to the post-war period. Husbands and wives thus viewed their roles as 'equal, but different'.

2 THE ART OF MARRIAGE: MARRIAGE AND MOTHERING DURING THE POST-WAR PERIOD

A wife's first duty is to make a happy and comfortable home for her husband and children. If she cannot do this and work too, she should put her home first and give up work. If she is not prepared to do this, she should not have married.

Mary Macaulay, *The Art of Marriage* (1952)

As Stephanie Coontz has argued, the immediate post-war period was a unique moment in the history of marriage. In Western Europe and the United States, the cultural consensus that everyone should marry and form a male breadwinner family was like a steamroller that crushed every alternative view.[1] In Britain, although the Second World War had inevitably disrupted the normal pattern of married life, it had done nothing to diminish the popularity of marriage, and the marriage rate quickly rose to above the pre-war level.[2] Following a brief rise in divorce petitions filed immediately after the war, the numbers sank rapidly from 60,000 in 1947 to 31,000 in 1950, and dropped again to a low of 23,000 in 1958.[3] During the ten-year period beginning around 1950, Roderick Phillips notes that virtually all the countries of the West experienced an almost stationary divorce rate.[4]

Since the 1970s historians have been critical of progressive, teleological accounts of marriage and the family.[5] They have uncovered contrasting pictures of 'families past', and suggest that it is misleading to assume that there ever was a time when home and family were 'all they were meant to be'.[6] John Gillis suggests that the notion that families were more stable in the past is a myth, and concludes that 'like antiques, family traditions have actually acquired their value by the passage of time and are more treasured today than when they were new ... the more things change, the more we desire to keep them the same'.[7] Research has indeed shown that beneath the harmonious surface, the two decades following the war were marked by a 'swirl of conflicting currents'[8] relating to fears for stability of the traditional family unit and shifting sexual mores.[9] Feminist scholars have interpreted attempts to reinforce traditional family life as rooted in the interests of state and nation, 'as episodic responses to perceptions of actual or incipient family failure during periods of military or economic crises'.[10] As such, they have been seen as disadvantageous to women who, as a consequence, have

30   *Desperate Housewives, Neuroses and the Domestic Environment, 1945–1970*

been resigned to an unpaid, low-status domestic role. Ann Oakley has emphasized the fact that beliefs underpinning the division of labour by sex rest on a number of inaccurate assumptions. Most inaccurate of all, she suggests, is the assumption that motherhood leads to necessary differences in the kind of economic roles the sexes can perform:

> [We] assume that because we in our society do things a certain way, they must be the best or only way of doing them [when] in actual fact, putting child-care in the hands of women alone is not natural – nor should we think of it as a rule which holds in all but a few insignificant and peculiar cultures. In fact, we have some strictly non-rational beliefs of our own about the ways in which sex, and particularly reproduction, determines the gender roles of male and female.[11]

These theories were based on important studies undertaken since the 1970s which illustrated how gender roles are influenced by culture. Oakley maintains that men and women are 'pressed by society into different moulds', and that it is therefore not surprising that they come to regard their respective roles as 'predetermined by some general law, despite the fact that, in reality, the biological differences between the sexes are neither so large, nor so invariable as most of us suppose'.[12]

Constructionist scholars have suggested that each society has created its own notions of sexuality and gender and that nothing is constant or unchanging through time. Gender roles are viewed thus as culturally determined by society and its discourses. In this chapter I will not disagree with these findings, but will instead redirect the analysis of marriage and the family in post-war Britain away from retrospectively judgemental accounts of the period. By drawing upon evidence from contemporary texts on marriage and parenting, this chapter will explore the belief system within which married couples experienced conjugal and parental relationships. It will thus provide the necessary context within which the oral history in the subsequent chapter is set. In so doing, it will illustrate how concepts were framed by the social, economic, political and religious forces of that time. I argue that previous scholars have underemphasized both the level of empathy shown to women in the domestic role and the considerable expectations placed upon men who were responsible for providing a secure emotional and financial environment for their families.

Marriage in Post-War Britain

Marriage before the industrialized era usually began as a property arrangement for those who were economically independent.[13] Historians have widely debated the rise of 'romantic love', and as Phillips notes 'historians have pointed to varying chronologies and to different social classes as being the purveyors of changed attitudes and practices'.[14] He rightly suggests that the increase of conjugal sentiment should not be considered in terms of the complete or absolute replacement of one set of criteria, attitudes or practices by a different set; but rather as a shift over time, as 'motives for marriage and the affective content of marriages varied from marriage to marriage at any given time'.[15] Nevertheless, during the late nineteenth and early twentieth centuries, the expectations of emotional fulfilment in marriage took on greater significance. The ideal of the companionate marriage post-1920s put greater emphasis on the wife's role as companion to her husband, as well as a producer of children. Thus, it was proposed that a woman's status within marriage would be raised.[16] The idea that man and wife would undertake complementary roles within marriage formed the basis of William Beveridge's *Social Insurance and Allied Services* (1942) which stated:

> Upon marriage, every woman begins a new life in relation to social insurance ... [the plan] treats a man's contributions as made on behalf of himself and his wife, as for a team, each of whose partners is equally essential ... in sickness or unemployment, the housewife does not need compensating benefits on the same scale as the solitary woman because her home is provided for her by her husband's earnings.[17]

The report recognized women principally as wives and mothers[18] and underpinned the importance of the traditional family. This was crystallized following the Second World War with the implementation of the National Insurance Act, The National Health Service Act and the Family Allowances Act (which was viewed as 'a cost effective means of adding to family income where it could do most good – in the housewife's purse').[19] Mathew Thomson has suggested that ideas from the British mental hygiene movement also influenced post-war welfarism: 'The argument that man had innately destructive drives which had to be controlled and directed constructively was an influential factor in the acceptance of a planned society'.[20] The war had been immensely destructive to the social fabric, and mental hygienists hoped that society could be organized to encourage the healthy development of ethical values. The ideas of 'experts' such as John Bowlby contributed to the promotion of a maternalist style of 'family values' at the heart of the welfare state.[21]

The practices and beliefs of post-war welfarism hence embodied a series of fundamental and essentially traditional assumptions about the family and motherhood.[22] These ideals provide the essential context to the experience and understanding of marriage and the family during the 1950s and 1960s. Indeed, the male breadwinner family was increasingly aspired to by families in all income brackets following the Second World War. As an ideal type, it achieved widespread acceptance among ordinary men and women and policymakers until the last quarter of the twentieth century and exercised considerable power in creating normative expectations as to male and female roles.[23] Nevertheless, appraisal of this social arrangement has been broadly negative in relation to its impact on the social and economic position of women. Jane Lewis, for example, notes that while women gained the right to vote on the same terms as men before the war, they remained second-class citizens, as the government's determination to minimize its own role and maximize family independence effectively structured women's lives.[24] Elizabeth Wilson proposed that 'the meshing together of the various aspects of the female condition may seem like an imprisoning net from which women struggle[d] to escape'.[25] However, the recollections from women interviewed for the following chapter suggest that to the contrary, women were not particularly inclined to examine their lives introspectively and their values and beliefs broadly paralleled those embodied in post-war welfarism. To them, complementary roles within marriage appeared not only as natural and familiar but also pragmatic.

Research undertaken in 1943 by Mass Observation into 'the psychological factors in home-building' indeed indicates that Wilson's description of the domestic role as an 'imprisoning net' was misplaced.[26] To the contrary, this report suggested that women perceived marriage and the acquisition of their own home as a route to 'freedom', largely due to the fact that a shortage of housing stock often entailed beginning married life living with parents, or at the very least sharing a bathroom with another family. Approximately half a million houses had been destroyed or made unfit for habitation during the war and the rate of new construction had decreased since the 1930s.[27] This was duly exacerbated by the surge in new marriages and the post-war baby boom. As a result, both men and women attached great importance to the symbolic importance of their own 'home'. In the words of one woman:

> I think the greatest part of any sense of security is derived from my own home and family life. In the three years of my married life, I have had to move a great deal and have spent several months at a stretch in other people's houses, which brought home to me the real strength of the desire always to have 'a home of one's own'.[28]

Wives who responded to this survey associated 'home' with 'relaxation, comfort, security, happiness and comradeship'. One woman noted that 'home' was 'everything ... I believe it is the building up of home-life that our future generation depends ... this setting is still the best ideal of life'.[29] Wilson also claimed that during the 1950s 'theoreticians, popularizing sociologists, doctors, vicars, schoolmasters and journalists engaged in prolonged and heated debates about the state of the family, without ever seriously discussing the position of women at all'.[30] To date, contemporary texts have been read largely in relation to their perceived inequalities toward women. Thus, the domestic role has been seen as one of oppression and the world of salaried work has been viewed as liberating.

The post-war period was undoubtedly influenced by the prevailing ideology in which women assigned value to the investment of time and energy in their families, and men were broadly accepting of their financial responsibilities. Nevertheless, it is also true that an underlying fear of family disintegration existed. Although the divorce rate may have declined, the anxiety surrounding it had not.[31] The origins of anxiety lay not only in the dislocation of war, but also in the decades leading up to it, in which pioneering sexologists and birth-control campaigners had begun to lift taboos on sex. The physician and sex-researcher Havelock Ellis, and the birth-control pioneer Marie Stopes increasingly proposed that women also had the capacity for sexual pleasure. These views were at variance with the Christian view of sexuality which had focused on sex within marriage solely as a means of procreation. This view was increasingly questioned and attempts were made to reconcile scientific research and religious doctrine.[32] The synthesis of medicine and religion is indeed widely evident in much of the prescriptive material on marriage and sexuality during the period which aimed 'to redefine the nature and purpose of sex, such that it became both positive and capable of its highest expression, only within marriage'.[33] Concerns over sexual morality were reflected in a series of commissions and investigations during the late 1940s and 50s. The Morton Commission on divorce, for example, undertaken in 1955, attempted to reconcile those who wished to liberalize divorce legislation with those conservatives who felt any relaxation of the law would lead to family decay. The principal recommendations were that the existing law, based on the doctrine of the matrimonial offence, be retained. Oliver Ross McGregor, social scientist and historian writing in 1957, was critical of the Commission, and the panic surrounding divorce. In his centenary study on divorce, he claimed that:

> Current discussions of divorce have been distorted by a misunderstanding of the character and origins of the new democratic family unit. Such misunderstandings feed the hypochondria of moralists who diagnose a diseased present because they worship a past they do not understand.[34]

Nevertheless, collective concern about divorce was evident in the inauguration of The National Marriage Guidance Council (NMGC) in 1938. This organization was founded by a group of doctors, clergy, social workers and lawyers who wished to foster a positive view of marriage. Its principles were based primarily on the assertion that marriage was 'a partnership for life ... the most important thing [was] to prevent, so far as possible, the desire for divorce'.[35] Jane Lewis notes that the NMGC's mission and structure was shaped by the social and political context, and in particular, the perceived breakdown of family life.[36] Its impetus originated from collaboration between medicine and religion, and from two individuals, Reverend Herbert Gray and Dr E. F. Griffith. Gray was a Presbyterian Minister and is recognized as the founding member of Marriage Guidance. His aim was to promote 'a positive and warm view of sexual relationships between men and women'.[37] Sex was nonetheless seen as an expression of 'married love'. Gray painted a positive picture of sexual fulfilment, mutual support and equality – interpreted as respect for their different roles.[38] Following the Second World War, a former Methodist Minister, David Mace joined forces with Griffith to develop proposals for a marriage guidance centre. The notion of wartime 'reconstruction' certainly included marriage and parenting, 'and the movement for marriage guidance gained strength as a publicly identified defender of marriage and the family'.[39]

The Council evolved quickly, and by 1948 there were more than a hundred marriage guidance centres.[40] It published numerous articles and books during these years and drew upon advice from authors with professional backgrounds who were concerned about marriage and family life. These texts and other handbooks on marriage are illuminating for the ways in which they reflect the essence of 'equality' as it was formulated in contemporary thinking. In one such publication, *Happy Ever After?* (1950), Hugh Lyon, dealt with the disquiet surrounding the future of the family. Lyon spoke of the paradox in which so much of what had turned out to be 'bad' was, in its origins, a reaction against something worse. The champions of easier divorce, he pointed out, had originally been moved by high ideals of marriage and a hatred of the cruelties perpetuated in the name of sanctity.[41] Fearful of the 'general deterioration, the increase of juvenile delinquency and the drift away from religion', Lyon's primary concern was that the status of marriage had been 'cheapened'.[42] It is interesting that the introduction begins with a scathing account of man's dominance over women, and Lyon's conviction in support of equality for women is notable. The message was not a critique of sexual equality. The emphasis was instead upon the solemnity of the marriage contract and his concern was that both men and women increasingly thought of marriage as 'an experiment which may or may not prove a success'.[43] The Christian doctrine of indissolubility was still very much in evidence. Nevertheless, Lyon was in support of both sexes and critical of many of the social problems that existed in post-war Britain such as the housing shortage and a decline in leisure time. These he regarded as detrimental to the quality of the marriage partnership.

In *The Stability of Marriage*, which was published in 1952, Alfred Brayshaw, who succeeded Mace as General Secretary of the NMGC, also acknowledged that the shift towards equality between the sexes had entailed a level of social disruption. However, he asserted that:

> While men and women are of equal value, they have essential differences of aptitude, outlook and function. Every modern marriage of thinking people presents husband and wife with the problem of reconciling equality with respect for difference.[44]

The influential judge and lawyer, Lord Denning, who was President of the NMGC in 1949, campaigned during the 1960s for a common law which would allow a deserted wife to remain in the matrimonial home. This resulted in The Matrimonial Homes Act (1967) which protected the wife's rights of occupation in such circumstances. Denning spoke in 1960 at the Eleanor Rathbone Memorial Lecture on the Equality of Women. In his paper, he articulated the complexities inherent in the notion of 'equality' as it was understood in post-war Britain. He noted:

> No matter how you may dispute and argue, you cannot alter the fact that women are different from men. The principal task in life of women is to bear and rear children. It is a task which occupies the best years of their lives. The man's part in bringing up the children is no doubt as important as hers, but of necessity he cannot devote so much time to it. He is physically stronger, and she the weaker ... these diversities of function and temperament lead to differences in outlook that cannot be ignored. But they are none of them any reason for putting women under the subjection of men ... she has as much right to her freedom. When she marries, she does not become the husband's servant, but his equal partner. If his work is more important in the life of the community, hers is more important in the life of the family. Neither can do without the other. Neither is above the other or under the other. They are equals.[45]

Denning also asserted that family law was, quite correctly, undergoing adjustments and developing new principles of 'partnership', under which family assets would belong to both parties. Gone also was the law which dictated that a wife must 'obey' her husband. He noted that: 'although law cannot make one love or cherish each other, nevertheless, if he or she so far disregards this duty as to make life intolerable for the other, he or she may well be found to have broken the law'.[46]

Theodore Bovet's contribution to marriage guidance also echoed this notion of 'equality'. Bovet, a qualified physician and psychoanalyst, wrote a number of texts on suffering and spirituality,[47] but also specialized in marriage counselling and relationships. In his 1958 publication, *A Handbook to Marriage and Marriage Guidance*, Bovet included a chapter entitled 'Men and Women', where he affirmed that they had been created 'to polarize and complete each other'. Within the union, he proposed, 'there need be no struggle for power ... They can both feel happy in fulfilling their own function with the help of the other'.[48]

Kenneth Walker, a British urologist who developed a professional interest in psychosexual problems and the relationship between mind and body, reinforced this theme in his book, *Sex and Happiness* which was published in 1963. He emphasized that women's equality had been positive for the institution of marriage because, 'the larger the field of their joint activities and shared interests, the stronger will be the foundations on which their marriage rests'.[49] He spoke of inspirational married women, such as the chemist and physicist Marie Curie, and Agnes, the wife of English surgeon, Joseph Lister, citing them as early examples of marital 'teamwork'. He posited that the secret of their happy marriages was that 'they shared so much together'. In successful marriages, he argued, 'couples look outward together in the *same* direction'.[50]

Such authors did not only point out the importance of equality within marriage, they also stressed the fact that individuals should be entirely free to choose to enter into a marriage contract in the first place – a notion described as 'full and free consent'. Authors impressed that all primary conditions of marriage must be fully 'understood and accepted by both parties' before the contract was made.[51] Free agency was defined as 'free of coercion or compulsion' and both parties should consider themselves to be 'legally and morally competent' in order to be able to make such a decision.[52] The explicit message was therefore that the decision to marry should only be made between two consenting individuals who had taken the time to consider their vocation within marriage and their equal, but different, responsibilities to one another and their families.

A Mass Observation study on 'The state of matrimony', undertaken in 1947 suggested that men and women, when questioned, imagined their roles broadly along these lines. Statistics taken from a survey of married women in London and Gloucester, and an additional smaller survey of urban areas, indicated the majority specified 'largely utilitarian and partly characterological' qualities in a partner. Men desired 'a home-loving wife and a good housekeeper' and women wanted 'well-defined character and personality'; men who were able to give wives 'comfort and security' and who were 'considerate, thoughtful and loving'.[53] Single people were also questioned about the perceived advantages of marriage and they were listed in rough order of precedence as: children; a home of one's own; companionship; and security.[54]

Mary Macaulay produced advice to young people during the 1950s and published the first edition of *The Art of Marriage* in 1952. In his foreword, Dr Herbert Gray endorsed Macaulay unconditionally and reassured readers that, 'as an experienced medical practitioner [she] writes with authority [and] is blessed with much sound common sense'.[55] Macaulay, who worked as a medical officer for the Family Planning Association and as a marriage guidance counsellor, warned that the young should have some idea of what they are going to require of their life's companion long before the time comes for them to make their choice. 'Deliberate thought about the future' she argued, 'is a point on which not enough emphasis is laid.[56] Her book fostered a warm and loving view of marriage and sexual relations, but has been widely misquoted. Wilson for example, has accused Macaulay of condoning the rape of a wife by her husband.[57] However, to the contrary, she was vehemently critical of unwelcome sexual advances by husbands, stating that intercourse, if the wife was an unwilling partner, was 'a desecration of marriage' and was 'dangerous to the whole future of the relationship'.[58]

In this and other contemporary texts on sexual problems within marriage, a level of support and understanding for women is evident that has been previously underemphasized. A NMGC publication in 1958, for example, although entitled *Sex Difficulties in the Wife*, suggested that one of the most important causes of sexual difficulty in marriage was 'the man's technique'. It stated that 'a man is something more than an animal, and if he acts like one in relation to his wife, then he must expect failure ... many a man who has complained his wife is cold to him has no-one but himself to blame'.[59] This handbook recommended that a lack of interest on the part of the wife may be a result of tiredness, illness or fear – or a lack of understanding by the husband. Readers were reminded that 'women need an atmosphere of complete harmony; grudge or resentment will make them hold back'.[60]

Literature published during the 1950s and 1960s was circulated with the desired aim of fostering healthy marriages in order that the divorce rate would decline. It embodied a notion of equality which arose as a result of contemporary anxieties about marriage and the family. These anxieties, in turn, originated from emerging views about sexuality and from the trauma and social dislocation of war. This view of equality rested upon a traditional division of labour that was seen to be beneficial not just to individual families but to society as a whole.

Mothering in Post-War Britain

As with marriage, post-war women entered into motherhood with a set of values and beliefs about 'mothering'. These were based on the assumption that, since women were biologically equipped for pregnancy, they would also be best suited to the care of a child. More recent histories have shown how our notions of motherhood and fatherhood are socially determined. John Gillis has argued that although the biology of conception, pregnancy and birth might be universal, 'maternity has no predetermined relationship to motherhood, and paternity no fixed relationship to fatherhood. Both vary enormously across cultures and over time.'[61] He has shown how, in pre-modern times, giving birth and giving nurture were often incompatible for demographic and economic reasons, as well as cultural ones. High rates of fertility and maternal mortality ensured that it was not always possible for all women who gave birth to 'mother' their children.[62] It was thus possible to imagine 'motherless' families. The absence of a patriarch in fact endangered families and, prior to the nineteenth century, custody of children following divorce or separation was invariably assigned to the father.[63] Ann Oakley has also shown that, today, other small-scale societies consider that 'the business of bearing and rearing of children belongs to a mother and a father equally ... the verb "to bear a child" is used indiscriminately of either a man or a woman'.[64] However, we do not necessarily gain a more accurate picture of the past by applying these more recent insights to our analysis.

The decades following the war bore witness to an increasing attention directed toward mother-love, mother-infant attachment and constant mother-care.[65] Ann Dally asserted that this notion of 'idealization' was based on illusion,

38 *Desperate Housewives, Neuroses and the Domestic Environment, 1945–1970*

and that the deliberate motive was to make mothers content with their lot in order that they could be controlled and, when necessary denigrated.[66] She went on to argue that:

> At the end of the war, the men came back. They wanted the jobs and they wanted wives to look after them at home. Many people felt that women needed controlling, if homes were going to be run and men served in the style to which they were long accustomed. Women had to be put in their place'.[67]

The reasons why attention came to be focused so entirely on the mother-child bond during this period are complex and Dally's interpretation underplays the impact of broad social changes that had been underway for over 100 years. Most importantly, this perspective assumes that a whole generation of mothers accepted the idealization of motherhood without question, simply because they were convinced by contemporary theorists and government propaganda. It therefore excludes the possibility that, following the horrors of war, many women may have gladly embraced the responsibility for 'mothering' and viewed it not only as important but also as desirable. Indeed, Richard Easterlin observed that families of the 1950s consisted of men and women who had grown up during the economic depression of the 1930s and experienced the dislocations of war. Such people were so touched by the effects of economic deprivation that when they married they felt stronger commitments to marriage and the family. Many of them, he argued, 'must have despaired of ever marrying, so that they regarded their eventual marriages as an acquisition not to be squandered or easily tossed aside'.[68]

As with marriage, the background to the beliefs and ideals of this period can be traced to industrial times. Symbolically, motherhood and fatherhood have switched places. Before the nineteenth century, thoughts of home conjured up father figures.[69] Slowly, over a period of 200 years, western European views of children and child-rearing began to change. Gradually, childhood came to be understood as a special and valuable period of life.[70] During the industrial period, unprecedented changes affected the form of family life and the new gendered division of labour effectively terminated the notion of the 'domesticated' male.[71] In addition to this, the nineteenth-century Factory Acts limited the hours of work outside the home for women and children. As Helen Jones notes, 'that women and children were lumped together in one category says much about the way women were viewed as indistinguishable from children'.[72] During the late nineteenth and early twentieth centuries, however, anxieties about the future health of the nation resulted in growing concern about maternal care. 'Healthy mothers produced healthy babies, so state and local agencies and activists invested in mother and baby welfare'.[73] As improvements in maternal health advanced with the discovery of sulpha drugs in the 1930s and antibiotics from the 1940s, the maternal mortality rate decreased. Mothers became more likely to survive and raise their own children and, as a result, the role increasingly became the object of idealization.[74] Furthermore, as antenatal care became increasingly medicalized, fathers became less involved with pregnancy. Due to the steady rise in hospital confinements from the 1950s, the father's role during birth was increasingly marginalized by medical routines.[75]

Thus, during the course of the twentieth century, a major cultural revolution took place. Child-raising came unhinged from any external goals, and, in this increasingly self-enclosed world of the nursery, the 'expert' loomed large.[76] There is now an expansive body of literature on the topic of advice to mothers from Hippocrates to the late twentieth century.[77] However, within the context of the post-war period, three experts in particular, John Bowlby (1907–90), Donald Winnicott (1896–1971) and Benjamin Spock (1903–98), deserve further attention here. At the end of the Second World War, Bowlby was commissioned by the World Health Organization to study the mental health of war orphans, children who had been hospitalized for long periods of time and children who had experienced evacuation. These children were often found to be emotionally withdrawn or autistic and frequently suffered from insomnia, lack of appetite and weight loss.[78] His most influential conclusion was that mother-love in infancy was of paramount importance to the mental health of a child: 'anxieties arising from unsatisfactory relationships in early childhood predispose the children to respond in an antisocial way to later stresses'.[79] His recommendations were primarily intended to bring about a reassessment of the methods used in caring for homeless children. However, Ehrenreich and English claim that Bowlby 'nimbly leaped beyond his database to the child *in* the home' and that he implied that maternal deprivation could occur wherever there was less than single-handed, full-time provision of maternal attention.[80] His theories fitted well with the views of some child-psychoanalysts in the United States who were concerned about children orphaned during the war,[81] and in Britain, it has commonly been asserted that Bowlby's views were influential in the closing of state nurseries following the Second World War. He has broadly been accused of influencing a whole generation of mothers to provide continuous twenty-four hour care of their children or otherwise risk the deleterious consequences of them developing delinquent personalities. Indeed, in one oral history account a woman claimed that she 'scanned through Bowlby to see if it was alright to go out for half an hour and certainly, below the age of three, you were not really meant to leave your child at all'.[82]

However, it remains open for debate whether or not the theory of maternal deprivation was developed and utilized, as feminist critics claim, deliberately to segregate and oppress women.[83] Denise Riley has shown, for example, that the reasons for the withdrawal of nursery provision following the war were complex and that the powerful rhetoric of the 'sanctity' of family life, in fact appeared to resonate with many of the desires held by ordinary women.[84] Bowlby himself argued that that the rationale behind his theories was indeed concern for the health and well-being of a generation of children who had experienced the social upheaval of war. He observed that while wartime reports told of disturbances in character resulting from war itself, they also showed 'the fundamental part played on their causation by rupture of the family'.[85] His interest in the mother-child bond was possibly also framed by his own distant relationship with his mother and his experiences during childhood – most of which was spent with a nanny. His principles also originated from concern about the treatment of hospitalized children. Alongside a colleague James Robertson, Bowlby observed two- and three-year-old children during a stay in hospital or nursery where there was no 'mother substitute'. Bowlby recalled that Robertson had been deeply impressed by the intensity of the distress and misery he was witness to while the children were away from home: 'no-one reading his reports, or viewing the film record he had made of one little girl, could be left unmoved'.[86]

Bowlby's theories were, above all, a reaction against a devaluation of family life and he argued for a greater appreciation of motherhood by society. Historians have paid little attention to the ways in which he in fact supported the family by, for example, recommending economic aid to mothers and by endorsing the provision of services for the care of parent's physical health.[87] In addition, he recommended the expansion of marriage guidance facilities in order to gain 'an understanding of why marriages fail'. Marital problems, he contended, were largely due to unresolved childhood problems: 'Personality difficulties stemming from childhood must be counted as the most frequent and weighty factors in marital maladjustment'.[88] Bowlby also emphasized the role of fathers and asserted that they were of equal importance because they were required to provide for their wives and families, in order that mothers could devote themselves to the care of children. Fathers were also required to support their wives emotionally.[89]

Bowlby's theory of maternal deprivation has now been discredited and was widely criticized, not only by feminist commentators who saw it as oppressive to women but also more recently by fathers' groups who argue that the concept of 'maternal deprivation' undermines the importance of 'fathering'. The organization 'Even Toddlers Need Fathers', for example, argues that his theories have had serious consequences for men following divorce where, under the British legal framework, residency and contact arrangements broadly favour the mother.[90] Bowlby's work has also been criticized in intellectual circles, most notably by Sir Michael Rutter who argued that although he had been correct in suggesting that early life experiences had lasting effects on child-development, a much broader range of factors such as discord and disharmony in the home, should be considered alongside the notion of 'separation'.[91] He also called for greater attention to the bond between father and child.[92]

These are valid criticisms. However, during the 1960s, when Bowlby was writing, the practical arrangements of marriage and parenting made it difficult for fathers to develop close attachments to their children since the prescriptive demands of their role resulted in long hours at work providing for the family. Bowlby also acknowledged in his work that it was possible for any individual to nurture attachment to a baby or small child. He stated clearly that 'The role of a child's principal attachment figure can be filled by others than the natural mother ... Provided a mother-substitute behaves in a mothering way toward a child, he will treat her as another child would treat his natural mother'.[93] Assessed within the post-war context, Bowlby's motives, however misguided, were perhaps not driven primarily by a desire to confine women to the home but instead by a genuine concern for the mental health of children. The oral testimonies presented in Chapter 3 will question the degree to which mothers were influenced directly by such theories. Only one woman interviewed had any knowledge of Bowlby, and this was gained during professional teacher-training in later life. Indeed, most women claimed to have used their common sense in child-raising issues, and the majority were not afraid to question expert advice when necessary. However, it is possible that these women were not aware of any direct, explicit use of such theories but that they were influenced indirectly by the pervasive way in which subtle messages were conveyed through television, radio and popular culture.

Bowlby's view, that 'anatomy was destiny', was reflected in the work of many contemporary theorists. Implicit in his view was the 'naturalness' of an exclusive mother-child relationship.[94] He combined ethological and psychoanalytical theories, but differed from Freud in that there was no mention in his work of essential 'drives'. Instead, Bowlby emphasized experience over fantasy and believed that:

> Attachment behaviour is regarded as what occurs when certain behavioural systems are activated. The behavioural systems themselves are believed to develop within the infant as a result of his interaction with his environment ... especially of his interaction with the principle figure in that environment; namely, his mother.[95]

For Bowlby, the corollary of this was that whenever a young child who has had the opportunity to develop an attachment to a mother figure was separated from her unwillingly, it would show distress. The sequence would typically be one of 'protest, despair and then emotional detachment'.[96]

The notion that mothers were the best people to care for and nurture young children is explicit in much contemporary literature. In contrast, men were seen as best placed in the work environment where they could provide for their families. There is little evidence to suggest that women believed the idealization of motherhood was contrived as a deliberate plan to limit their opportunities to those related to the home. On the contrary, many of the women interviewed for this project articulated their concerns about twenty-first century women, who, due to their financial commitments, have no choice but to work outside the home and are no longer afforded the luxury of remaining in the domestic role full-time. During the 1950s and 1960s there was no research available to suggest that alternative family forms would produce well-balanced individuals. As even Lewis acknowledges, when social and political commentators of the period were writing, 'there were few thorough criticisms of John Bowlby's ideas about the perils of maternal deprivation to draw on'.[97]

Another paediatrician and psychoanalyst who focused on the mother-infant dyad was Donald Winnicott. Winnicott, like Bowlby, also maintained that the individual's interpretation of its relationship with its mother and family members became the basis for later relations with others. He is renowned for his research into 'transitional objects' – the familiar inanimate objects (security blankets) that children use to stave off anxiety during times of stress. Winnicott worked for forty years at Paddington Green Children's Hospital, and his experience with children informed his theories. His stated aim was to educate parents, particularly mothers, 'to provide the environment that is appropriate to the age of the infant, toddler or child'.[98]

Once again, the reoccurring theme in Winnicott's work was the importance of familial stability to both the small child and to wider society. He asserted that 'the family is an essential part of our civilisation [and is] something that deserves our detailed study'.[99] Between 1940 and 1950 Winnicott gave a series of radio broadcasts on the theory and practice of childcare, within which both the practical and emotional aspects of childcare were explored. However, it was not just the responsibilities of the mother that were highlighted. Winnicott argued that:

> Fathers come into this too, not only by the fact that they can be good 'mothers' for limited periods of time, but because they can help protect the mother and the baby from whatever tends to interfere with the bond between them ... the father is needed at home to help mother to feel well in her body and happy in her mind. A child is very sensitive to the relationship between the parents ... I suppose this is what an infant or a child would mean by 'social security'.[100]

Speaking directly to mothers, Winnicott reassured them that their job was worthwhile and urged that society found appreciation for the 'ordinary good mother'.[101] In his postscript to the published papers from the broadcasts he reiterated the importance of parenting to wider society:

> In the last half century, there has been a great increase in awareness of the value of the home. We know something of the reasons why this long and exacting task, the parent's job of seeing their children through, is a job worth doing; and in fact we believe that it provides the only real basis for society ... If this contribution is accepted, it follows that every man or woman who is sane; every man or woman who feels to be a person in the world; and for whom the world means something; every happy person, is in infinite debt to a woman.[102]

Thus, women could be assured that their contribution to society was fundamental to the task of 'reconstructing' post-war Britain.

The theory of instinctive mother love signalled a decisive shift in thinking from interwar behaviourist theories such as those promoted by Frederick Truby King. The orderly and regimented approach of the behaviourists had fitted well during difficult periods of depression and wartime when children were seen as 'raw material' to be hammered into shape. Their natural impulses for play and food were viewed as something to be suppressed, and pre-war advice had been to administer a strict four-hourly feeding schedule and give minimal fuss or attention in between.[103] In contrast, following the war, there was an increased awareness of the emotional sensitivities of children. The child's spontaneous impulses were now understood as good and sensible; 'the child actually knew, in some sense, what was right for itself'.[104] It was within this context that Dr Benjamin Spock published his first edition of the *Common Sense Book of Baby and Child Care* in the United States in 1946. During his year in paediatric residency, 1931–2, Spock conceived the idea that a doctor specializing in paediatrics would benefit from psychological training. This appeared revolutionary at the time, although Spock felt that it was a common-sense approach that would enable doctors to offer the appropriate advice on issues such as thumb-sucking, toilet training, fears and sibling rivalry.[105] Spock was concerned about the lack of understanding within medicine about such issues and felt that the advice given to parents was unsatisfactory. He recalled, for example, that: 'Paediatricians just used traditional answers like the one for thumb-sucking: "it's a bad habit". You try to break the habit by painting nasty stuff on the baby's thumbs ... I knew these things were wrong, but I didn't know what was right.'[106]

Spock eventually combined Freud's psychoanalytical theories with his own knowledge of physical and psychological child development. His recommendations also centred on the importance of maternal affection, while allowing the child ample room to express its wants and needs.[107] The naturalness of mothering was certainly made explicit in the opening words to his manual which read: 'Trust yourself. You know more than you think you do ... bringing up your child won't be a complicated job if you take it easy [and] trust your own instincts'.[108] By the third edition printed in Britain in 1973, Spock was still guarded in relation to advice on working mothers. He acknowledged that 'some mothers have to work [and] usually their children turn out all right, because some reasonably good arrangement is made for their care. But others grow up neglected and maladjusted'.[109] He further admitted that some mothers with a professional training may wish to work 'because they wouldn't be happy otherwise'. In these circumstances, Spock claimed that he 'wouldn't disagree if the mother felt strongly about it'. However, he reaffirmed that:

> You can think of it this way: useful, well-adjusted citizens are the most valuable possessions a country has, and good mother-care during early childhood is the surest way to produce them ... The younger the child, the more necessary it is for him to have a steady, loving person taking care of him. In most cases, the mother is the best one to give him this feeling of belonging.[110]

Spock was hugely influential. Hays notes that in America his manual sold twenty-two million copies between 1946 and 1973; one for almost every first-born child.[111] He undoubtedly had a sizeable impact in Britain also. However, as the following chapter will illustrate, among the middle-class readership there appeared to be a split between two extremes; while one half declared that his advice could be relied upon; the other half was reluctant to accept professional advice at all.

Like Bowlby, Spock has also been criticized for urging women to remain in the traditional, maternal role. Furthermore, critics have argued that he fostered a generation of undisciplined children. As Sharon Hays has noted, twenty years after his book was first published, Spock was widely charged with responsibility for the moral failure of the generation then coming of age. His recommendation of 'maternal indulgence', many suggested, had resulted in a generation of spoiled, hedonistic children.[112] However, Spock's theories were initially cultivated by a disapproval of medical education and the manner in which it was 'dedicated exclusively to the laboratory sciences'. Spock was concerned that this approach 'encouraged students to forget that their future patients were human beings', thereby making them 'impersonal'.[113] He claimed that he differed from other paediatricians because it was the ordinary, everyday problems that he considered to be the problems of greatest interest.[114]

The theories of Bowlby and Spock must be viewed within the post-war political context and as a product of their time. During 1946, the British government began to regard communism and the Soviet Union as an increasing threat to world peace. In 1947, these worries led the Labour government into the decision that Britain should develop its own atomic bomb.[115] In reality, until the atomic bomb became available, Britain remained entirely dependent on America where the threat of communism loomed even larger. The communist ethos, as portrayed by the press, represented everything that Americans were against. Religion had been abolished; all life centred on production, and, perhaps worst of all, 'the sanctity of family life had been violated. Muscular women swept the streets while their children were raised by the state.'[116] Indeed, in his book *Masters of Deceit*, published in 1958, J. Edgar Hoover, described communism as a threat to 'the happiness of the community, the safety of every individual, and the continuance of every home and fireside'.[117] Spock claims that he did not vehemently endorse or oppose communism. However, he was critical of the resulting American hysteria about communism; and during the late 1950s he became involved with the National Committee for a Sane Nuclear Policy (SANE).[118] He campaigned publicly for a test-ban treaty and disarmament, primarily because of his concern that the development of nuclear weapons might lead to children, not only in America, but around the world, dying of cancer and leukaemia – or being born with mental and physical defects from fall-out radiation. He saw it as 'a paediatric issue'.[119] Spock agreed to advertise for SANE in national newspapers and posed for a photograph in an emotive picture of him looking down anxiously at a trusting one-year old. The caption read 'Dr Spock is worried', and it went on to decry nuclear arms testing for fear of its irresponsible effects on the next generation.[120] Indeed, the oral testimonies in the subsequent chapter at times reflect these wider tensions and illustrate how some women feared for the safety of their families and the future of their children.

Other influential writers on marriage and the family strongly echoed the theories of instinctual mothering and its importance for the well-being of the child. Writing in 1967, Douglas Hooper and John Roberts, two lecturers in mental health from the University of Bristol, undertook an investigation into the causes of subnormal, delinquent behaviour. They argued that the family had become increasingly important as civilization had become more industrialized and specialized.[121] Hooper, a highly respected clinical psychologist and counsellor, worked with the NMGC for several decades and was eventually elected vice-president in 1997. His lifelong interest in family dynamics was central to both his personal and professional life; by the time of his death he and his wife had celebrated their diamond wedding anniversary.[122] Together with Roberts, he argued that the social and cultural pressures of the mid-twentieth century had intensified the degree of importance with which society has invested in the family group. They asserted that 'the interaction between family and the infant, more particularly between mother and infant, is the area in which disorders occur' and that the absence of a parent, or a prolonged stay in hospital 'can have drastic effects on the way in which the family functions'.[123] Printed advice in marriage handbooks also laid great emphasis on the biologically determined bond between mother and child. Bovet, writing in 1958, described the relationship as 'primordial unity; bound together like the trunk and limbs of a body ... the bond can never be close enough'.[124] He attempted to explain this difference in biological term, proposing that:

> One of woman's chief tasks is to bear and rear children. To enable this, she has a natural relationship with everything that has life or soul ... man on the other hand, whose vocation is to protect and feed the family, has a special relationship with inanimate objects which he can take to pieces and put together again ... this ability is at the bottom of that typically male thing 'logic'. Women possess an instinctive certainty to a large extent lacking in men.[125]

Bovet stressed the degree to which both parents were responsible in different ways for the success or failure of their children as future individuals. He proposed that 'a child that has enjoyed a harmonious and peaceful home life, full of a sense of its mother's love, can never be defenceless in the face of evil ... it has, once and for all been given a sense of security'.[126] Hugh Lyon, writing for the NMGC, also contended that young children needed love and security and a home without nagging, bitterness or open hostility between parents, which, he argued 'strikes a deadly blow at a child's instincts of loyalty and destroys her security'.[127] Angela Reed, also writing on behalf of the NMGC in 1963, concurred, reminding newly married couples that 'however high or low your ideals are, whatever your views – you will influence your children'.[128]

It is notable that much of this advice came from women themselves. With particular reference to the topic of work outside the home, women writers usually expressed concern in relation to possible negative effects upon the family. Reed openly admitted that the domestic role could be frustrating and monotonous and noted that it was becoming more acceptable for a wife to undertake paid work. However, she reminded her readers that 'the whole question will crop up again when a baby is born'. Doubtful about the advantages of day nurseries, her preferred option was for women to undertake voluntary activities. Her recommendations included the Women's Voluntary Service, the Citizens Advice Bureau and the Towns' Women's Guild.[129] According to Reed:

> Home should be the centre of a mother's world, but not its boundary. [You must] be ready to take advantage of the activities that are going on around to make your life full and interesting ... it means deciding what kind of life you aim to lead, and then accepting the consequences of that decision without looking back over your shoulder at what might have been.[130]

She also warned that a mother may experience negative effects from paid employment, since she may worry unduly about the arrangements put in place for her child and may feel cheated of the rewards of being a mother. To Reed, these emotions were highly likely, since she maintained that 'we receive satisfaction from any human relationship, only in return for what we give to it, and children usually grow to love the person who looks after them'.[131] Mary MacAulay was even more emphatic and warned her readers that 'There is no career which is of equal importance with that of bearing and rearing children ... a woman who considers the care of her home and family an inferior task and feels her children are a bother or a distraction cannot make a success of it'.[132]

Conclusion

Gillis may well be correct in suggesting that our construction of motherhood is a reflection of our need to find, through symbol and ritual, a sense of nurture and protection that mothers themselves can never fully provide.[133] It may also be the case that, while various periods in history have been gripped by anxiety about family life, perhaps no one family form has ever been able to satisfy the human need for love, comfort and security.[134] Post-war theories of mother love and the importance of maternal supervision undoubtedly bolstered the traditional domestic role for women. However, it is important to remember that these ideals were fostered during uncertain times, following a world conflict that had involved unprecedented suffering and hardship on the part of the civilian population. As a result, renewed significance was assigned to notions of 'the family'.

Constructions of roles relating to marriage and parenting have been interpreted as a deliberate conspiracy to ensure women remained in an unpaid, dependent role. From this perspective, motherhood has been 'used by the state for political purposes', and mothers have had to 'bear the burden, not only as child-rearers but also as scapegoats'.[135] However, it is at least possible that the prevailing domestic ideology was, in part, a collective attempt (among women as well as men) to build a new beginning in all areas of life. Indeed, male writers often emphasized 'equality' of the sexes, and female authors usually supported the notion that men and women were 'equal but different'. Substantial pressure was also placed upon men to fulfil their roles with responsibility and commitment. This was often explicit in the literature and is exemplified in the writing of Hooper and Roberts:

> Although [we] rightly emphasize the very important role that the mother plays in the development of the infant, this in turn is dependent on that of the father. Thus, we can say that the family as a whole relies on the continuing and efficient function of the father ... his relationship with the mother and his ability to provide for the material aspects of the home are essential for the child's well-being.[136]

Published literature from the post-war period therefore indicates that there was a certain acceptance that 'individuals should develop a sense of social solidarity ... and a willingness to sacrifice private interests for the larger welfare of society as a whole'.[137]

The following chapter will analyse the experiences of housewives and mothers interviewed for this project. It will propose that, while not always easy, the domestic role was one that women valued, largely in accordance with the beliefs and ideals of post-war theorists.

3 THE HOUSEWIFE'S DAY: PERSONAL ACCOUNTS OF HOUSEWIFERY AND MOTHERING

> Running a home may seem unspectacular and ordinary, but making a success of it, so
> that the home is a happy one for all who live in it, is creative work to rank with the best.
> Kay Smallshaw, *How to Run your Home without Help* (1949)

Since the 1970s, historians have written widely about the tensions women have experienced between homemaking and employment. The origins of this area of debate can be traced to the controversy surrounding the conscription of women workers during wartime. Historical debate has been based largely on the acceptance or rejection of the thesis that 'war promoted social change for women', an area explored in depth by scholars including Penny Summerfield, Denise Riley, Arthur Marwick and Viola Klein.[1] Marwick and Klein, along with Richard Titmuss, collectively viewed the war as important in giving women greater self-confidence and a more public, visible role. Commentators of the 1950s and 1960s made an 'essentialist' identification with women and their socio-biological functions as wives, mothers and homemakers, and conceptualized change from within this category.[2] Thus, it was argued that their status was raised from within the existing separate spheres. However, since the 1970s, scholars have claimed that the notion that women were more naturally suited to mothering and homemaking continued to reinforce the practices of undervaluation and discrimination.[3] The criteria used to measure progress in equality have been dominated by job opportunities, equal pay and political power – largely in terms of women becoming more like men. However, in 1986, Harold Smith claimed that many women viewed wartime changes as undesirable. Drawing attention to the unpleasant and life-threatening experiences that many people experienced during the war, Smith was critical of academic studies that focused on women and work, which, in his view, encouraged 'a distorted view of war's effect by neglecting the largest category of females – housewives'.[4] He went on to consider the ways in which 'greater independence' was also accompanied by 'greater stress and anxiety, separation from loved ones and loss and damage to homes'.[5]

Summerfield has more recently undertaken an extensive oral history project among women with wartime experience. In her analysis she acknowledges that previous histories have been overly simplified. She argues that the polarity of opinion within the debate exists because academics on both fronts have been guilty of ignoring evidence, or denying readings that might suggest a more ambiguous and contingent picture of women's desires and preferences.[6] Summerfield now employs a new theoretical approach in which she examines the discourses available to women in reconstructing their lives. This has resulted in an appraisal that more accurately reflects the diversity of experience among women.

In their earlier work on women in the Second World War, both Summerfield and Riley made extensive use of Mass Observation surveys and Wartime Social Surveys. The original post-war researchers had asserted that the majority of women wanted marriage and domesticity rather than paid work after the war. However, Summerfield claimed that there were inconsistencies between the survey's own data and the conclusions drawn.[7] She argued instead that 'the women surveyed either definitely wanted to carry on in full or part-time paid work or felt that their decisions would depend on a number of other factors'.[8] When women expressed a clear wish to return to domestic life, Riley even questioned their ability to reveal what they really wanted, and she urged that 'post war journalists and sociologists tended to accept the wishes attributed to women to return home as true – and to confirm or lament this wish, but not to scrutinize the original attribution'.[9]

Summerfield now warns against generalizing about women's subjective responses. However, it is not clear whether or not she now rejects the conclusions drawn from her early work on Mass Observation material. Certainly, the contentious notion of 'false consciousness' is still central to many feminist analyses. Speaking in 2002 on the topic of discrimination, Ann Oakley, for example, questioned women's ability to evaluate their own experiences, claiming that 'the beholder's eye is often only half-open; acceptance of inferiority comes as part of the package, and there may be very little point in recognizing subjugation when there are few chances of escape'.[10] In Coontz's recent appraisal of *The Feminine Mystique*, she too suggests that women who wrote to Friedan expressing their disapproval of her book were unwittingly confirming the strength of the 'mystique'.[11] The danger with this approach is that it has been used to devalue the choices made by others. It also assumes a straightforward power relationship between oppressor and oppressed, when, in fact, 'the story of power is not a simple story'.[12] Judy Giles has recently offered a more productive way forward in which she fosters a wider understanding of home 'that neither pathologizes nor pities the millions of women for whom domesticity is a primary concern and an actively created space'.[13]

Although a number of important surveys of family life were undertaken during the post-war period in Britain, they tell us very little about how middle-class women felt about their role as housewives and mothers. Peter Willmott and Michael Young undertook the now well-known study *Family and Kinship in East London* in 1957 which gave illuminating insights into the effects of new housing estates on communities. However, the study focused upon the working class and was concerned primarily with the effects of new housing estates on extended family networks. It broadly concluded that kinship networks were surprisingly resilient, despite the considerable upheaval placed upon families moving from inner-city communities to new housing estates. Although some young married wives felt isolated by the lack of public spaces and the distance between them and their wider kin, many were content with their spacious, modern houses.[14] Undertaken some years earlier, Robert and Helen Lynd's *Middletown: A Study in American Culture* (1929) also examined patterns of family life in Muncie, Indiana, which they described as a 'typical' American city. Their overarching theme was class, and they focused upon the impact of industrialization on values and personalities; in particular the social divisions between working and business classes. Despite rapid industrial change, the Lynds' conclusion in this study, and in *Middletown in Transition*, published in 1937, was that much continuity could be found in family life. Although family sizes were smaller and divorce was more common, most people lived in a traditional family unit. For men, the primary concern was to provide for the family and the responsibility for looking after the children rested with women. By and large, women approved of this arrangement.[15]

The two oral history studies of women in the twentieth century undertaken by Elizabeth Roberts also focused upon working-class women.[16] Nevertheless, it is interesting that Roberts acknowledged that her work could not be classed as feminist, since her view was that women's hardship was caused by poverty, not patriarchy. In a response to a review of the first of these books, she noted that 'the respondents I was fortunate enough to interview were survivors and had been forged in the fire of very hard lives. They did not regard themselves as victims and I could not patronize them by promulgating this view'.[17] Young and Willmott's later work, *Family and Class in a London Suburb* (1960) is more useful, since its focus was upon middle-class families in the London suburb of Woodford. However, their attention focused less upon the feelings of wives and mothers, and more upon the blurring of class boundaries and the consequent effects on mother/daughter relationships, aging parents and friendship networks. It is nonetheless valuable for its discussion of the division of labour within the home and for its analysis of the trend towards home-ownership. In their studies of both working-class and middle-class families, Young and Willmott concluded that the home was increasingly becoming a more comfortable and inviting place to be. It was thus becoming the 'focus' of family life.[18] The oral histories in this chapter are set within this context and suggest that not all women viewed their role in a negative light. Many negotiated a role for themselves that brought them respect and satisfaction. A significant number of women also proposed that men were the ones to be disadvantaged by their role, since conforming to the acceptable stereotype of 'the breadwinner' resulted in them missing out on a great deal of family life. Additionally, they experienced the considerable pressures of supporting a family financially.

In the oral testimonies that follow, women were questioned at length on all aspects of their domestic lives and their responses are organized around a number of key themes: education and aspirations, practical management of the home and mothering. They were also questioned about the levels of satisfaction/ dissatisfaction associated individually with paid employment, childcare and housework in addition to a general assessment of their role. The intention was to establish to what extent satisfaction with life in general was connected with the acceptance or rejection of domesticity. The findings are considered alongside material from social surveys on women's attitudes towards work and home and articles and letters published in the popular press.

Education

In 1944, the Butler Education Act raised the school leaving age to fifteen and created the Ministry of Education. The new tripartite system consisted of grammar schools, secondary technical schools and secondary modern schools. At the centre of the new education policy was the concept of 'equal opportunity'. For the first time, all students, regardless of their background, were given the opportunity to sit an exam at the age of ten/eleven which would determine their academic ability. Those that passed the new Eleven Plus exam were entitled to a grammar school education. Fee-paying grammar schools were also abolished in an attempt to free places for intelligent children of poorer means.[19] In reality, it is far from clear that the ideals underpinning these policies brought about 'equality of opportunity'. Michael Sanderson has pointed out that the tripartite system was far from 'balanced' – 56 per cent of schools were allocated secondary modern status, whereas only 15 per cent became designated grammar schools, and only 7 per cent became technical schools.[20] Seventy-five per cent of pupils failed the Eleven Plus exam and ended up in 'residual' schools; the assumption was thus that three-quarters of children were already academic failures by the age of eleven.[21] Nevertheless, many children from working-class backgrounds were able to take advantage of an education previously denied them. This opportunity was a common feature among respondents in this cohort of interviewees. Jean Hill, for example, was born into a working-class family in Middlesex and felt that, as a child, the label of 'middle-class' was 'way above her economically and socially'. She described herself as 'of the generation of the Butler Education Act', and went to grammar school in 1944. 'I, in the eyes of other people around me,

The Housewife's Day 53

took a step up because I went to grammar school ... it was a great achievement to get into grammar school'.[22]

Attendance at grammar school often brought its own problems for working-class families who could often ill-afford the cost of school uniforms and additional items. Kath Greenham, like Jean Hill, was the only one in her family to excel academically. Born in 1927 in Stoke on Trent, Kath remembered helping her father deliver vegetables from his grocer's cart after school. She described feeling uncomfortable about the obvious material differences that existed between her and other pupils from school:

> I went to high-school, and I felt that if the girls from high-school, who'd got houses with bay windows – I think I was a bit of a snob really – because I used to think they'd look down on me if they saw me sitting on a cart ... I got a grant because we couldn't afford really – I had to wear my uniform as my Sunday best. My school shoes had to do for Sunday.[23]

Young and Willmott also noted in their study of working-class families, that grammar schools were often divisive because children were removed from familiar peer groups and lost contact with old friends. Older relatives also often objected, describing it as 'not right'.[24]

For girls, it appeared as though a grammar school education was viewed primarily as a sign of status for the family and not in terms of providing a career opportunity. Jean recalled that 'the impression I got was by me going to grammar school, gave our family status ... they wanted me to do well but that's what it gave them'. She went on to say, 'Didn't even think about going to university. Didn't even enter the question'.[25] This sentiment was expressed by the majority of respondents and was reflected in the testimony of Christine Calderwood who was born in 1937 and eventually became a nurse. She agreed that university was not considered an option.

> There was absolutely no expectation that girls would go to university. I was in the top stream at grammar school ... and that was supposedly the top people. But no one, at any time, ever suggested that I would be able to go to university. And there were three careers which you could do: secretarial, nursing or teaching.[26]

Gwen Collins was born into a middle-class family in Cardiff in 1919. She entered the secondary phase of education as 'a scholarship girl', prior to the Butler Education Act of 1944. She later passed the 'open clerical' exam and joined the civil service at seventeen. Gwen remembered her parents' values had been formulated during the unemployment of the 1930s and this strongly influenced her father's views on the importance of education:

> He was very keen on education, although we were a very large family, there were six of us, there was no question that the girls shouldn't have exactly the same education

54   *Desperate Housewives, Neuroses and the Domestic Environment, 1945–1970*

> as the boys ... but, there wasn't an expectation to go to university. I remember a girl at
> school getting a scholarship to Cambridge and we had a half-day holiday because that
> was really unusual. It just seemed to be the sort of thing, when I was young, to go into
> the civil service, because there was such a lot of unemployment wasn't there – before
> our time, and there was a necessity to get a job.[27]

That British women were rarely afforded the opportunity to go to university seemed unremarkable to them. These women, many of whom were evaluating their experiences as graduates of degrees gained in later life, did not see their young adult lives in terms of a 'missed opportunity', but on the contrary as 'normal' viewed within the expectations of that time. Most viewed a grammar school education as a route into an 'acceptable' occupation and as a foundation for future family life. In addition to this, many noted that their experience proved invaluable in later years when guiding their own children through the education system. Ann Shepherd, for example, another respondent from a working-class background who gained a place at grammar school, remembered that her mother emphasized the importance of educating girls: 'she thought that a girl being educated was not a waste of time, because, she said, if a woman is educated, you educate the children'.[28] Gwen Collins recalled how, as a result of her schooling, she went on to place great importance on her children's education: 'And I was very thankful that I'd had the education that I'd had – that I was able to work with Latin problems and that sort of thing. I think that is very important.'[29]

Certainly, these women were drawing on post-war discourse in which domesticity featured prominently in the life plan. However, in many cases, responses simply revealed a common-sense, pragmatic approach, in which life choices were simply guided by circumstances. This was particularly so for those women whose education was disrupted by the Second World War. Eileen Roberts, for example, grew up in Lewisham in London and missed out on much of her secondary education:

> I didn't go into secondary school until I was thirteen because everybody was evacuated ... from the time that the war started, we used to do half day in the morning on the radio, and then in the afternoon you took it in and they marked it. But you didn't go to school for two years ... when I was thirteen, the Germans came across and dropped bombs and machined the children in the playground. Forty children and eight teachers died. My best friend was buried for three days. It was a traumatic experience. It was terrible.[30]

Eileen's evaluation of her life was thus framed by the experience of trauma and loss. It is perhaps understandable that her high regard for family life in later years was inspired by a sense of appreciation for having survived the war when many others close to her had not. As Judy Giles has argued, for such women, 'physical existence is fragile and precarious ... modernity for them signified cleanliness, health and belonging, and was made materially manifest in clean bodies and clothes, fit, healthy children, the ability to purchase domestic commodities, and a comfortable house in the suburbs'.[31]

Only three of the respondents obtained a university degree. Two were born and educated in the United States and later migrated to England. Girls were much more likely to gain a college degree in the United States, and, although they were unknown to each other, their experiences were strikingly similar. Barbara Vicary was born in Chicago in 1931 and moved to England with her husband and two small children in 1964:

> And when I came to England, I found that the women here – a few exceptions, but very few, and they were the ones that were ten years younger – had not had a university education. And therefore I had much more in common with the men. The different [school governing] boards I went on, I was often the first woman, and certainly the first American. But I think the reason was possibly, that I'd had more education, I don't know ... both my parents were university graduates, so I never thought about not going on for a university degree myself and I never thought of my children not going on to it.[32]

Diane Braithwaite married an Englishman and moved to England in 1962. She felt that a college education 'was the norm' in America. Nonetheless, as in Britain, a degree was seen largely as a foundation for appropriate employment until marriage. Women had no real aspiration for life-long career:

> Generally I think they regarded a liberal education for girls as almost a kind of 'finishing' thing. It was almost a social status thing, that you had a college education. Men would find you more acceptable as a mate if you had that kind of thing behind you ... my mother didn't go to university, but she always felt bad that she hadn't. So it was definitely a goal.[33]

When asked whether or not American women expected to continue with a career after marriage, Barbara replied: 'No ... I assumed that I would work until I had children. I happen to think it's very important for mothers to be at home when they do have children. So I didn't plan to work after that if I didn't have to.'[34] Diane concurred: 'I don't think the women that I knew thought that they needed to have a career. They probably thought they might do something when the big child-raising commitment was over – which I think was kind of my feeling'.[35]

The third respondent to have attended university was British. However, despite her university education, Barbara Rogers maintained that her ultimate wish was to stay at home to raise her family. She married in 1962 and had four children:

> Although I had a university education, I chose to stay at home without paid work for almost twenty years ... although I was an only child and very academic up to getting married, I never felt guilty about staying at home, and now I feel privileged to have been able to do it. When the children were all at school, I intended to do a teacher training, and indeed, had the opportunity. However, life was too good, and I stayed home until the youngest was thirteen.[36]

56 *Desperate Housewives, Neuroses and the Domestic Environment, 1945–1970*

The consistency in the accounts of British women educated at grammar school during the late 1940s and 1950s, following the implementation of the Butler Education Act, is remarkable. However, the account of one younger woman whose grammar school education took her into the 1960s is revealing. Her testimony indicates that girls' expectations for a career changed greatly during a ten-year period. Born and raised in the Lincolnshire Fens, Faith Lawson left grammar school after A Levels at eighteen in 1963. Her experience is in contrast to those born earlier:

> I travelled thirty-two miles a day across the fens by bus ... [the] education was totally different, so classical ... very academic and the whole thing 'push, push – achieve marks' ... and the headmistress – she was called Mrs Driver! Interesting name! And she was academic – terribly important that girls achieve ... and the expectation of what you did, I mean they wanted everybody to go to university, they all knew who had done well and that was the aim. And so you had university – which I didn't do – nursing was OK as long as it was one of the good hospitals like St Thomas's or Guys, and then after that it was 'a bit of a shame'.[37]

It is notable that Faith was the only respondent to refer to herself as 'ambitious'. Her testimony suggests a shift in expectations during the early 1960s, which presented a new set of challenges to a whole generation of women. New opportunities driven by success in education left Faith with an impossible choice during a period where family life and a career were still mutually exclusive:

> The pressure was there for me to achieve as that's the way I'd gone and that was supported by my family. And then, against this was this other part of myself – which was the female part – the sexual part, which pushed you to have a relationship ... and marriage for me, the fear of it was that it would be forever ... you could easily have several children, because at that time, the pill and all of that was hardly talked about – just beginning to be at the end of the 60s. You know, I am ambitious, I have worked terribly hard to get where I am ... that on its own would have been OK – put this other angle into it, which was sex and babies and marriage and I could feel this distinct pull ... at that time it was a clear-cut choice. It wasn't both.[38]

Nevertheless, the testimonies of two other women who were born later in 1943 and 1950 suggest that, despite this tension, the traditional domestic role was still an attractive option. Jane Davy was born in 1950 and educated at a grammar school in Lincoln. Asked about her decision to be an 'at home' mum, she emphasized, 'there was never any question that I would stay at work when I had the children'.[39] Judith Morgan was born in 1943 and had an exceptionally ambitious mother who worked full-time as head teacher of the local primary school. Her parents placed great importance on academic achievement; however, Judith felt that for her it had been disadvantageous to have two parents simultaneously pursuing a career. Speaking about her mother, she recalled:

The Housewife's Day   57

> Her career was very important to her and she was very good at what she did. But you
> always got the feeling that the children in school actually saw more of her than we did
> ... I suppose with the effect it had had on me, personally I had no intention of working
> and having children ... I wanted to enjoy my family.[40]

The limited options available to girls following the war were thus generally seen as acceptable and there appears to be little evidence of dissatisfaction. This is particularly so for those who had traumatic experiences during wartime. Inevitably, as educational and occupational opportunities opened up gradually for women during the late 1960s and early 1970s, a conflict began to emerge between the important values associated with the family and those increasingly associated with personal fulfilment and the growing consumption of commodities. Ina Zweiniger-Bargielowska has rightly noted therefore that: 'While Oakley's analysis struck a chord in the specific circumstances of the late 1960s and early 1970s, particularly among middle-class women, there is no reason why this approach should be equally valid or relevant to other historical periods'.[41]

Domestic Life

In 1963, John and Elizabeth Newson suggested that middle-class mothers may have aspirations to an active intellectual life and that, 'for such women, the period when her children are very young may be a time of frustration and despondency'.[42] The evidence from this oral history project does, on occasions, indicate that there was a level of isolation among respondents during these years, particularly from those who moved house regularly in order to follow a husband's career. A survey undertaken of the National Housewives' Register in 1966 showed that 77 per cent of members had no relatives living nearby and that only 9 per cent were natives of the town in which they lived.[43] Understandably, most women who were interviewed for this project found homemaking irritating at times and despite the introduction of household appliances the consensus was that housework remained 'hard work'. However, once again, this appeared unremarkable to the women interviewed. Many of them compared their experience to that of their husbands, generally viewing life at home as less demanding than the working world outside the home. Chris Richards, for example, married in 1949 and saw herself as 'fortunate' to be able to stay at home to look after her two children:

> I think I was fortunate. I never had to work. I was an 'at home' wife ... my husband
> always had very demanding jobs and he was away a lot – the stress was more with him
> than with me. I'd hoped I wouldn't have to work, I didn't enjoy work.[44]

The same sentiment was evident in Betty Sanderson's account. Betty was born in Sussex in 1929, and, following a private education, became a school teacher. She declared that she 'had no desire' to return to work after the birth of her children and described herself as 'one of the lucky ones': 'I've always been very conscious that I have been fortunate, that I didn't have to work for financial reasons – and the fact that I felt I was doing a worthwhile job'.[45] Frances Wilson, another academically able student, was happy to give up work to look after her children. In her view, it was her husband who 'kept the family going':

> He was my breadwinner. I never went out to work outside the home, it was accepted. As far as I was concerned, that's what it seemed to be, that you gave up work when you had your children – it didn't worry me, I didn't want to. I wanted to be at home with the baby. That was my job. It was my profession.[46]

Barbara Rogers was also keen to emphasize the advantages of the housewife's role. She recalled that, 'the best aspects of domestic life was doing what I wanted, when I wanted and being with my children constantly until they went to school. [I] considered my life idyllic ... I felt the role was made for me'.[47]

This attitude was often conveyed by women who were consulted in wartime surveys about future aspirations. Many married women genuinely saw life within the domestic sphere as advantageous. Conversely, war work was often seen as an interruption to family life. Among those interviewed for a survey in 1944, for example, there was 'no doubt that a large majority ... looked forward to settling down and making a home after the war ... a minority of less than a quarter were ready to continue in their present work. Most of these were women of thirty-five to fifty, unmarried or widows'.[48] One woman commented:

> Of course when we get married, I shan't want to work. I shall want to stay at home and have children. You can't look at anything you do in the war as what you really mean to do – it's just filling in time until you can live your own life again.[49]

Economic factors were cited most commonly as the reason for continuing with paid employment and most women only considered working after the war if circumstances meant that their husbands could not find work. In the words of one woman: 'I'll go right home after the war, unless they make us stay. I suppose most of the married women will go back home – but it depends which of you is unemployed – the woman's got to work if the man is unemployed.'[50]

Mass Observation diarist Edie Rutherford even expressed dismay at the prospect of working in industry following the war remarking that:

> I shudder at the thought. Willing though I am to do my bit, the memory of crowded trams, standing around waiting for them in the dark and cold, scrambled meals, no time to do a thing properly. I just hate and dread the thought of all that again.[51]

Jean Bills, who was interviewed for this project, recalled that her mother had been sent to work in a munitions factory during the war. She told Jean that she 'absolutely hated' the experience and that she was 'very fortunate' that she became pregnant and did not have to stay there. Jean remembered her mother talking about the women who worked in the factory and that 'she was horrified by the conversations that went on – absolutely horrified, and couldn't escape quick enough'.[52] A Mass Observation survey that reported on the aspirations of teenage girls in 1949 is also illuminating. Of those interviewed, 68 per cent were 'looking forward to marriage'. For many, this was the 'only future they desired', and those for whom marriage was so important 'seemed to be looking forward, not so much to romance, but domesticity'.[53] One sixteen-year-old shorthand typist, discussing marriage and children, stated that she was 'looking forward to it' because she was 'homely'. Another sixteen-year-old girl who had come from a large family felt that she already 'knew it all by heart' and would 'like to try out [her] experience in her own life'.[54]

Although a number of women in this oral history sample described their husbands as 'head of the household', there is little evidence that these women saw themselves as oppressed. They evaluated their position as part of a team effort. Their responses clearly reflected the practices and beliefs of post-war welfarism. Beveridge's social insurance plan assumed a man's contribution would be made 'on behalf of himself and his wife, as for a team, each of whose partners is equally essential'.[55] Indeed, many directly acknowledged the advantages of their position and the 'trade off' for less worry and responsibility. Christine Calderwood gave up her nursing career to travel abroad with her husband who worked in the oil industry. At first she missed her independence. However, she remembered:

> It was fun. We had tremendous parties and there were lots of sports facilities. Most people we knew, they just accepted that you got certain advantages with it – you got nice holidays, you got plenty of money and [for some] you had help in the house.[56]

Val Parker's father had been a Colonel in the army and her education had been disrupted during the war. She undertook a variety of jobs until she met her husband who was also in the armed forces. She recalled that the army lifestyle was at times difficult and that the frequent house-moves were disruptive. Nonetheless, as a wife and mother she noted that she had a great deal to be thankful for:

> In your home you were secure, you were controlling your own environment ... when you had to go out to work you had traffic, you had challenges, you had maybe difficult bosses, and so you couldn't just say – well, I'm off for a lie down now! So I did feel that men had much more demands made on them.[57]

During the 1960s, married women writing in to the popular weekly magazines also regularly endorsed the benefits inherent in the domestic role. One housewife from Warwickshire writing to *Woman's Realm* in 1968, for example, argued that full-time wives and mothers were able to benefit from freedom and flexibility

60 *Desperate Housewives, Neuroses and the Domestic Environment, 1945–1970*

that was not possible during employment. She condemned those who criticized the housewife's role and reminded readers that employment had its drawbacks:

> As a working girl, I'd like to know what's so stimulating and interesting about most jobs, and just how many interesting people one really meets at work. At least a housewife can go for a walk, take a lunch break when she wants, and order her work to suit herself. If these housewives looked back to their working days, I bet they'd remember that they were generally bored to tears waiting for five pm.[58]

Another woman writing to *Woman's Own* in 1960 described how she felt about the marriage partnership:

> After three happy years of marriage, I'm sorry for wives who like to wear the trousers. Although I am strong-willed, with decided ideas on how a home should be run ... it suits me perfectly well for my husband to be boss ... it relieves me of a lot of unnecessary worry and I am only too glad to have a husband who accepts responsibility.[59]

At times, women vehemently rejected any assumption that dual roles were oppressive to women. One housewife contributing to the letters page of *Woman's Own* in 1960 declared that she was 'insulted' at any suggestion that men were superior to women. She argued instead that, within marriage 'we are just different – and if we sometimes seem to be wearing the trousers, it's not because we want to, but because we have to. We'd much rather sit back, be ourselves, and let the men get on with running the world.'[60]

Some of the respondents interviewed for this project reacted with surprise when asked whether or not they would have liked to work during their young married lives. Their reply was that the tasks undertaken at home were indeed 'work'. The consensus was that, since modern labour-saving technology was expensive and often considered a luxury, housework and cooking were still time-consuming. A Mass Observation survey carried out in 1952 had attempted to quantify the amount of time British housewives spent shopping. It found that, on average, women spent one hour shopping every weekday and nearly two on Saturdays.[61] Edna Goodridge married in 1950 and had two sons, the first of whom was born in 1954. She explained why regular shopping was not a luxury, but a necessity:

> I didn't have a fridge until 1962 and that was agony in the summer when it was hot. I had a marble – an old-fashioned wash stand on a shelf in the pantry to put all my things on and try to keep them cold. And of course you'd have to go out to the shops more or less every day to get anything that might go off. To keep the milk from going sour, well – it was dreadful.[62]

Doris Carter was born in 1915 and married in 1945 when her fiancé returned from war. Although she only had one child, Doris also looked after her elderly mother who lived with them. She remembered that her husband returned home each day for lunch and, like many families, this meant that they ate their main meal at midday. This entailed shopping and food preparation which would invariably take up most of the morning. Talking to her mother, Doris's daughter remembered that she would visit the shops every morning: 'you'd have to go and buy the stuff and have the dinner on the table by 12 o'clock, which is really early. I remember you saying that you'd never get it done on time!'[63]

Jean Hill and Val Parker were at pains to emphasize that there were no ready-made items and that home-cooked food took time to prepare. Both women recognized that cooking good, wholesome food was an essential aspect of caring for the family:

> If you think about the food our children ate, it was real food, wholesome food. And you cooked, and you didn't think twice about cooking a meal ... you did a pudding, proper dinners and proper puddings ... parents of today are dealing with food that contains the most peculiar things.[64]
>
> Pastry was made from scratch and vegetables came with earth and slugs on them, possibly from one's own garden. Like many other wives, I also did a cooked breakfast, so there wasn't a lot of time between washing up from that and starting lunch.[65]

Most wives settled into a daily routine that included housework, cooking and washing, with a couple of hours spent 'taking children out' in the afternoon. Cleaning was perceived as something that 'you just got on with'. Although Ann Oakley argued, later in the 1970s, that 'a majority of women who are housewives fail to realize that housework is unproductive, arduous and petty',[66] a number of women interviewed for this project claimed to quite enjoy it. Eileen Roberts, for example, married a general practitioner and the family lived above his surgery. She supported him in his role in addition to caring for their five children. During her interview she remembered that a close friend had employed a woman to clean for them, referred to as a 'daily':

> She came from the morning right through to the evening, but I never really wanted that. Because I really quite enjoyed being at home and having housework. I enjoyed the housework. I mean, I got fed up obviously, like we all do – but it wasn't a terrible drudge for me.[67]

Washing was seen as the most time-consuming task and most women began married life and motherhood without a washing machine. Gwen Collins retained a keen sense of humour in her account of life before modern detergents:

> I had three boys with rugby kit and playing rugby twice a week – with all this kit to wash without any help. And the thing that used to annoy me was when you scrubbed and rubbed and bleached and boiled and then [the kit] turned out to be someone else's![68]

It is interesting that the women interviewed, while industrious, did not think it necessary to ensure that their houses were immaculate. Angela Holdsworth, writing in 1988, claimed that post-war women increasingly feared the criticism of other housewives. She included oral testimony from women who claimed that the appearance of their homes, their prams and their children had to be 'manicured into order'.[69] However, the majority of women in this project were not influenced by social pressure to keep their homes pristine. Although the importance of 'white' nappies featured regularly in the accounts, by and large spending time with children took priority. Katherine Stead was married in 1958 and had five children. At one point, she had four children under the age of five and remembers it being 'a very busy experience'. However, she declared that she 'was not house-proud at all':

> I got satisfaction of having a nice line of washing [but] I always had the theory that if you kept the floor clean and tidy, people didn't look higher than that! And if they saw a reasonably clean floor, they missed the fact that everything was a bit dusty and not as it should be ... I've always enjoyed cooking, so I never minded cooking meals.[70]

Ann Coles married at eighteen and also had five children. She explained that she had never been domesticated:

> I only had three weeks after being married before becoming a mother. So I never established any kind of domestic routine. And what routine there was revolved around the baby ... I remember being very comforted by a letter in the woman's page of the *Guardian*, where a woman had written in and said 'I know when it's time to wash the floor, it's when both feet stick!'[71]

Kath Greenham's husband died very young, leaving her alone to bring up their three daughters, then aged eight, thirteen and fifteen. She always considered that spending time with the girls was preferable to household chores:

> Well I'm not very tidy! But you see I was more interested in the children ... My sister came to me and said, 'I'll do your housework for you if you'll read stories to my children' – I preferred doing that you see ... And I remember one incident – when you filled a twin tub with a hose, you put the tap on, and Jill called me into the room. And I ended up reading poetry with her until she said 'Mummy! What's that water coming under the door?'[72]

In most cases husbands did not help with the housework; however, many respondents pointed out that, given the long hours they spent at work, it would simply not have been practical to expect men to undertake household tasks. Moreover, some women claimed not to want them to help. Christine Calderwood claimed that she 'never really wanted him to really. Probably because I never expected it.'[73] Nevertheless, there were a surprising number of men who took on more than was expected of them. Jean Hill's husband would turn his hand to 'anything': 'He would do any job that I could do in the house. The only job that I could do better than him was the ironing. But he did it, and you know he'd change the babies, he looked after them.'[74] Margaret Windsor led a somewhat atypical life, in that she returned to teacher training college when her children began school. She felt that many financial sacrifices had been made in order for her to receive a grammar school education, and she wanted 'to put something back in the pot'. She negotiated tasks in the home with her husband, and they agreed between them:

> I had a cleaning lady for quite a bit of the time. But I think, between us we talked about things we liked doing, and there are certain things that he enjoyed and I didn't enjoy. Alex was always out in the garden – but that's because I didn't like doing that. There was no 'this is man's work, this is woman's work'. We did always talk and discuss. We used to have family conferences with the two little kids![75]

A Mass Observation Bulletin in 1948 reported that attitudes towards men helping with domestic chores were slowly changing, concluding that there was a growing acceptance that 'men should help a bit in the home'. Although there was still a clear distinction between suitably 'masculine' and 'feminine' tasks, only one in twenty-five men interviewed felt that they should not be called upon for domestic duties. One man freely acknowledged that 'the fact that a man is at home shows that he has finished his own work – that there is still housework to do shows that his wife has more to do than he has'.[76] The report suggested that decisions about who should undertake the various household tasks were not based on assumptions about gender; rather: 'sex has little to do with it. It's a matter of health, strength and time available.'[77] Later in 1960, Young and Willmott also found that although husbands worked long hours, they were increasingly helping with household tasks. Not only did they undertake much of the 'heavy work', carrying coal and lifting rubbish, they also helped with lighter tasks such as washing up and vacuuming. Increasingly, families were buying their own homes which also resulted in men investing more time and money in maintenance and decorating. Young and Willmott concluded, 'The husbandman of England is back in a new form ... an improver not of a strip of arable land, but of the semi-detached family estate at thirty-three Elsmere Road'.[78]

For most wives, it did not occur to the majority of women to dwell on 'what might-have-been', for this was simply 'what there was'. Drusilla Beyfus, the journalist and broadcaster, noted in her study of marriage in 1968 that older couples 'tended to accept matrimony as part of the air they breathed – not to think about it particularly'.[79] This very much echoed in the interviews. Val Parker, for example, remembered:

> It sounds weird, but you just got on with what you were doing at the time. I'm sure you know yourself; you are so busy with young children that you don't stand back and get a perspective on it. Things come along so quickly with young children – worrying about schools and keeping them safe and that sort of thing.[80]

When asked to recall the negative aspects of their lives as wives and mothers, women often described health problems, and many of them remembered having a difficult childbirth or an unsympathetic midwife. Others encountered physical difficulties following birth. Eve Raddon remembered 'the worst bit' was when her husband contracted tuberculosis shortly before the birth of her daughter. She described this as 'pretty gruelling' and 'very upsetting'. Indeed, she emphasized that, looking back, this was the only thing about her life that she would change.[81] Other women wryly remarked that it was not always easy being confined in the home on a rainy day with lots of small children; however, they argued that these were minor aggravations that did not cause serious discontent. The ups and downs of daily life were regarded as commonplace and were accepted as a normal facet of domestic life.

Creative Activities and Support Networks

Social surveys undertaken by Hanna Gavron, Judith Hubback and Viola Klein during the period indicated that a significant number of educated, married mothers expressed an interest in going out to work. Extra 'pocket' money for non-essentials was cited as the most common reason; however, many housewives indicated that it would be desirable to meet new people for mental stimulus.[82] Hanna Gavron also commented on the loss of confidence and isolation experienced by mothers of small children.[83] While it is true that a notable number of women experienced a degree of isolation in their role, the overwhelming majority of respondents interviewed for this study made an explicit choice to explore other avenues of creativity that did not necessarily involve paid employment. Articles in women's magazines regularly promoted the benefits of friendship outside the domestic arena and recommended new hobbies or volunteer work. In 1960, writing his regular column for *Woman's Own*, psychologist Denis Harley argued that no woman need fall into a 'drab routine'. He suggested that housewives should seek interests outside the home and his advice to those who were 'bored' was that 'the remedy is in your own hands'. Harley urged women to 'write down a list of qualities, talents and characteristics you think you have' and to 'list the activities you like doing best'. With this information, he argued, women should be able to match their interests to one of the many clubs or organizations that existed in local communities. He advised all mothers and wives to rekindle their interest in books and, above all, to keep in touch with old friends.[84]

For the women interviewed for this project, such activities played a key role in their lives, providing companionship, a sense of belonging and, most of all, an avenue for mental stimulation. Most respondents expressed a general preference for activities that would reinforce the beliefs and values that underpinned family life and traditional gender roles. Christine Calderwood recalled that:

When you first give up work, you know it's absolutely dreadful. You know, I felt like a lost soul in a strange country, knowing no one, absolutely nothing to do all day. I was bored out of my mind. It took me at least eighteen months to get used to it, and after that, I never looked back. I had all my interests ... we used to have classes and we arranged so many things for ourselves. We learned history and organized wonderful parties for the children in the school holidays. And there was a lot of charity work to do in most countries.[85]

Eileen Roberts became involved with the Pre-School Playgroup Association. Her husband was a general practitioner and, in 1967, she opened a playgroup in the basement of her home beneath her husband's surgery. Eileen advocated creative stimulation for women from within the mother/wife role. In her view, the experience changed her life:

It was absolutely amazing. It was as much for the mums ... making them understand that there is a value of being at home ... I feel very, very strongly that women should stay at home with children, until they are five at least. Where people find staying home with kids 'a waste of time' is beyond my thinking, because for me, it's the most important thing you can do. You make or break these people.[86]

Jill Faux, writing recently about her experiences with the Pre-School Playgroup Association, described the ethos of the organization as being essentially about parental involvement and parental growth. As such, it provided an opportunity for mothers with young children to meet to get to know each other and improve parenting skills:

I learnt a lot about children and was much happier at home with my own kids. I could now organize play activities for them which kept them occupied and I could get an intellectual satisfaction from watching them develop through the play I was offering them – which made the whole business of having them worthwhile! Before that, I wouldn't say it was a bore, but I wasn't aware of what was happening so I found it much more difficult to get that kind of satisfaction out of it.[87]

Katherine Stead joined her local branch of The National Housewives' Register and initiated a babysitting circle. 'I found I needed more stimulation than just reading children's books to them every evening. And we got some more meaty topics – and that was good.'[88] Other women too noted that they felt 'intellectually frustrated' and found that the Housewives' Register provided an important outlet for gaining self-confidence.[89] Not all the interviewees were members of the Register during their young married lives, but joined other organizations instead, such as The Townswomen's Guild and The Inner Wheel.[90] Mass Observation surveys from the period also indicate that many women were finding meaningful activities with which to entertain themselves. The Townswomen's Guild was often cited.[91] For some, the Church provided a social network and support; others met like-minded women through their children. Eileen Bailey joined the local choral society and the drama group of the Women's Institute. Referring specifically to her husband's extra-marital affairs later on in her marriage, she noted that her Christian faith had enabled her to cope: 'I couldn't have coped if I hadn't had some other interests. And I couldn't have coped if I hadn't been a Christian either.'[92]

Not all respondents joined outside organizations, and some actively chose to keep themselves usefully entertained at home. Gwen Collins, for example, described herself as 'bookish' – always wanting to read: 'I always had a thing – a bar – against the kitchen window so that I could have a book behind when I was washing napkins and things'.[93] Frances Wilson, pregnant with her first child, moved from her birthplace in London to a new housing estate in Leeds:

> So, I was in this still-being-built estate; you'd occasionally see someone moving around in a house which was occupied, so it was a bit lonely. But I read *Middlemarch* and did my exercises and relaxed every afternoon, and went to antenatal classes where I met some other women. But I was perfectly happy.[94]

A support network of wider kin did not exist for the majority of these interviewees. Most had moved away from their relatives, usually as a result of their partner's employment, but on occasions through personal choice. By and large, this was not seen as a cause of inconvenience. In a few cases, a family network did not exist in the first place, as was the case for Margaret Windsor whose father died when she was ten months old: 'My mother died two years after my first daughter was born ... and there wasn't a "rest" of the family, because I'd got no siblings'.[95] Provided they had the support of their partners these women saw coping alone as normal:

> I had sisters and brothers, but they were all doing their own thing, and when the first child was born, they were all doing things in the war ... Jack's parents lived in Durham and we lived in London, so they came down once a year ... they were very fond of the children, but they weren't really anything very much to help. I don't think, in a way, we expected it.[96]

Although these women built up a base of friends in a variety of ways, relationships were often superficial. It was certainly seen as unacceptable to discuss personal matters with others. A common remark was 'I didn't want people knowing my business'.[97] Unsurprisingly, many respondents noted that housewives had 'difficult days'. These were seen as unremarkable and only 'difficult' in a general sense – akin to the ordinary ups and downs experienced by everyone. During days that did not go to plan, many women recalled the support of 'one good friend' (or a small group of exclusive friends), with whom it was possible to discuss anything. Katherine Stead, for example, remembered that:

> The saving grace really has been one good friend ... she had a large family as well and one day a week we had each other's family. So one day a week we had nine children!

But it gave the other a day off. And if things were going wrong, if you were fed up with husbands – anything – you'd pick up the phone. And we had a coded message; we'd pick it up and say 'I need a cup of coffee!' [Laughing] And you'd immediately know there was a problem.[98]

Eileen Roberts described a similar situation:

After we'd been in practice about four or five years, [my husband] joined partners with a doctor down the road … she'd got six kids … they were like cousins to each other … we used to help each other reciprocally, you know, she'd have the kids sometimes.[99]

The two women who were born and educated in the United States noted that the introverted disposition of British women caused them a degree of difficulty upon their arrival in England. Barbara found she naturally gravitated towards other ex-pats: 'the people I had most in common with were the Americans, and I enjoyed my friendships'. When asked whether British women were receptive to her friendship, she responded: 'On the outside, yes. And I didn't realize that I wasn't being taken in as I would have been in an American family friendship. That was my own stupidity! I knew the English were reserved!'[100] Their accounts suggest that housing estates in America were more neighbourly and both women had difficulties integrating with British women. Speaking about life before she left the United States, Diane recalled:

Women would get together and have coffee mornings and there would be a lot of bonding. I thought that would be quite nice. But of course it didn't happen, even on a new estate in England, because people are much more inward looking and the gardens were all fenced off. In America, gardens would run together. There'd be no delineation, in fact it's against the law in some places to have fences … in England, you had to make an effort, you had to go and knock on somebody's door … so it was a different pattern for me, and I would have needed to take the initiative, which I didn't. I mean, I was in my twenties then, so we're talking about somebody who was fairly green.[101]

Whereas Barbara actively sought integration into the community by applying for a school governor's position, Diane found taking the initiative more difficult:

I think some of the problems were self-atrophy. The more I stayed at home, the more reluctant I was to do anything to get myself out. I think I could perhaps have been more of a mover and shaker, and taken the initiative … I could have formed a connection with the church – I think there was a Mother's Union in the first place we lived in … so I think that would have helped some of the isolation. I think there were resources out there that I just didn't go out and find.[102]

The experiences of these women illustrate how some wives understandably found their role isolating at times. However, by and large they did not feel it appropriate to aspire to a career outside the home until their children were much older. Instead, they sought intellectual and social stimulation from alternative sources.

Mothering

As the previous chapter has shown, notions of mothering and ideas about 'the family' were underpinned by a range of assumptions about women and maternity. Contemporary beliefs accentuated the importance of a stable conjugal relationship, and promoted it as the best environment in which to bring up children. The evidence from this project illustrates that women also bought into these ideals. Without exception, these women placed the care and nurture of their children as their priority in life.[103] It is striking testimony to such principles that, within such diversity of experience, similar sentiments were expressed by the interviewees. Their beliefs and values were clearly influenced by a dominant discourse that accentuated the importance of the mother–child bond. However, it would still be fair to argue that these women believed that the labour of child-rearing was the most worthwhile of all. The sense of 'responsibility' for the next generation was a common sentiment in their accounts. In Betty Sanderson's view:

> A mother's role is really a provider isn't it – a provider of love and everything for their well-being. I always have felt very strongly that it is a parent's duty to bring up their children so that they are equipped to leave home as young adults ... I'd say that the way we brought our children up, we did to our best ... how else could we? We had to be true to our beliefs. I wasn't a very introspective mother, or person – consequently it was what I was there for, I was fulfilling my role.[104]

A number of respondents expressed their fear about the unstable political environment and the Cold War. During a period in which repeated political and military crises threatened world peace with the potential for nuclear destruction, their greatest concern was for the safety and well-being of their children. Joanna Bourke has argued that, for many people, the Cold War was more frightening than the Second World War because, for the first time, it introduced the possibility of total annihilation.[105] Joan Talbot distinctly remembered this climate of fear:

> I tell you one thing I remember very well. There was – you know, at the time of the Kennedy crisis, we had to go to something called 'one in three' lectures, and that was the only time I think I've ever been frightened. Not for myself, but for the children ... it was ludicrous, you had to find an indoor room and make it gas-proof ... at that time, I really was frightened for the children. Quite honestly, knowing you couldn't do anything about it.[106]

Chris Richard's husband visited the Soviet Union during the period. She too remembered being anxious about this: 'I had two kids and it was Cold War time. You heard all these stories of them not getting home again and I was terribly worried about it.'[107] Similar concerns were voiced by Margaret Lincoln. Married in 1951, Margaret had no children of her own, but remembered her sister-in-law being fearful of the prospect of nuclear war: 'she had two children, and the Cold

War was on at the time. She was saying how worried she was that she was going to be blown up, and what was going to happen to the children.'[108] These accounts echo those provided by women who were traumatized by events of the Second World War. Given the backdrop of uncertainty, family life was seen as something fragile and precious, to be appreciated and, above all, guarded.

In 1964 Margaret was unexpectedly required to adopt her nephew and niece, and her experience is also testimony to the ways in which the familial environment was considered to be of paramount importance to a child's emotional development:

> I had to give them a base, to start off with almost eroding what they'd got and put in a new life – very hard work because they actually rebelled. But the social services lady ... said that 'every child needs a frame, and it will knock the frame to find whether it's secure'. She said 'and you'll be the frame'. She said 'you'll have to be very firm', and I was. And they've both grown up as they should have done, and not got into any trouble at all.[109]

When asked what effect this had had on her life, she remembered that it had inspired a complete life-change which, at times, had proved to be very hard work. Nevertheless, she explained that the children bestowed upon them a new sense of purpose:

> I'd been married for sixteen years and then I had these two children, and I learned how to be unselfish. Because we'd become wrapped up in one another, you know and I think it taught me to be unselfish. You know, when you've got the flu and you're going around and you have to think of them rather than of yourself – and you're getting up in the middle of the night when one of them's saying 'there's a spaceman under the bed' or something [laughing]. All those things are the best.[110]

Some women commented on how they had been rewarded for their devotion by adult children who expressed appreciation for their parents' commitment. Gwen, for example, was married shortly before the war. Her husband was on active service and she had to bring up her first child alone for four years:

> And then he went away, and I didn't see him for four years. I brought the child up by myself. And one day since, somebody said something to me about this when [my son] Martin was there, and he said 'yes, but didn't we have a lovely time'. And I was really touched by that because I never thought about the child appreciating the mother being there all the time, and playing and reading, and all the things I did with him.[111]

The consensus among those interviewed was broadly that it was important for mothers to stay at home full-time until their children reached school age. However, some women emphasized that 'mothering' was just as crucial during teenage years. Eileen Bailey emphatically stated 'I think your children need you at all ages. And a lot of people say, oh I'll go to work when they go to school, but

70   *Desperate Housewives, Neuroses and the Domestic Environment, 1945–1970*

I think they need you just as much'.[112] This is not to say that the women in this sample all remained at home exclusively until their children were grown up. A number did small part-time jobs, and of course the majority undertook other activities for pleasure outside the home. Those who did work outside the home emphasized the importance of being back before the child returned from school.

It is notable that given society's dominant belief in the mother–child bond, a small number of respondents did not feel that mothering came instinctively to them. However, their responses were often ambiguous in this respect. Barbara, for example, claimed that she was 'not a natural mother' and 'had to work at it', but at the same time recounted numerous occasions upon which she had clearly used her own instinct to reject 'expert' instructions from health professionals, who, she felt, were giving unhelpful advice. Even those who claimed not to be particularly maternal described themselves as ultimately 'loving' and 'caring'. The majority of interviewees indeed felt that mothering, while not always easy, was intuitive. Rose Courtenay had two sons, one in 1958 and one in 1961. In her account, she affirmed that 'when you're a mum, you just have this rush of love when they're born'.[113] Frances Wilson remembered being 'worried' about whether she would love her first child. However, she soon discovered that loving him came naturally:

> There's a photograph of me holding Sam when he was first handed to me ... and the expression on my face says it all, I'm totally in love! There was never a problem. Knew I wanted to breastfeed; that was immediate.[114]

Approximately half of the interviewees referred to child-expert manuals, with opinions falling at two extremes. Dr Spock was the only author mentioned, and those who found the information helpful were usually women who had little experience with babies – perhaps because they had been an only child. For these mothers the book was often described as their 'bible'.[115] However, others disagreed with his ideas, claiming that there was not enough structure, discipline and routine in his advice. The majority of women felt they did not need advice at all. Katherine Stead recalled that:

> I had a friend who read it from cover to cover, passed it on to me and I don't think I really read it at all. I couldn't tell you anything that was in Spock, but he was the thing that kept being brought up.[116]

Contemporary surveys echo this split in opinion with regards to the relevance of child-expert manuals. Fifty-two per cent of women interviewed in 1950 for a Mass Observation investigation into 'Babies and Children' claimed that they had never read childcare books. Many of them used their own intuition and did what they thought best, not being afraid to disagree with expert theories. Among those who sought advice, the general consensus was against 'rigid application of expert advice'.[117]

A general acceptance of a mother's ultimate suitability (innate or otherwise) for the role was conveyed by the interviewees. As a result, many women commented on how fathers were marginal to family life and excluded from many 'hands on' tasks. Although it was viewed as acceptable for a father to entertain children, they were not expected to participate in tasks such as bathing or feeding. Christine Calderwood recalled that 'it was 1964 when Elizabeth was born and it was just getting to the stage where men might just occasionally push the pram around the sports field – if pushed'.[118] Katherine Stead too remembered that 'you certainly never saw fathers picking up children from school ... because if you are working you can't do that sort of thing. So it was the normal thing to have to do anyway, for the woman'.[119] Diane Braithwaite described the arrangement she had with her husband who sometimes worked from home:

> He used to work at home one afternoon a week ... and that was my afternoon off. He just did things with the babies. It was just the beginning of the hands-on fathers, but he had no model for that because he said that his father didn't. He was a loving father, but it just wasn't expected and just wasn't done.[120]

There was thus no sense that these women particularly resented the lack of input from their husbands in this way. It was largely viewed as unavoidable since men were usually absent from the home environment during week days. During evenings and weekends men were expected to act within social norms and undertake household and childcare tasks that were deemed 'suitable' for men, such as mowing the lawn and 'occupying' the children for short periods of time.

Many of the letters published in weekly periodicals reflected happy memories of mothering. One woman submitted her own poem entitled 'Remembering', in which she looked back upon her life as a mother:

> *Remembering*
> Once our house was filled with noise
> Shouting, laughing girls and boys.
> Muddy footprints on the floor
> Fingerprints around the door.
> Discarded toys left on the stairs
> Misused clothes with rips and tears.
> Now that all have grown and wed
> A tidy house is here instead.
> Now no noise disturbs our ears
> But how we sigh for those past years.[121]

These feelings were very much reflected in Eve Raddon's testimony. She remembered finding it 'a real wrench' when her children left home for university and felt that she 'blotted out a lot of it' because thinking about them all at home upset her.[122] Thus, although the accounts of family life provided by these women illustrated how mothering was hard work, it is clear that most of them remembered it with great fondness.

Conclusion

In this chapter it has been suggested that it would be productive to place these oral testimonies within the context of their time, acknowledging both the disadvantages and advantages of women's role in the home. The women interviewed were perhaps responding with hindsight to the second-wave feminist discourse that implied they had 'wasted their time'. A defensive tone is certainly evident in many of the accounts where women asserted that they were not victims. Many contended that they were able to exert influence in numerous ways within marriage and family life. Feminist values have influenced society to the extent that a number of respondents initially assumed that the objective of this research would be primarily to illustrate the discontent and disillusion among women of this period. Betty Sanderson, for instance, was concerned that she 'hadn't been a very good person' to interview, since she was unable to provide any real discontent with her role.[123] This was also echoed in the testimony of Barbara Rogers, who recalled, 'I had people saying I had wasted my education, but I never felt guilty about staying at home and felt it was the right thing to do at the time'.[124] While it is possible that given different opportunities some women may have made different choices, this should not detract from the experience of many who look back on their lives as genuinely happy and successful. Gwen Collins indicated that women generally had realistic expectations about life and were simply inclined to accept the circumstances in which they found themselves. She remarked, 'we weren't trying to "find ourselves" or whatever it is you've got to do – "find your identity", or whatever you've got to do today!'[125]

In some cases, women contended that there were indeed real choices available to them. Katherine Stead, for example, always 'wanted' a large family. When asked if she regretted forsaking her career, she replied:

> I don't think I resented it because I'd brought all this on myself, and you can't blame other people for your own actions. I hadn't been forced to do anything that had got me in that state and I was very lucky because I loved my husband dearly ... he put up with a very pig-headed woman![126]

A number of women went on to undertake degree courses when their children had grown up and by and large felt that they gained more from doing this later. In this sense, they felt that they had indeed 'had it all', but 'not at the same time'. Christine Calderwood, for example, went to university as a mature student after her children had left home. She had no doubt she would have succeeded at university at eighteen. Nevertheless, she maintained that 'I probably wouldn't have got as much out of it ... I found it very exciting having children of my own – interesting and different ... I think it's very positive, wouldn't have missed it for the world'.[127] Frances Wilson also gained a degree after her children had grown up. She followed this with a ten-year career in social work. She declared: 'I'd managed rearing my children and having a professional career – I think that was quite neat!'[128] Edna Goodman simply remarked that 'there's time enough. You can catch up with your life when the children are older. I'm proof that you can.'[129]

It is also interesting that a number of women claimed to have swapped roles with their husbands in retirement – in some cases taking control of many aspects of the relationship. G. M. Carstairs, Professor of Psychological Medicine in Edinburgh, writing on the topic of gender roles in 1962, suggested that 'the coming of old age does something to redress the balance. Then it is the husband who finds himself idle and useless, while his wife's role continues and may be enhanced.'[130] This situation is also reflected in the testimony of Val Parker who observed that:

> As the years went by and, I don't know, I matured – whatever – I began to think, well, I'm actually much better at managing the finances than he is, and so I gradually took over, and by the time he died I did everything, the direct debits – a lot of the financial decisions.[131]

Chris Richards described a similar set of circumstances and suggested that, by retirement she had developed a more assertive attitude within marriage:

> You see, it's only since we retired ... I don't know, I think you just come to a stage in your life, and of course you're going to be together a lot and you can't have somebody ruling the roost all the time. I mean, he was always a lovely husband, but he was the dominant one. And it's worked since we retired – I've just had a couple of good goes at him! I even swear now which I've never done![132]

Therefore, although women often felt that their husbands were 'head' of the household, the power dynamics within relationships were complex and multifaceted.

This chapter has examined domestic life, as experienced by the women in this cohort of interviewees. It has shown that many married women were happy to endure and enjoy both the positive and the negative aspects of their position, in the belief that they were undertaking a worthwhile role. The findings would certainly suggest that Judith Hubback might not have been speaking on behalf of the majority of married women when she claimed in 1957 that 'brains are a distinct handicap to a woman's prospect of happiness and contentment'.[133] In Britain, for the most part, discontent with the domestic role grew gradually towards the end of the 1960s as new educational and professional opportunities became available. Until then, serious dissatisfaction was largely confined to those women who were perhaps untypical of the average housewife. Drusilla Beyfus's eclectic investigation of marriage, for example, includes an account from the journalist Baroness Joan Bakewell who was a Cambridge graduate. Her views at that time were broadly in line with those of Friedan. With disdain, she argued that 'the whole feeling that a woman's role is concentrating on embroidering cushion covers ... and nappy rash, is all wrong. Sure, I worry about nappy rash, but I solve it and get on to something else'.[134] However, her husband, although totally supportive of her career, was at pains to mention later that 'there are times when she gets tired and wants a simpler life. She certainly woke up that way this morning.'[135] Indeed, a Mass Observation investigation undertaken in 1957 into the experience of housewives noted that commentators frequently assumed that the domestic role was mundane; yet they had failed to consider that many women were content within it:

> It is fashionable to look upon housewives as an underprivileged group, overworked, underpaid and undervalued – legitimately dissatisfied with their lot ... to the contemporary eye, her domestic day of varied, overlapping activities may look muddled and wasteful. That she should prefer it that way is a point rarely considered.[136]

The following chapter will explore the psychiatric landscape during the 1950s and 1960s. Historically, developments during this period provided the impetus for new research into the activity of neurotransmitters in the brain and led to modern biochemical theories of psychiatric illness. The new research was driven largely by the somewhat accidental discovery of new drugs that proved capable of altering mood. However, very little was known about brain chemistry and the theories that emerged could not be substantiated with certainty. The sources examined illuminate a range of contemporary concerns surrounding the classification, diagnosis and treatment of mental symptoms, and illustrate how categories of mental illness were reconceptualized to include an increasing list of symptoms that often related to the problems of daily living. The articles suggest that, despite the increasing credence afforded to biochemical notions of mental illness, research frequently indicated that there might be an association between dysfunctional relationships and the onset of mental symptoms. Centrally, many of the articles include evidence from women who were interviewed about their life circumstances. While they repeatedly recounted memories of traumatic past events or alluded to difficult personal relationships, they rarely appeared dissatisfied with opportunities available to them within their role as homemakers.

4 LIGHTENING TROUBLED MINDS: MID-TWENTIETH CENTURY MEDICAL UNDERSTANDINGS OF AFFECTIVE DISORDERS

> As a general practitioner, I experience great difficulty in fitting my patients into the arbitrary classifications of depression which appear both in psychiatric literature and in the glossy pamphlets produced by the drug companies ... A few [patients] present with symptoms of anxiety, but on the whole they appear to be essentially normal individuals who, sometimes in response to some form of stress ... or sometimes without any discoverable cause, become depressed. It therefore hardly seems correct to label these patients as suffering from atypical, neurotic, hysterical, reactive or anxiety depression.
>
> D. C. Morrell *British Medical Journal*, 20 January 1962

In January 1962, a general practitioner, D. C. Morrell, wrote the above letter to the *British Medical Journal* (*BMJ*) articulating his concerns about the current system of classification for depressive and anxiety states. He went on to express deep concern about the ways in which powerful drugs 'which were by no means devoid of side effects' were being used widely without the existence of uniform, precise diagnostic criteria.[1] The difficulties highlighted by Morrell in his letter reflect some of the concerns that developed during medical debates of the 1960s about the diagnosis and treatment of minor affective disorders. This chapter will draw on contemporary clinical research to examine the medical theories and treatment of neurotic and depressive states during the late 1950s and 1960s. As clinicians began to direct attention towards the less severe categories of mental illness, various theories were put forward about the causes of anxiety and depression from psychiatrists, psychologists, psychosomatic theorists and (to a lesser extent in Britain) from psychoanalysts. These debates were played out in the medical press, and, although women continued to appear more frequently than men in statistics for neurotic and depressive disorders, the 'desperate housewife' did not play centre stage in medical discourse.

Mid Twentieth-Century Psychiatry

Prior to the twentieth century, British psychiatry had been dominated by asylum-based care of individuals affected by severe psychiatric illness.[2] However, by the 1950s, caring for the mentally ill in large institutions came under increasing criticism. Edward Shorter has described the problems facing psychiatry on the eve of the Second World War:

> In the first half of the twentieth century, psychiatry was caught in a dilemma. On the one hand, psychiatrists could warehouse their patients in vast bins in the hope that they might recover spontaneously. On the other, they had psychoanalysis, a therapy suitable for the needs of the wealthy people desiring self-insight. Caught between these unappealing choices, psychiatrists sought alternatives. Some of these alternatives proved to be dead-ends and were discarded. Others became the basis for a new vision of psychotherapy; still others laid the groundwork for the revolution in drug therapy that would take place after World War II.[3]

In 1946, the newly inaugurated National Health Service inherited the system of large-scale asylums, and moves were made to integrate mental health services into mainstream health care. Although the Mental Treatment Act of 1930 had promoted the concept of voluntary treatment, in reality most psychiatric patients before the Second World War had been 'certified' for institutionalized care. The 1959 Mental Health Act eventually abolished the distinction between psychiatric and general hospitals and promoted treatment without certification. Increasingly, patients were treated voluntarily and not under compulsory order.[4] Individuals who were receiving inpatient care were likely to undergo one of a range of physical treatments that had been developed for psychosis and depressive states. Electroconvulsive therapy had been introduced in the 1930s for the treatment of deep depressive disorders and prolonged sleep therapies were administered for schizophrenia. Prefrontal leucotomy was at first regarded as a major advance in therapy, but proved to be damaging to the patient's personality.[5] Roy Porter has described early twentieth-century developments in psychiatric care as 'violent, invasive and frankly experimental' but also suggests that treatments signalled the 'desperation of well-meaning psychiatrists to do something for the masses of forgotten patients in asylums'.[6] However, by the end of the Second World War, psychiatry was beginning to promote greater sympathy and understanding for patients with psychiatric illness.[7] This shift in approach was influenced greatly by the large numbers of psychiatric casualties from both world wars which raised the possibility that there might also be numerous people in the community at risk of mental illness. It certainly provided the field of psychiatry with credibility in identifying and caring for the mentally ill.[8]

During the 1950s and 1960s, community psychiatry came to be seen as the way forward in the treatment of mental illness. The motives underlying the decline of mental asylums have been extensively debated by historians. Many see the introduction of new psychopharmaceuticals as central to the trend towards de-institutionalization. Mickey Smith, for example, maintains that new drugs offered real hope for relief from mental illness and that, while not innocuous, they stimulated a move away from asylums and were also instrumental in reducing suicide and alcohol abuse.[9] Others have been less complimentary. Andrew Scull, for instance, has suggested that the 'therapeutic achievement' of the first psychoactive drugs has been exaggerated. He argues instead that the new welfare state came under pressure to curtail institutional costs. The drugs, he suggests, merely facilitated a policy that was already underway by 'reducing the incidence of florid symptoms among at least some of the disturbed, thus easing the problems of managing them in the community'.[10]

The history of post-war psychiatric disorders has undoubtedly been dominated by the discovery of these new drugs. Most historians mark the discovery of the antipsychotic effects of chlorpromazine (marketed in Britain as Largactil) in 1952 as the most important development in the story of psychopharmaceuticals. However, as Shorter has shown, 'in terms of medication, there have always been drugs to soothe the mind and tame the agitated spirit'.[11] Indeed, prior to the pharmaceutical revolution of the mid-twentieth century, alcohol, opiates, cannabis and cocaine have all been used both for medicinal and recreational purposes to alter mood and alleviate pain. Hypnotic barbiturate drugs that were discovered at the turn of the century were widely used as sedatives for anxious and agitated individuals.[12] In fact, Shorter argues that their uptake was 'enormous' and that more than sixty versions, from a variety of manufacturers, were available by the 1940s. Both in and out of psychiatric units, the drugs were used for a broad range of conditions and were widely overprescribed.[13]

Amphetamines were also important players in the treatment of depressive disorders long before their more recent indication for use in children with what is now diagnosed as attention deficit disorder. Marketed by Smith Kline and French during the 1930s as a decongestant inhaler (Benzedrine), the drug was soon used for treating depression because of the way in which it increased energy and concentration levels. Depressed people who were also 'anxious' were unsuitable for the drug, since amphetamines heighten anxiety; however, Smith Kline and French sought to overcome this problem by combining amphetamine with a barbiturate sedative as a 'combo' drug, which, they argued, made patients 'relaxed yet cheerful and talkative'.[14] As Nicolas Rassmusen has shown, 'this combination would one day become a blockbuster'.[15] Amphetamines were also widely used by the military during the Second World War as performance enhancers and to combat exhaustion. As Rassmusen indicates, the drug had 'many lives' because of the wide range of psychological and physiological effects it has on the mind and body. Dexedrine, the brand name for another amphetamine molecule, for example, was widely marketed for weight loss. The use of the drug for this purpose fitted well with shifting understandings of obesity which was increasingly seen to have an 'emotional' or psychiatric cause, in contrast to the old notion that being overweight was caused by a slow metabolism.[16] Ultimately, as was to be the case with many of the later drugs, problems arose with dependence, harmful side effects and illicit misuse.

Despite these early pharmaceutical innovations, it was nevertheless the discovery of chlorpromazine that was critical to the foundation of psychopharmacology, since its use led to the synthesis of new antidepressant drugs and anxiolytics used for nervous problems.[17] The tranquillizing effects of chlorpromazine were discovered largely by accident. Research into the compound was initially undertaken to investigate its antihistamine properties. However, in the process, it was observed that chlorpromazine produced 'disinterest and quietness' as a side effect.[18] Although this drug was later to be associated specifically with the treatment of schizophrenia, during the mid-1950s it was reported as being useful for 'almost every psychiatric condition'.[19] In much the same way as with chlorpromazine, serendipity played a part in the discovery of many of the compounds later synthesized for use in psychiatry. The group of antidepressant drugs known as the 'tricyclics' is a further example. While investigating a compound similar in structure to chlorpromazine for treatment of schizophrenia, psychiatrists in Switzerland noticed that the drug produced agitation in patients. This led to further investigations in depressed patients. The new drug, imipramine, was the first of the tricyclic antidepressants and became associated with treatment for endogenous depression.[20]

Likewise, the antidepressant effects of iproniazid, a compound belonging to another large group of drugs, the monoamine oxidase inhibitors (MAOIs), were discovered as a side effect during its use in tuberculosis. Clinicians using the drug to treat patients with tuberculosis noticed that they became euphoric, even though they were still ill. It was eventually established that the compound resulted in mood improvement among the chronically ill and functionally impaired patients on psychiatric wards. The drug was soon established as effective for use in depression.[21] In 1952, reserpine, another antipsychotic drug, was isolated from the dried root of the plant Rauwolfia Serpentina. Once again, its sedative effects were discovered during research into its antihypertensive properties. This drug paralleled the discovery of chlorpromazine and was used extensively by the National Health Service due to the fact it was less expensive.[22]

Although the new drugs made an impact on those with severe mental illness, they were less appropriate for use in those with mild or moderate emotional disorders in primary care.[23] As historians of psychiatry have noted, during the mid-century, the threshold for the diagnosis of affective disorders was lowered dramatically. Psychiatrists became increasingly interested 'in the kinds of patients previously seen by family doctors, or not seen medically at all'.[24] In addition to anxiety disorders, clinicians began to speak of 'minor depressions': mixed, neurotic, reactive and endogenous forms of the illness. Developments in primary care and the introduction of the minor tranquillizers must be seen within this context and the 'therapeutic vacuum' that existed.[25] In the United States, where office practice was more common, meprobamate, marketed as Miltown, became the most popular drug prescribed in primary care. This drug was found to relax muscles and reduce anxiety without unwanted sedative effects and by the late 1950s it became one of the most widely prescribed drugs in the world.[26] In Britain, prescriptions of meprobamate, marketed as Equanil, rose sharply during the late 1950s and early 1960s.[27] As pharmaceutical companies began to recognize that an increasing number of people were seeking medical advice for anxiety and depression, competing companies began research into this new and lucrative market.

The benzodiazepine compounds were developed as a result of these endeavours, and the first of this range, chlordiazepoxide (Librium), soon overtook meprobamate as the most frequently prescribed drug in primary care. Both doctors and patients quickly accepted Librium's superiority over the other tranquillizers, and three months after it was approved, it became the most prescribed tranquillizer in the United States.[28] The second of this group of compounds to be discovered was diazepam (Valium) which was released for use in Britain in 1963. An important distinction had thus emerged between the two categories of medication. Chlorpromazine and reserpine on the one hand became known as the 'major' tranquillizers; whereas, meprobamate and the benzodiazepine compounds, by virtue of their ability to relieve anxiety without sedation, were soon described as 'minor' tranquillizers. These medications were prescribed for a wide range of non-specific emotional disorders, largely due to the fact that by the early 1960s there was little or no agreement on diagnostic categories or disease classifications, no suitable control populations and no standardized outcome measures that might have enabled a systematic investigation of the efficacy of treatment.[29]

From a medical perspective, the move away from asylum-based care and the introduction of seemingly efficacious drugs were positive developments in the field of mental illness. However, during the 1060s, there was disquiet among some psychiatrists and social commentators who began to question many of the assumptions upon which modern psychiatric theories rested. As a result, the movement known as 'anti-psychiatry' was formulated during the late 1950s and early 1960s. Proponents of this perspective included: Ronald Laing (1927–89), Michel Foucault (1926–89), David Cooper (1931–86) and Thomas Szasz (1920–). The term 'anti-psychiatry' was coined by Cooper, while Szasz and Laing distanced themselves directly from the expression. Nonetheless, they all questioned the scientific foundations of psychiatry and argued that it had been used primarily to control those who deviated from societal norms. In his controversial book *The Myth of Mental Illness* (1961), Szasz questioned the disease model of psychiatry, proposing that mental illness was a linguistic phenomenon because 'behaviour' cannot be a 'disease' – only the body can predicate disease. Laing, in his essay *The Politics of the Family*, first published in 1971, wrote: 'Man does not always need bars for cages. Ideas can be cages too. Doors are being opened in mental hospitals as chemical constraints become more effective.'[30] These critics argued that conditions such as schizophrenia were not organic diseases to be treated with physical methods. On the contrary, they maintained that symptoms were a response to difficult environmental circumstances and they promoted therapy in a safe environment, away from electroconvulsive therapy and other treatments. In 1965, the radically experimental therapeutic community, Kingsley Hall, was established in London by Laing and his colleagues, to provide natural healing and to research the causes of mental illness, in particular, schizophrenia. It was nonetheless viewed as controversial. The ethos that promoted 'respect for personal freedom' meant that residents were allowed to 'regress' physically and mentally and live according to their own natural rhythms. As a consequence, Kingsley Hall was 'noisy, unpredictable, at times dangerous, ecstatic and often unclean ... a place where treatment was not offered in any conventional sense.'[31]

The roots of this emphasis on social causes can be traced much earlier to the 1920s and 1930s and the mental hygiene movement. Born of a more general concern for the mental health of the population as a whole, and influenced by the United States, the National Council for Mental Hygiene was formed in 1922.[32] Mental hygiene turned everyday life into a potential subject of psychological medicine.[33] Many forms of disordered behaviour were thought to be caused by an inability to adapt to the demands of ordinary living. Thus, moral education, social responsibility, healthy relationships and happy marriages were to be engendered throughout the population.[34] As Nikolas Rose has noted, a wide range of social problems were reconstrued as:

> symptoms of mental disturbances, having their origin in minor troubles of childhood, themselves arising from disturbances in the emotional economy of the family. Hence, the minor problems of childhood – lying, quarrelling, bedwetting, temper tantrums – became significant, not in themselves, but as signs of major social problems to come.[35]

The language of mental hygiene, Rose argues, 'made it possible to conceptualize a range of new institutions such as child guidance clinics, as the fulcrum of a comprehensive system for the inspection and treatment of all those pathologies now described as "maladjusted".'[36]

In 1920, the Tavistock Clinic was founded in London under the leadership of Dr Hugh Crichton-Miller (1877–1959), initially to explore the traumatic effects of First World War 'shell-shock' victims. Its vision was extended 'to provide systematic major psychotherapy on the basis of concepts inspired by psychoanalytic theory, for out-patients suffering from psychoneurosis and allied disorders'.[37] The therapeutic approach emphasized that the patient was 'a product of his environment and his own history' and thus 'the aim was to understand the child as the father of the man and the parents as conditioning the new generation of children'.[38] Henry Dicks, who wrote a history of the Tavistock Clinic, argued that with its emphasis on the whole person, it went some way in making the British psychiatric world safe for psychoanalysis. However, despite its multidisciplinary team that covered all aspects of personality study, it struggled to escape being 'tarred with the Freudian brush'.[39]

The resistance to Freudian psychoanalysis in Britain is well known, and a strong neurological basis for psychiatry persisted.[40] Some time earlier, the leading psychiatrist James Crichton-Brown had even described psychoanalysis as a 'deviant' therapy – philosophically incoherent and cruel. Thus, the psychological therapies that did develop tended to focus on practical, re-educative methods that centred on the external and the physical.[41] Mathew Thomson has recently pointed out that there were a number of other clinics and hospitals that emerged as innovators for psychotherapy, such as the Medico-psychological Clinic in London and the Lady Chichester Hospital in Sussex.[42] However, he argues that, although these experimental clinics provide important examples of psychological thought in medicine, 'the total reach of the phenomenon was very limited: no more than several thousand individuals a year, compared to the numbers languishing in mental hospitals – some 120,000 by 1930'.[43]

In an attempt to explore the troublesome relationship between psychological, social and biological factors in disease, psychosomatic theorists also contributed to the debates on mental illness. These theories were founded upon work of late nineteenth- and early twentieth-century stress researchers Walter Cannon (1871–1945), Hans Selye (1907–82) and Harold Wolff (1898–1962)[44] who all variously attempted to explain possible links between the pressures of life and sickness. As Herbert Weiner has shown, psychosomatic theorists mid-century espoused a range of different approaches. Helen Flanders Dunbar, the first editor of the American journal *Psychosomatic Medicine*, proposed that individual personality characteristics tended to be associated with certain conditions; hypertensive patients, for example, tended to be 'shy and perfectionist', but with 'volcanic eruptions of feeling'.[45] Franz Alexander, another key figure in the development of the psychosomatic movement, fostered a psychoanalytic model whereby different diseases were thought to be caused by specific unconscious conflicts. Hypertension, in Alexander's view, was thus understood to be the result of a patient's fear of their own 'repressed' aggressiveness.[46] In Britain, the Scottish physician James Halliday was more interested in the physical, socioeconomic and familial environment of the patient. He argued that interpersonal,

82   *Desperate Housewives, Neuroses and the Domestic Environment, 1945–1970*

social and cultural factors played a significant role in the aetiology and treatment of ill-health.[47] As Weiner has shown, these theories struggled to become a dominant force as medicine increasingly adopted a reductivist, quantitative approach. In practice, as Thomson illustrates, the ongoing popularity of pills and potions throughout the post-war period also indicated a reservoir of popular demand. Medicine, with the authority of science behind it, began to capture this market. Furthermore, general practitioners found the drugs something of a panacea for those intractable problems that they encountered on a daily basis – problems that they often recognized as psychological, but found themselves ill-equipped to solve through lengthy psychotherapy.[48]

The remainder of this chapter will examine papers and correspondence from the medical press during the late 1950s and 1960s to explore contemporary ideas about the classification, aetiology and treatment of affective disorders. It will argue that, although the competing biological and psychological approaches fostered very different views about the aetiology and treatment of mental illness, many of the case studies from both indicated a possible association with dysfunctional personal relationships and the onset of symptoms. Most importantly, there appears to be no evidence to suggest that patients themselves regarded the lack of opportunities afforded to them from within the domestic role as the cause of psychological symptoms.

Classification of Affective Disorders

Although there was general agreement between psychiatrists, physicians and general practitioners that affective disorders constituted a sizeable public health concern, there was much debate about the appropriate method of quantifying symptoms and categorizing disorders. Many articles during the 1950s and 1960s examined these difficulties. Writing in the *Journal of Mental Science* in 1962, two influential psychiatrists Neil Kessel and Michael Shepherd explained:

> The difficulty is largely one of definition. As most people experience emotional conflict of some sort, the concept of neurosis can be widened so readily as to rob it of much value for medical purposes. Epidemiological enquiries have been hampered by disagreement about the nature of neurosis and by the lack of screening techniques. Formal morbidity surveys have proved difficult to conduct and their results still harder to interpret.[49]

Shepherd established the General Practice Research Unit at the Institute of Psychiatry during the late 1950s. His main objective was to use epidemiological methods to study mental disorder in primary care, where, under the conditions of the British NHS, information was obtainable about the health of the bulk of the population.[50] Shepherd worked with Kessel to promote the importance of the general practice in the treatment of psychiatric illness. They observed that family doctors were often required to detect psychological disturbance in a setting of general morbidity and noted that 'the majority of neurotic patients present physical, rather than psychological complaints and are disposed to receive somatic diagnoses and treatment'.[51] The report on Psychological Medicine in General Practice (1956–8) had also noted that GPs were the people best placed to manage the great majority of psychological ailments and a number of influential GPs began to express a special interest in the area.[52] C. A. H. Watts was one of these. He worked in a large general practice in a mining district of Leicestershire and published two key texts and numerous articles based upon his experience of treating patients with depression and neuroses.[53] Despite their unified aim in providing a framework for diagnosing and treating mental illness, these physicians did not always agree with one another on the classification of symptoms. Watts, for example, acknowledged that the topic was a 'complicated' one, but proposed a simple definition that could be easily adopted by GPs. He also argued that, from his experience of patients, depression could simply 'come out of the blue' – not necessarily related to organic disorder or psychological upset.[54] However, Shepherd, whose mentor had been the distinguished psychiatrist Aubrey Lewis, vigorously promoted the understanding of not only biological, but also psychosocial factors in mental illness.[55]

Ultimately, diagnosis rested upon the subjective judgement of the clinician since there was no standardized means of measuring the clinical state of a depressed patient. Nonetheless, a number of methods were developed to assist with the diagnosis and measure the severity of conditions. One of the most widely recognized methods was developed by Hans Eysenck (1916–97), a German-born psychologist who moved to England during the 1930s. Mathew Thomson has noted that Eysenck attempted to assert the appeal of a 'psychology of science' over that of 'meaning and mysticism', previously associated with psychoanalysis. His was a psychology that 'rejected any spiritual or ethical pretensions ... it was a science'.[56] Eysenck developed a 'theory of personality' in which he claimed that individuals had a tendency towards one of two personality factors: 'neuroticism', which was described as a propensity to experience negative emotions; or 'extraversion' which was typified by an ability to enjoy positive emotions – especially social events.[57] This method, known as the Maudsley Personality Inventory, was developed by Eysenck during his appointment at the Maudsley Hospital, and (in collaboration with his wife Sybil) was later developed into the Eysenck Personality Inventory. It was closely linked to others methods developed by co-workers which included the Cornell Medical Index and The Hamilton Rating Scale for Depression.

The Cornell Medical Index had been created in 1949 as a means of collecting both medical and psychiatric data on patients. It originated from Cornell University Medical College in New York and comprised a set of 195 questions related to all aspects of health, health habits and family history.[58] One component of this questionnaire was concerned with mental health and comprised fifty-one questions related to mood and feelings. The test was generally well respected 'as an indicator of the presence and severity of emotional disturbance'.[59] However, the opportunity existed for bias and ambiguity since interpretation of results was based largely on the knowledge and experience of the clinician. The Hamilton Rating Scale was developed in 1960 by Max Hamilton, as a means of rating the severity of depression. Hamilton undertook his psychiatric training at the Maudsley Hospital and later became interested in psychology, statistics and theories of personality. His rating scale was developed for use in patients who had already been diagnosed with affective disorder or depression and consisted of a questionnaire related to the presence or otherwise of somatic and emotional symptoms.[60] Results were based on observations made by the clinician and by the responses of the patients.

Medical debates about the diagnosis and classification of conditions rarely included references to gender. When they did appear they were limited to the occasional reference to premenstrual tension and the menopause and the ways in which various depressive states exacerbated hormonal problems. Instead, discussion largely centred on the description of symptoms that could be seen in both men and women. Increasingly through the 1960s, symptoms of 'nerves' and anxiety were subsumed under the more general heading of 'depression'. However, a heated debate developed around the existence, or otherwise, of two distinct depressive states. The 'endogenous' form of the condition was characterized by early-morning waking, appetite disturbance and loss of libido. Symptoms were usually quite easily recognizable and embodied the more 'classical' aspects of melancholic depression such as feelings of guilt and hopelessness alongside a generalized sense of emotional indifference. The other form of the illness was referred to variously as atypical, exogenous, neurotic or reactive depression. Atypical depression was thought to be more likely to occur as a result of life stresses, and usually in people who were previously quite capable of dealing with environmental pressure. This condition was typified by subtly different symptoms. For example, patients with endogenous depression tended to wake early in the morning, whereas those with atypical depression often experienced difficulty getting to sleep. Most importantly, atypical depression usually included anxiety as an additional dimension.

The debate on classification was reviewed in a paper published in 1963 by Kiloh and Garside, two lecturers in psychological medicine at Durham University. They argued that, despite semantic confusion, it was essential that a distinction was made between the two forms of depressive illness. As with many of the academic papers on this topic, arguments for such a distinction were usually framed by the prevailing biological notion of mental illness and the conclusions were duly based upon the efficacy of drugs in clinical trials. Imipramine, for example, appeared to alleviate symptoms of endogenous depression:

> Patients diagnosed as suffering from endogenous depression made a significantly better response to the drug than those regarded as showing neurotic depression ... it was thus felt that results suggested that endogenous and neurotic depressions were distinct nosological entities.[61]

Other clinical trials appeared to support this contention and showed that patients with atypical depression responded more positively to the drug phenelzine (one of the MAOIs, marketed as Nardil). The British psychiatrist William Sargant (1907–88) wrote extensively on this topic and argued that there had been what amounted to a 'total revolution in treatment'; nonetheless, the success of physical treatment, he claimed, depended on 'the proper selection of patients'.[62] Sargant trained at the Maudsley Hospital and later became founder of the Department of Psychological Medicine at St Thomas's Hospital, London. During the early 1960s, he worked alongside his research registrar, Peter Dally (1923–2005), undertaking extensive studies into the effects of antidepressants and anxiolytic drugs.[63] Dally, known later for his groundbreaking work on eating disorders, was less exclusively devoted to physical methods and later advocated a combination of drugs and psychotherapy. However, Sargant was a pioneer of physical treatment in psychiatry and is remembered for his sometimes controversial use of ECT, sleep therapy and psychosurgery. He asserted that electroconvulsive therapy was still preferable in cases of serious endogenous depression but promoted the use of phenelzine for use in depressions that included symptoms of anxiety.[64] Others too reported success with the drug, and claimed that the beneficial effect of phenelzine in depressive illness was due to its sedative action in relieving anxiety.[65]

Nevertheless, not all physicians endorsed the distinction between categories of depressive states; nor did they agree on the finer points of diagnosis. The study by Kiloh and Garside was replicated by a group of Australian psychiatrists in 1967, who found that depressive states 'did not appear as two separate entities'.[66] They argued that 'the clinician's knowledge of the syndrome caused him to elicit such symptom clusters when interviewing the patient'; and further that, 'the same type of depressive illness occurring in different groups of patients could present with different clusters of symptoms'.[67] In another paper, Costello and Selby maintained that there was in fact little difference in the sleep patterns between endogenous and atypical depression.[68] Increasingly, physicians attempted to overcome such difficulties by prescribing a tranquillizer alongside an antidepressant:

> Anxiety and depression almost always are intermingled. Anxiety may cause depression as a secondary effect, or it may appear during a primary depression as a secondary effect ... since many patients with depression also show considerable anxiety or agitation, it is common practice of the authors to give a tranquilizer as well as an antidepressant.[69]

Given the confusion over diagnosis, some clinicians were cautious about the use of chemical treatments for affective disorders. In a response to the letter from D. C. Morrell cited at the beginning of this chapter, A. L. Sanderson, a psychiatrist from the Maudsley Hospital wrote:

> I fear that Dr Morrell is doomed to disappointment in his plea for clarification of the concept of depression ... The present diagnostic classification of depression suffers from two major weaknesses. In the first place it is based on symptoms and has all the limitations inherent in such a system. Secondly, psychiatry, in trying to imitate the diagnostic formulations of general medicine, has cast the classification of depression in a quite inappropriate and rigid mould.[70]

While Sanderson acknowledged that a biological cause might account for some cases of affective order and that new drugs had opened up 'great possibilities', he urged caution in this respect and suggested that individuals reacted in unique ways to psychological pressures. Depressive states, he argued, could therefore be more readily understood as evidence of reactions to environmental stress.[71]

Aetiology of Affective Disorders

In observing that both biological and environmental aspects might influence the onset of symptoms, Sanderson's comments epitomized much of the mid-century debate on the causes of depression and anxiety. Broadly speaking, in Britain most debates were constructed within the framework of two opposing perspectives. Neuropsychiatrists usually emphasized the influence of biochemical factors in depressive illness and many claimed that the disorders were possibly caused by genetic abnormalities. Other psychiatrists, general physicians, behavioural therapists and some GPs working within psychiatric medicine stressed the relevance of environmental pressures. Editorial articles in the medical press often promoted an amalgamation of the two theories and suggested that, while some individuals were constitutionally predisposed to depressive states, environmental stress over a prolonged period might also trigger the onset of affective disorders. A report by the working party of the Council of the College of General Practitioners, for example, reasoned that, while such conditions often responded well to modern treatments, 'a change in a patient's attitude to his social environment or personal relationships is needed far more often than a variation in blood chemistry by the use of drugs'.[72] Michael Shepherd, who contributed widely to this debate, argued that the two perspectives should not be mutually exclusive. He argued that psychology should be used to provide a bridge between the biological and the social.[73]

During the 1960s and 1970s, psychosomatic theorists also attempted to explore psychosocial variables that could increase vulnerability to illness.[74] These efforts were built upon research into the effects of specific life events and the invention of the 'life chart' by the Swiss psychiatrist Adolf Meyer (1866–1950).

Meyer hoped that his chart would provide a means for physicians to investigate whether or not the onset of medical disorders coincided with 'important environmental incidents'.[75] Meyer's research provided the framework for the work undertaken by two psychologists, Thomas Holmes and Richard Rahe, who published their *Social Readjustment Scale* in 1967. Within this system, units were allocated to different life events and attempts were thus made to quantify individual life stresses. Ordinary life events were included in order that the accumulation of a range of circumstances could be considered. As a result, Holmes and Rahe argued that 'the magnitude of life changes was significantly related to the timing of disease onset and to the seriousness of the illness experienced'.[76]

Many of the psychiatrists who were sympathetic to the importance of environmental factors in mental illness undertook research into the effects of childhood experiences, family life and interpersonal relationships. A large amount of research was undertaken on the topic, the vast majority of which provided evidence to suggest that these factors impacted significantly on an individual's sense of well-being. Although these ideas were clearly influenced by contemporary theories that advanced a heightened awareness of family psychodynamics, it is interesting that patients themselves often identified the family as the site of disorder. One study, for example, investigated the occurrence of 'psychogenic, stress or tension' headaches that were not caused by organic disease. Women cited in this research often recalled that their headaches had arisen in conjunction with marital problems.[77] Some researchers focused directly upon the phenomenon of neurosis in married couples and families.

A collaborative study in 1962 by a London general practitioner, Anthony Ryle, and psychiatric social worker, Madge Hamilton, examined the prevalence of neurosis in fifty married couples. Ryle, the son of John Ryle, Professor of Social Medicine at Oxford University, had a special interest in psychiatric disorders, and noted later that his attitude towards psychiatry had been shaped by his father who sought 'to study the ultimate as well as the intimate causes of disease'.[78] Anthony Ryle worked in a large group practice in Kentish Town and went on some years later to develop Cognitive Analytic Therapy which, he proposed, helped patients to 'recognize and control damaging ways of acting'.[79] Among their cohort of patients during the early 1960s, Ryle and Hamilton considered the possibility of a correlation with childhood experience and current social and marital adjustment.[80] Evidence on this occasion was obtained from three sources: the general practice records of Anthony Ryle; interview notes from a psychiatric social worker interview with the married couple; and finally from the results of the Cornell Medical Index questionnaire completed by the married couples. Ryle described his patients as 'urban working class'; however, it is still possible to draw parallels with other studies of common psychological disorders. Firstly, there was evidence to suggest that women experienced symptoms more frequently than men, and the authors claimed that this was possibly because they reported a higher rate of adverse childhood experience than men. Secondly, there was a significant correlation between poor marital adjustment and neurotic illness among both sexes. Further evidence of this was reflected in the incidence of symptoms in seven women who were ultimately excluded from the study because they divorced or separated. These women consistently scored in the 'neurotic group'. Finally, the report suggested that when neurosis occurred in both the husband and wife together, it was unlikely to be due to 'the selection of mates from similar backgrounds', and could more effectively be explained 'as an effect of one individual's disturbance upon the other'.[81] The authors argued that, while no firm conclusions could be drawn from a study of this size, there was some indication that mild, common neurotic illnesses of a type seldom presenting a serious clinical problem were not only associated with poor economic achievements, but also with unsatisfactory relations in social and interpersonal spheres.[82]

This research continued in 1963, when the authors, aided by a physician from University College Hospital, investigated the possible links between neuroticism and marital history.[83] In this instance, the couples' marriages were rated on a sliding scale from those that were 'good', showing evidence of a high level of warm, positive feeling, to those that were 'acrimonious', exhibiting stress and open conflict. Factors that were associated with marital adjustment were also explored, such as: age at marriage, length of marriage and the level of dominance/submission between partners. 'The general marital adjustment rating was intended to record the extent to which the marriage fulfilled the overall social, emotional and sexual needs of the partners'.[84] Their findings offer interesting insight into the effects of personal relationships upon psychiatric disorders. Firstly, the number of women affected by neurotic tendencies was once again marginally higher than the number of men. The authors reiterated that this might be connected to the fact that a greater number of women reported memories of childhood trauma. It was tentatively suggested that either the impact of such disturbance was greater for girls, or that the degree and length of exposure to disturbed family situations might be greater for girls. It was therefore not surprising, the authors argued, that couples who recalled emotionally secure childhoods were significantly more likely to go on to experience satisfactory marriages. Secondly, the research suggested that neurosis in women was also significantly correlated with a poor marital rating. Where marriages were rated as 'male-dominated', both partners were susceptible to neurosis; however, where marriages were rated as 'female-dominated', the number of men likely to experience neurosis as a consequence was not significant. The study concluded that:

> There seems little doubt that family influences in childhood play an important part in determining the occurrence of neurosis. This paper presents some evidence to suggest that the adult relationship of marriage both reflects the childhood experience of the couple and may also play an independent role in the production of neurosis.[85]

Lightening Troubled Minds

Although the individuals in the sample were interviewed at length by a psychiatric social worker, and, in addition to this, gave their own personal assessment of their marriage in a questionnaire, at no time was any reference made to dissatisfaction with the domestic role and its requirements. Had the negative assessment of domestic chores and mothering impacted to any significant extent on a woman's experience, it is likely that it would have been included as a factor to be associated with marital adjustment. The marriages were also rated in terms of dominance and submission. Although twenty-three of the eighty-seven couples interviewed described their marriages as 'male-dominated', forty-nine of the eighty-seven couples rated their marriage as in 'a state of equilibrium', with neither partner 'imposing his or her needs, wants or interests at the expense of the other'. Furthermore, fifteen out of the eighty-seven couples assessed their marriages as 'female dominated'.[86] It is therefore by no means certain that any significant number of married women felt themselves to be dominated in marriage. Even those marriages described as in a state of 'equilibrium' were variously rated as 'average' or 'bad', based on levels of emotion given and received and on sexual matters. Ryle and Hamilton explicitly noted that the objective of their research was not to investigate the effects of economic and social status on marriage. Therefore, although the sample focused upon working class couples, their research raised important questions about the emotional dynamics of marriage and their effects on mental health more broadly.

In a later article, published in 1966, Anthony Ryle once again called for further academic attention to the psychological effects of intimate relationships between adults. He reiterated that 'neuroticism' appeared to be related to low levels of affection received:

> Psychiatric illness and psychosomatic disorders may be linked with the individual's experience of love and security and with domination/submission conflicts, not only as they were experienced or perceived as a child, but also as they are enacted in current relationships, particularly in marriage.[87]

Ryle put forward a prototype of what he described as a 'marital patterns test', designed for use in psychiatric studies of patients. This, he hoped, would aid psychiatrists in measuring aspects of relationships based on affection given and received in addition to levels of domination.

His findings were substantiated in 1967 when, using the same research methods, he undertook a larger study of 112 families in London. Once again, individuals who were affected by neurosis repeatedly recalled adverse experiences in childhood. Ryle also reiterated that there was an association between poor marital adjustment and mental symptoms, particularly in wives, and that this was true even for those who did not recall emotionally insecure childhoods. Once again, individuals had completed their own assessment of their health and family issues using the Cornell Medical Index. Ryle also discussed a number of

90   *Desperate Housewives, Neuroses and the Domestic Environment, 1945–1970*

aspects related to family life, including the ability of the husband to provide for the family and the wife's role as housekeeper. Nevertheless, dissatisfaction with domestic life among women was not evident. Instead, Ryle stressed the importance of the ability to communicate ideas and feelings and sexual adjustment within marriage. He emphasized that balance in relationships was 'central to psychological stability' and concluded that: 'it may be more valuable to look upon much psychiatric illness as a form of, or as failure of, communication between the individual and those around him'.[88]

It is striking how contemporary medical discourse about the environmental influence on mental illness frequently highlighted the importance of familial relationships. Numerous studies were undertaken to investigate the underlying situational causes of anxiety and depression. Although many of these papers were focused on psychiatric hospital inpatients, their findings are illuminating because a number of commentators drew attention to the importance of marital relationships. Many of these studies included the views of the patients themselves, and, without exception, none of the women included in interviews referred to the structural aspects of domestic life in negative terms. In one example, Gordon Langley, a Senior Hospital Medical Officer from Wickford, Essex, reported on a study of forty-eight inpatient 'neurotics' who were asked to complete a questionnaire about their attitude to 'life difficulties'.[89] The women questioned rated 'family interpersonal difficulties' (IPD) as the commonest source of stress. Where this existed, 'the person concerned was most commonly the spouse, then, in descending order of frequency: children, parents, siblings and in-laws'. Men also rated family IPD at the top of their list, alongside insomnia. However, they also emphasized financial and practical difficulties. The paper acknowledged that there was always the possibility that physiological mechanisms were a cause of illness and that pharmacological treatment could be helpful. Nevertheless, it concluded that 'the frequency and importance of family interpersonal difficulties and the frequency with which close family members are involved, tends to confirm the general impression that neurosis is a family affair'.[90]

Housewives themselves were the primary focus of one report written by a registrar from the Department of Psychiatry, St George's Hospital, London. Writing in the *BJP* in 1964, A. H. Roberts described a follow-up investigation of a group of forty-one housewives who had been admitted to the psychiatric unit between 1946 and 1962.[91] These women had become housebound *by* their phobic anxiety symptoms, and in no way did the report suggest conversely that they were experiencing symptoms because they were housebound and trapped by their domestic role. Indeed, it was emphasized explicitly that:

> Notes were selected in which it was clearly recorded as one of the principal characteristics of the patient's illness, that she was unable to leave her house alone because of the phobic anxiety symptoms.[92]

The women were contacted by letter and interviewed either by the author or by a psychiatric social-worker. In all cases, anxiety was the major feature of the symptomatology and, 'without exception, they all had panic attacks'. It was the 'fear of reoccurring symptoms of panic' that caused the women to feel that they were unable to leave their homes. When questioned about the onset of symptoms, 60 per cent of patients interviewed were able to recall, without prompting, the anxiety-provoking circumstances related to their first panic attack. Initial triggers included: serious physical illness, a sudden redundancy in the family and the strain of having a sick child in hospital. Notably, women also talked about sexual difficulties within marriage and infidelity. One patient recalled that her friend's husband had made sexual advances toward her which resulted later in the friend attempting suicide. Another woman remembered receiving a letter giving details of her husband's infidelity; and another recalled that she experienced her first panic attack 'while travelling to meet her husband, at a time when she was living with another man – her husband having broken her jaw on a similar occasion in the past'.[93]

These women, it was noted, usually had a family history of neurotic illness or alcoholism and that 'characteristically, the patients had always been anxiety-prone, worrying individuals'. Their personality types might thus have predisposed them to anxious behaviour. Nevertheless, all recalled a specific period of 'heightened anxiety, reactive to some clearly threatening or distressing event'. During their stay as inpatients, all the women had received psychotherapy; and some had been given a further combination of treatment with either imipramine or ECT. The author emphasized that the prognosis depended greatly upon circumstances post-discharge and cited the case of one patient:

> Symptoms developed for the first time when her husband was unfaithful, these ceased when she was admitted to hospital and the husband broke off his relationship with the other woman. They recurred five years later when he was again unfaithful, then ceased and have never recurred since she separated from him.[94]

Similar investigations were also undertaken in the United States and the findings were regularly published in the *British Journal of Psychiatry*. One paper of note appeared in 1968, in which a group of psychiatric patients was studied for the effects of different life events. The results were compared with a control group of 'psychiatrically well' individuals who were matched in terms of age, race, social class and marital status.[95] The patients in the control group were recruited from a list of people admitted to the general medicine unit for conditions unrelated to psychiatric disorder. Life histories were taken from both groups relating to a wide range of circumstances and events including: births and bereavements; work and financial history; interpersonal relationships and marital history; and 'any other important or stressful occurrences preceding or during illness'. The

92 *Desperate Housewives, Neuroses and the Domestic Environment, 1945–1970*

analysis of life events in both groups revealed a similarity in the area of bereavement, indicating that the death of a loved one was not necessarily likely to result in an individual being susceptible to the development of mental illness. In this case, the results were also similar in respect of separation from parents during childhood and also in terms of work stability. However, when examining the area of interpersonal difficulties, there were much greater discrepancies between the two groups. The authors wrote:

> Compared to the controls, psychiatric patients had a higher incidence of instability in their interpersonal relationships, especially during the year prior to admission when their illnesses were already underway. The more frequent changes of dwelling in this group also stemmed from this factor.[96]

The authors acknowledged that the experience of psychiatric illness could possibly cause interpersonal discord at home and that it would be difficult to establish which factor was the precursor. However, there was a significant level of infidelity noted among partners of the psychiatric group, and it might follow that discord within marriage affected patients' sense of well-being. Other clinicians also debated whether or not the 'stress' experienced was a result of psychiatric illness rather than a cause of it. In the words of one psychiatrist from the Royal Edinburgh Hospital:

> It is quite difficult to date the onset of depressive illness and ascertain whether, for example, a depressed patient lost his job because of his depression, or became depressed because he had lost his job. Secondly, the dating of the onset is often obscured by those many cases where the personality and the illness merge imperceptibly, the one into the other.[97]

Nonetheless, in his ensuing examination of 105 depressive patients, this author believed that there was good reason to argue that 'depressive illness has the effect of removing the individual temporarily from the noxious environment, thus allowing repair to the organism'.[98] He also remarked that it was likely to be the cumulative effect of a number of environmental stresses that would result in the onset of depressive illness.

Other researchers investigated cases of mental illness where both partners in marriage were affected. A series of papers appeared in the 1960s exploring this phenomenon and the similarity of symptoms between partners. The aim of these studies was to test the hypothesis of 'assortative mating'; the name given by psychiatrists to the process whereby one partner who was predisposed to mental illness would instinctively seek out a partner with similar tendencies. The alternative possibility put forward by commentators was that one partner's behaviour would influence the otherwise normal behaviour of the other. This was described variously as either the 'interactive' or 'contagion' hypothesis. In

Lightening Troubled Minds 93

one study, the case notes were examined of seventy-four married couples who had both received inpatient psychiatric care.[99] The aim was to establish the frequency with which the pairs experienced similar conditions. The sample was divided into groups that distinguished between the onset of illness prior to marriage and the onset of illness post-marriage. As a result of dividing the case notes in this way, the findings of this investigation did not support the assortative theory, since, for it to have been so, 'the degree of diagnostic concordance among the couples who fell ill before marriage should be at least the same as that found in pairs with a post-marital onset'. However, this prediction was not supported since, 'only twenty-six percent of the premaritally ill group were diagnostically concordant, compared with forty-four percent of the post-marital group'.[100] It was acknowledged that the theory of predisposition could not be dismissed entirely; nevertheless, it appeared that the assortative hypothesis could not be used to explain symptoms of neurosis in this study.

In order to further illuminate these findings, the paper then proceeded to deconstruct a number of variables relating to the marital and family histories of the couples. Based on follow-up notes, the author attempted to assess the quality of the marriages and rated them on a sliding scale from 'good' to 'bad', in terms of: positive satisfaction; friction and dissatisfaction; infidelity and separation/divorce. Only nine of the fifty-seven couples were assessed as having 'good' marriages; thirteen were described as 'average'; twenty as 'poor', and fifteen as 'bad' – 'indicating the generally low standard of these marriages'.[101]

There is no doubt that there were numerous drawbacks associated with research of this kind and these were acknowledged by the author. There was, for instance, no way of confirming that the results were representative of 'ill pairs'; the number of couples utilized was too small to prove any statistical significance. Furthermore, data had been extracted from existing records, and quite some time had passed since the primary diagnosis had been made. A further consideration was that the sample excluded cases that had not received inpatient treatment. There was thus a dearth of information on the possibility of interactive behaviour among couples that did not seek help for less severe categories of affective disorder. Nevertheless, as the author remarked, the investigation was concerned solely with the qualitative features of sick couples and, with caution, many of the findings could be accepted with confidence. Most importantly, references made to the areas of married life that were a cause for concern were largely those of a sexual and emotional nature. There appeared to be no evidence to suggest that, for women, the domestic experience itself impacted significantly upon their mental health, as many feminist authors were beginning to suggest.

Research on twin siblings also provided a means of investigating the effects of environment on mental health. Neville Parker from the Medical Research Council's Genetics Unit at the Maudsley Hospital undertook a detailed study of two pairs of monozygotic twins, and revealed that, where one sibling of a twin pair developed psychiatric disorder, the other sibling remained free of symptoms.[102] He argued consequently that 'personalities of similar endowment develop differently as a result of special experiences and stresses'. Marital infidelity featured regularly as a life stressor mentioned by those in the group of psychiatrically ill. One woman recalled that her husband 'went off with another woman'; another remarked that her marriage had 'proved most unhappy'.[103]

Much of this work directly contradicted earlier research on neurosis, marriage, assortative mating and mental illness in twins undertaken by the psychiatrist Eliot Slater. Slater, who became well-known for his work on the influence of genetics on mental illness, argued conversely, that neurotic individuals were constitutionally predisposed to neurosis.[104] His study, *Patterns of Marriage* (1951), was undertaken with psychiatric social worker, Moya Woodside, on a cohort of hospitalized 'neurotic' soldiers during wartime. They were compared with a control group of soldiers who had been admitted to hospital for physical illness or injury. Slater and Woodside argued that 'nervous symptoms run in families in a way that can only be put down to heredity'.[105] A neurotic temperament in either partner was thought to have deleterious consequences to the marital relationship and it featured significantly as a cause of unhappiness. The authors stated that 'again and again, we find that neurotic parents come from a neurotic family' but did concede that it was difficult to disentangle the effects of heredity and of early environment. Nevertheless, they remained emphatic that the personality of the individual affected the quality of the marriage, and not the other way around. Slater's conclusions were not surprising given his status as a genetic psychiatrist and his involvement with the Eugenics Society. Much of his later work on twins also suggested that heredity played a major part in the predisposition to mental illness, although he also conceded that environmental circumstances were central to whether or not disease became manifest or not.[106] Whatever his conclusions, it is interesting that the wives interviewed for Slater's work during wartime did not mention domestic duties and mothering as a cause of unhappiness. They were drawn from a working-class background and the authors acknowledged that their findings were difficult to compare with other studies of middle-class families since working-class people revealed 'very different attitudes and values, conditioned by the different environment'.[107] Nevertheless, the women interviewed for their project noted that it was the quality of temperament that was important in a partner and that children 'ranked highest as a cause of happiness in marriage'.[108]

While not dismissing the effects of environmental influences, during the 1960s, other psychiatrists also emphasized the probability of a genetic predisposition to mental illness. Alistair Munro, for example, Lecturer in Psychiatry at the University of Leeds, argued in 1966 that, 'there is a good deal of evidence that [depression] is due to a specific genetic abnormality'. Nevertheless, he noted that 'the mode of inheritance of the condition remains controversial'.[109] Others attempted to provide evidence for the physiological origins of affective disorders by emphasizing somatic symptoms. In one lengthy article published in 1965, John D Pollit, physician in psychological medicine at St Thomas's Hospital, London, argued that a clear distinction should be made between conditions 'showing somatic symptoms based on disturbed physiology' and those 'in which such changes are absent'.[110] The former, he observed, included symptoms that often formed a recognizable pattern (similar to those described by others as endogenous depression) such as loss of weight, loss of appetite, impotence, menstrual changes, early-morning waking, lowered blood pressure and lowered body temperature. These cases tended to appear 'independently of psychological stress' and the symptoms occurred as result of 'alterations in biological rhythms, metabolism and autonomic balance'. For these reasons, Pollitt suggested the use of the label 'depressive functional shift' as a means of distinguishing this condition from other feelings of depression that could simply be understood as a normal reaction to psychological stress. Symptoms associated with the 'functional shift' were said to be caused by a disturbance in the hypothalamus which, the author noted, was 'responsible for homeostasis, the regulation of certain biological rhythms (such as sleep), metabolism and the autonomic nervous system'. These views were constructed within the context of Darwinian theory that presumed emotional expression to be a response designed for self-defence. Thus, Pollitt speculated that the hypothalamus played an important part in the adjustment of the individual to stressful life situations.[111] Predisposed individuals were likely to be those of an 'obsessive or anal-erotic character' and those who had the capacity to inhibit emotion. The condition was also thought to be more common in the elderly. In cases of depression precipitated by environmental stress, the full functional shift thus only developed in predisposed individuals. Pollit also reasoned that the greater incidence of depression in women in Western culture might be explained by the fact they live longer and are subject to additional endocrine disturbances during menstruation, pregnancy, the puerperium and the menopause.[112]

Neuropsychiatrists put forward an alternative construction of mental illness and contended that biochemical changes were an important cause of depressive illness. In many cases, they argued that the efficacy of pharmacological treatments provided clear evidence that biochemical disturbances were responsible. Most research centred on the function of catecholamines (adrenalin, noradrenaline and dopamine) and the indoleamine serotonin, all of which were known neurotransmitters in the central nervous system.[113] This was largely with reference to the MAOI and tricyclic groups of antidepressants, both of which were thought to promote the concentration of serotonin levels in the brain.[114] Alec Coppen, neuroscientist from West Park Hospital in Epsom, remarked that there was evidence that biochemical disturbances were possible in three main areas:

amine metabolism, electrolyte distribution and adrenal cortical activity.[115] The evidence for this, he remarked, had been clearly demonstrated by the success of physical treatments – ECT and psychotropic medications. Other physicians suggested that the measure of the basal blood-flow in the forearm could give a physiological index to anxiety.[116] Writing in an original article in 1967, Henry Miller, a neurologist from the University of Newcastle Upon Tyne, reminded clinicians that psychiatry was one of the most difficult branches of medicine, since it was at base, neurology without physical signs: 'where disturbed cerebral function is manifest not in the easily elicited and fairly objective physical evidence of the neurological clinic, but in the subtler fields of altered mental processes and changes in behaviour'.[117] Based on experience acquired in the management of more than 2,000 cases during nearly two decades of private consultant and general hospital practice, Miller maintained that both environmental theories and theories of personality were inadequate ways of explaining the aetiology of affective disorders. Writing with specific reference to endogenous depression, he remarked that the 'infrequency' of cases precipitated by emotional stress should be emphasized. Moreover, he argued that theories of personality were based upon the 'rather unsatisfying subjective assessment of immeasurable qualities, lacing any "normal" standard of reference'.[118] To Miller, 'the most exciting clues to the physical basis of depressive illnesses' had emerged from the previous ten years research in neuropharmacology. Thus, he agreed with Coppen that the evidence favouring the catecholamine and indoleamine theories was encouraging. He concluded that 'the hypothesis cannot yet be regarded as firmly proved, but it is generally compatible with clinical and pharmacological evidence'.[119]

Debates about affective disorders also identified men as being more frequently predisposed to alcoholism. Many psychiatrists noted the disparity between numbers of men and women presenting with neurotic illness, with women consistently featuring more regularly in statistics. On a number of occasions, research provided evidence to suggest that the apparent deficiency in affective disorder diagnoses in men might be made up by alcoholism.[120] Articles that appeared throughout the decade suggested that men might be more likely to deal with life pressures by abusing alcohol.[121] In one paper, it was explicitly noted that the male alcoholic 'is basically, and most centrally, a neurotic ... alcoholism should be treated as essentially neurotic expression'.[122] It is perhaps not surprising that difficult relationships were implicated as triggers for problem drinking. Men who began drinking early in life, the authors argued, were more likely to have experienced a range of unsatisfactory life experiences, including difficulties in the areas of professional and family relationships.[123] In another article, Charles Smith, a lecturer from the Department of Psychiatry at the University of Edinburgh, reported on a therapeutic group that had been organized for the wives of alcoholics. Testimonies from the women in the group revealed that, as wives, many had admitted to extramarital affairs. Moreover, many of them expressed the need to 'keep secrets' from their husbands, for fear of 'upsetting the precarious equilibrium' even further.[124]

The historian's role is not of course to evaluate the validity of either environmental or biochemical explanations of affective disorder, and, as these debates illustrate, there was considerable diversity of opinion among clinicians. Nevertheless, the discussion about the aetiology of psychiatric illness provides little evidence to suggest that aspects of domesticity such as housekeeping, cooking and childcare were perceived to be pathogenic. Genetic theorists sought to account for the higher numbers of women affected by looking for ways in which they might be genetically predisposed. One paper, for example, indicated that healthy males might transfer some protection from affective disorder to their sons but not to their daughters, whereas, the daughters of affected women appeared to be at greater risk of developing illness than sons.[125] Neurologists proposing biochemical factors as the most important cause of affective disorders put forward possibilities related to a woman's reproductive potentiality: menstruation, childbirth and the menopause. Those who aligned themselves with environmental theorists provided myriad examples of research whereby women themselves were given the opportunity to analyse their own circumstances and events that might have caused emotional stress. Many of them observed that aspects of their relationships with others provided cause for concern. Relationships with husbands came under scrutiny and women often appeared to be dissatisfied with emotional and sexual aspects of their partnerships. The levels of affection given and received within marriage appeared to be particularly important, as did the levels of security and nurture experienced as a child. None of the women referred directly to isolation or stultification in relation to their role as housewives. Indeed, many of them were single women who were thus less likely to have assumed a full-time domestic role, and others recalled the onset of symptoms before their marriage union.

Treatment of Affective Disorders

Psychiatrists who were committed to physical treatments for anxiety and depression promoted the use of various psychopharmaceutical preparations and, where appropriate, continued to defend the use of ECT.[126] The late 1950s and early 1960s were characterized by cautious enthusiasm in relation to the discovery of the therapeutic effects of the tranquillizers chlorpromazine, reserpine and meprobamate. While this was regarded as welcome progress for psychiatry and mental illness, previously seen as 'the traditional poor relation of physical disease',[127] there was concern that enthusiasm might be running ahead of evidence.[128] The effects of the antipsychotic drugs were seen largely as relevant to the more severe forms of personality disorder and some psychiatrists argued that the available drugs proved unconvincing in the treatment of neuroses. There was greater optimism surrounding the treatment of depression. Gradually during the 1960s, the possibilities opened up for symptomatic treatment not only of severe endogenous depression, but also for the category thought to be 'reactive', and characterized by anxiety. William Sargant commented in 1963 that there were numerous patients with milder, atypical forms of depressive illness and that large numbers of treatable cases of depression were being seen by general practitioners and physicians. He argued that:

> Depressive illnesses are now the most easily treatable and also have the highest potential for recovery of all types of mental illness. Patients can nearly always be helped out of an attack of depression, most of them fairly speedily, if only the correct diagnosis is made and the appropriate treatments are given.[129]

Sargant continued to promote the use of ECT for endogenous forms of depression. However, he conceded that it could now be used alongside the tricyclic group of antidepressants. Although calls were made for further research, those affected by reactive depression appeared to respond favourably to the MAOIs.[130] Sargant and Dally noted particularly that many patients affected by anxiety states had previously been 'driving, capable people, sometimes occupying positions of responsibility'.[131] As will be shown in Chapter 6, the pharmaceutical company William Warner, manufacturers of the brand Nardil (phenelzine, a MAOI), were quick to draw upon this idea and suggest that their product was the preferable choice for use in the patient of 'previously good personality'. This was despite inconclusive results in placebo-based drug trials.[132]

During the 1960s, barbiturates were still prescribed to patients with sleep disorders. Long-acting barbiturates were used as sedatives and short-acting ones were used in anaesthesia. In many cases, these drugs were still seen as 'safe, reliable drugs'.[133] Nevertheless, concerns had been mooted for over a decade about the risks of overdose and dependence. For example, a leading article in *The Lancet* in 1954 had attempted to raise awareness about the 'harmful potentialities' of the barbiturates and recommended 'restraint in prescribing'.[134] This prompted numerous responses in the subsequent issue, where physicians expressed concern in agreement over their addictive properties and also about the alleged practice of indiscriminate prescribing.[135] Likewise, an editorial in the *BMJ* in 1954 discussed the dangers of the addictive properties of barbiturate drugs. In this instance it was observed that phenobarbitone was being prescribed for anxiety-related disorders 'two or three times more often' than other psychotropic medications.[136] By 1962, Enoch Powell, Health Minister, raised concerns about the rising number of prescriptions for tranquillizing drugs. He told parliament that the net cost to the NHS had been £1.6 million in 1960 and that this had

Lightening Troubled Minds 99

risen to £2.4 million by 1961.[137] Concerns were also voiced about the overprescribing of meprobamate. It was announced in parliament that, during 1961 in England and Wales, a total of 870,000 prescriptions were written for this drug alone, at a cost of £320,000 to the NHS.[138]

Numerous letters appeared during the mid-1960s raising further concerns about the practice of combining antidepressant drugs. While Sargant's conviction was that various antidepressive compounds could be mixed safely provided that the doses were correctly adjusted, other psychiatrists urged extreme caution due to isolated cases where atypical reactions had been observed.[139] Particular concerns were also raised about the MAOIs which were soon found to react seriously with certain foods causing potentially fatal hypertension. They were also found to be contraindicated with the drug phenylpropanolamine which was used in many simple cold and flu remedies to relieve nasal congestion.[140]

Later in the decade, the benzodiazepine compounds became the favoured pharmacological treatment for anxiety-related disorders. Commentators suggested that their calming effects were 'unique' and indeed 'remarkable', in particular because they did not cause drowsiness in the same way as barbiturates.[141] In comparison with other drugs such as chlorpromazine and meprobamate, these compounds were rated highly for moderate or long-standing anxiety.[142] Although studies in the early 1960s indicated that there was a potential for dependence if benzodiazepines were used in high doses for a prolonged period, they continued to be used widely throughout the decade and into the 1970s. Malcolm Lader argues that the existence of physical dependence in patients taking high doses was established right from the initiation of benzodiazepine use. However, he suggests that little notice was taken of negative reports partly because of the widespread perception of their safety:

> During the 1960s, the medical profession realized that the benzodiazepines were surprisingly safe in over-dosage, compared to their predecessors, the barbiturates ... So impressed were British doctors that they mounted a campaign under the auspices of the British Medical Association to phase out the barbiturates. Implicit in that initiative, in the mid-1970s, was acquiescence in the growth in use of the benzodiazepines.[143]

Since anxiety was a frequent accompaniment of depression, it became common practice for benzodiazepines to be prescribed alongside either tricyclic or MAOI antidepressants.[144]

Articles during the early 1960s that reported on clinical trials of these drugs are especially illuminating, since they regularly featured case studies of individuals and included details about their life circumstances. Sargant and Dally noted in 1962 that atypical depressions sometimes overlapped with, and were sometimes indistinguishable from, illnesses often labelled as anxiety neurosis.[145] They argued that the MAOI 'Nardil', either used alone or in combination with the benzodiazepine 'Librium', could be effective in treating anxiety states. This appeared to be particularly so in patients 'of previously good personality' who had 'broken down, only after great stress'. Although environmental circumstances may thus have triggered symptoms of anxiety, for mainstream psychiatrists, pharmacological treatment was still seen as appropriate. The case histories cited by these authors are revealing since the 'severe or prolonged stress' often related to difficulties in relationships. In one instance, a forty-two-year-old farmer's wife was found to respond favourably to Nardil:

> [She] gave a four year history of headache and generalized pains in the face and abdomen. All her teeth had been removed without effect. She had a constant feeling of anxiety and bouts of weeping and depression. She felt exhausted, was emotionally labile ... symptoms tended to be worse in the morning and late at night.[146]

The authors confirmed that no organic cause for these symptoms had been found, despite repeated examinations. Doctors prescribed a variety of tranquillizers and sedatives, without effect. Previously, the woman had been a conscientious, lively woman 'who had looked after her family well and helped her husband in his work'. However, it transpired that 'her husband was a heavy drinker, more interested in his farm than his wife'. In addition to this, 'the sexual side of the marriage had never been satisfactory'. The woman entered into an affair with one of her husband's employees and 'the arousal of satisfying sexual feelings for the first time conflicted with the sense of guilt she felt for what had occurred'. Psychotherapy enabled her to break off the affair, but the symptoms continued. Another woman was referred with symptoms of phobic anxiety. Her personal history included an attempted sexual assault at the age of seventeen. This resulted in the fear of going out alone and symptoms of claustrophobia when travelling on buses and trains.[147] The other example given was of a man who developed an 'acute state of anxiety' following serious organic illness.[148] These two patients were described as 'less stable in their autonomic responses' and responded positively to the combination of Librium and Nardil.

The pharmacological treatment of affective disorder thus became entrenched during this period. As Callahan and Berrios have commented, psychotherapeutic methods proved impractical in a primary-care setting and 'experts failed in the challenge of balancing specific training in psychotherapy with the realities of the primary-care environment'.[149] Tensions also existed between providers of different 'psychotherapies'. During the 1950s and 1960s, psychotherapy became synonymous with psychoanalysis and suffered from negative criticisms and declining confidence.[150] Joseph Wolpe, for example, an early pioneer of behaviour therapy, strongly criticized the practice of psychoanalysis and claimed in 1964 that its proponents had failed to provide adequate scientific evidence for its efficacy: 'they have adduced no acceptable support for their theory; beguiling themselves with surmises, analogies and extrapolations'.[151]

During the 1960s, behavioural therapists applied the principles of 'modern learning theory' to the treatment of neurotic disorders. Fundamentally, these principles assumed that human responses to situations and stresses are learned and that, therefore, there can be 'no neurosis underlying the symptom, but merely the symptom itself'.[152] Neurotic symptoms were defined by therapists as 'conditioned autonomic responses' and treatment involved counter-conditioning, or, re-educating the mind to react differently to stimuli. Wolpe described the process:

> If a response antagonistic to anxiety can be made to occur in the presence of anxiety-evoking stimuli, so that it is accompanied by a complete or partial suppression of the anxiety responses, the bond between these stimuli and the anxiety responses will be weakened.[153]

The alternative hypothesis put forward by psychoanalysts regarded symptoms as merely 'the manifestation of some unconscious and repressed complex ... the "complex" itself is seen as the illness, and the symptom cannot be cured in any permanent form without uncovering the complex'.[154] During the 1960s, Eysenck and Wolpe, among others, were regular contributors to the *British Journal of Psychiatry*, in which they put forward their ideas about the efficacy of behavioural treatment in phobias. It was regarded as useful in the treatment of 'simple' phobias; those that related to one object or situation. However, it was often thought of as less efficient in complex cases where a more generalized level of anxiety was present. Eysenck believed that disorders of a dysthymic character (those that were characterized by depression, anxiety or phobia) responded to 'reconditioning' to produce a more rational response which would weaken and ultimately 'extinguish' the anxious reaction. Conditions that brought about behaviour that was socially ostracized (such as alcoholism, fetishism and, during the 1960s, homosexuality) were thought to respond effectively to 'aversion therapy'. This consisted of 'the pairing of the stimulus in question with strong aversive stimuli producing sympathetic reactions'.[155]

Case studies included in academic reports once again revealed a variety of environmental traumas and also illustrated the pathogenic potential of difficult interpersonal relationships. In 1964, Wolpe argued that behaviour therapy could be helpful in complex neuroses but was mindful that treatment might take longer than in simple phobias. The examples given included 'Mrs Y, aged fifty-six' who had a case of complex neurosis, arising from her life history. An only child, Mrs Y had rarely seen her father and had endured a 'harsh and brutal' mother who 'beat her frequently and confined her alone in an upstairs room'.[156] Another woman, 'Mrs Z', aged thirty-six, had become traumatized when her husband had deserted after she had been diagnosed with tuberculosis. A further example was 'Mr T', a young eighteen-year-old man who developed anxiety from being made to sleep in bed with his sister until the age of fifteen. His sister was two years older than him and 'Mr T' had developed guilty feelings over the sexual arousal he experienced as a consequence of sleeping in such close proximity to her.[157] Another article cited similar case studies and included: a forty-two-year-old woman who was dissatisfied with her marriage; a twenty-two-year-old single woman whose mother had died when she was ten; a twenty-five-year-old married woman whose mother had been 'highly strung and beset by fears'; and a thirty-two-year-old single man whose father had been a long-term depressive.[158]

Alongside the formal methods of 'psychotherapy', in many primary-care settings there also existed a more informal and unofficial practice of supportive therapy that took place during regular surgery consultations. Callahan and Berrios note that there is no data available on the effectiveness of informal physician-patient discussions on the course and outcome of emotional disorders. Nevertheless, the oral history testimonies in Chapter 5 suggest that many general practitioners attempted to provide informal counselling sessions. Although these were brief and often took place within the six minute allocated consultation time, there is evidence that a sympathetic attitude (sometimes in combination with prescribed pharmacological preparations) enabled patients to understand their symptoms and ultimately work towards changing difficult life circumstances. Michael Balint, a Hungarian psychoanalyst who moved to England during the 1930s, promoted this simple and pragmatic method of psychotherapy and placed great emphasis on the importance of the doctor–patient relationship. Alongside his wife Enid, Balint set up groups for general practitioners in London which were coordinated by a qualified psychiatrist. Their aim was to help doctors understand the psychological aspects of their patients' problems and thus avoid any breakdown of communication between the two. The Balint Society was formed in 1969 to continue their work.[159] Arguably, GPs trained in such a fashion were more receptive to psychological therapies.

The situation in Britain differed greatly from that in the United States, where office-based psychotherapy dominated. Explorations of the clinical practice in both countries indicate that there was a wide divergence in the use of therapeutic techniques. One comparison of clinical practices undertaken in 1967 demonstrated that a high percentage of American clinicians were involved in private practice; however, the majority of British psychiatrists were engaged mainly in hospital-based NHS treatment.[160] The investigation therefore suggested that, in Britain, there was 'a much greater emphasis on physical techniques', whereas in the United States 'there was more reliance on psychotherapy'. Even within American psychiatric hospitals, clinicians used physical techniques, including modified electroplexy, less frequently than their British counterparts.[161] Sargant argued that these differences were largely due to the differences in working environments, and to 'the greater influence of psychodynamic theory on American teaching departments'.[162] Other commentators emphasized that all psychiatric services must be set within the country's socio-cultural context. Thus, 'the prevailing psychodynamic orientation [could] be understood only in relation both to the economic structure of American medicine and to the attitudes of a relatively sophisticated public with a widespread interest in the concept of "positive mental health".[163] Nevertheless, the publication of this article prompted a number of American psychiatrists to retort that psychiatric residents had developed growing optimism towards the use of psychopharmacological agents during the 1960s.[164] Sargant's view that 'Freudians were reluctant to accept tranquilizing drugs' was thus rejected. Instead it was duly emphasized that teaching departments had 'allowed drugs to gain recognition and acceptance'. However, psychopharmaceutical treatment was usually seen as an adjunct to psychotherapy.

Conclusion

This chapter has explored key themes and developments in the psychiatric classification and treatment of affective disorders during the period following the Second World War. Medical debates illustrate that, by the 1960s, although there was cautious acceptance of the notion that some individuals may be biologically predisposed to certain disorders, many practitioners were also open to the idea that environmental factors could trigger illness. A wide range of environmental stresses were thought to influence such cases and these naturally included serious lifetime traumas such as bereavement and abuse in childhood. Although practitioners were drawing on theories from a range of different perspectives, much of the research indicated that disordered personal relationships were an important precursor to mental disorder. Contemporary theorists were evidently drawing on prevailing notions of 'the family' as a site of disorder, however, academic articles often included case studies where life histories were analysed not only by medical staff but by the patients themselves. Within these life histories there is no convincing evidence to suggest that women found the day-to-day aspects of domestic life and mothering to be stultifying or dissatisfying. When asked to comment on 'marital adjustment', respondents referred to dysfunctional emotional and sexual relationships and not aspects of domesticity and mothering. Many of the women patients were in fact young and unmarried; although we cannot be certain that these young women did not have some domestic responsibilities, the case studies suggest that they were not primarily homemakers. Other case histories indicated that men also experienced psychiatric symptoms related to environmental stress, and statistically they featured more regularly in some categories of mental disorder, in particular schizophrenia and alcohol abuse.

The following chapter explores the experiences of the oral history respondents who endured symptoms of nervous anxiety and depression. Their testimonies broadly reflect the findings of psychiatrists and clinicians who were undertaking research on psychiatric illness.

5 NOT SOMETHING YOU TALK ABOUT: PERSONAL ACCOUNTS OF ANXIETY AND DEPRESSION

No amount of direct medication can be effective, unless women can also be brainwashed into deluding themselves that their monotonous and unremitting drudgery in the home is for any purpose, or doing any good.
Germaine Greer, *The Female Eunuch* (1970)

During the mid-twentieth-century, psychiatry 'widened its net' to include the treatment of, not only the more severe categories of mental disorder, but also neurotic disorders: depression, anxiety and phobias.[1] Increasingly, the 'problems of daily living' were redefined as medical conditions. Agnes Miles has noted that there has been a rising expectation that all human problems should be amenable to solutions by science and medicine. Unhappiness has become medicalized; doctors have replaced the clergy – medical problems seem more acceptable than social ones.[2] An extensive range of behaviours are listed in the Diagnostic Statistical Manual (DSM), and in the equivalent used in Britain, the International Classification of Diseases (ICD). In 1952, the DSM listed 112 disorders; this figure had expanded by 1994 to 374.[3]

This process has not been undertaken overtly; instead, the expansion of medicine has been largely 'an insidious and often undramatic phenomenon, accomplished by medicalizing much of daily living by making medicine, and the labels "healthy" and "ill", relevant to an ever increasing part of human existence'.[4] During the 1960s, Thomas Scheff, the key proponent of labelling theory as related to mental illness, held that society creates a set of rules about behaviour that are deemed as 'normal'.[5] Those who exhibit behaviour that falls outside these norms are labelled as deviant. Individuals who are assigned a label or diagnosis for their symptoms are thus inclined to assume a new social role as 'deviant', and increasingly begin to behave in accordance with the sick role. Patients are also more likely to seek a positive diagnosis because a label implies that the condition is understood and treatable.[6] 'Sickness' therefore becomes something of a self-fulfilling prophecy. Scheff's views have been widely criticized, primarily

– 105 –

because he underplayed the possibility that psychiatric symptoms, or 'primary deviance' as he called it, might be caused by biological or hereditary factors. His most vocal critic, Walter Gove, who also wrote with authority on the subject, argued that the 'social reaction' or 'labelling' theory does not adequately explain the initial act of deviance which might plausibly 'reflect a serious disturbance'.[7] Scheff remains a staunch critic of the current medical model of mental illness, although he now concedes that an interdisciplinary approach is needed because, 'in human conduct, particularly, the vital processes seem to occur at interfaces, in the intersections of the organic, psychological and social systems'.[8] More broadly, critics of the medical model contend that it offers no solution to the social problems which may trigger psychiatric symptoms. Thus, if no attempt is made to address environmental influences, the symptoms are likely to recur. From this perspective, psychopharmaceutical treatment is viewed simply as a means of alleviating symptoms and not as a solution to the cause.

Motivated in part by the insights put forward by Michel Foucault in 1967, in *Madness and Civilization*, many scholars have also suggested that the medical model of mental illness has been utilized as a tool for social control.[9] Thomas Szasz argued in 1962 that those labelled as 'mentally ill' were in fact those that 'lacked contribution' to social welfare, either by ineptitude, stupidity or lack of resources. These individuals were thus at variance with dominant values in culture.[10] Ronald Laing and others associated with the critique of psychiatry that took place during the 1960s maintained that psychiatric treatments were inhumane and that mainstream approaches did not view patients' problems within their social context.[11] More recently, Nikolas Rose has proposed that the psychological sciences have attempted to 'render human subjectivity into science as a disciplined object'.[12] Procedures such as tests, scales and assessments have thus been employed to codify, mathematize and standardize as 'a psychological schema for differentiating individuals'. Thus, 'the human individual has become calculable and manageable'.[13]

Symptoms of anxiety and depression in women have been widely viewed as inherently related to the unfulfilling nature of domestic work and other disadvantageous aspects of the female role. Agnes Miles suggested that 'the home can become, for the full-time housewife, a setting which, by its peculiar strains, "drives her mad"'.[14] According to Miles, doctors act as agents of society and maintain the status quo by 'adjusting' their female patients to their domestic roles, without considering that the role itself might have caused the illness.[15] It is this aspect of the debate on mental illness that will be explored more fully in this chapter. Historically, it has long been documented that women appear to be more likely to experience certain types of mental illness than men. During the twentieth century, greater numbers of women are treated in psychiatric hospitals, outpatient mental health services and with psychotherapy. In 1967, a major study found 'more mental illness among women than men from every source of data'.[16] However, there remains discussion about whether the statistics simply reflect the fact that women are more likely than men to report symptoms, or, whether they reflect substantive differences in the health experiences of both sexes.[17]

Walter Gove provided an important contribution to the feminist debate on women and mental illness during the 1970s and 1980s when he provided a reappraisal of the theories of American psychologist Phyllis Chesler. As one of the first academics to draw attention to the harrowing plight of institutionalized women, Chesler had claimed in the early 1970s that 'women who reject, or are ambivalent to the female role, frighten both themselves and society'.[18] In her research on psychiatric treatment, she concluded that, during the 1960s, women began to experience higher rates of neurotic and psychotic illness. Gove took this premise and sought to distinguish between the numbers of women and men receiving psychiatric treatment and the real incidence of mental illness. He applied what he called 'a precise definition of mental illness' to his analysis and excluded those who experienced personality disorders or substance or alcohol abuse.[19] His conclusion was that:

> When single women are compared with single men, divorced women with divorced men, and widowed women with widowed men, these women do not have rates of mental illness that are higher than their male counterparts. In fact, if there is a difference within these marital categories, it is that these women have lower rates of mental illness.[20]

Gove's central argument was that married women were more likely to develop psychiatric symptoms than men from all marital categories. His research focused on the domestic aspects of a married woman's life, and he argued that a number of difficulties associated with the role combined to increase the likelihood of the onset of mental illness. However, Gove's work was based upon many assumptions, and the oral testimonies in Chapter 3 would suggest that his analysis is misleading. Gove suggested, for example, that 'it seems reasonable to assume that a large number of women find their major instrumental activities – raising children and keeping house – frustrating'.[21] Nonetheless, he acknowledged in his footnotes that this assumption was based on the writing of authors such as Friedan and Myrdal and Klein, and that he had been 'unable to locate any systematic evaluation of this assumption'.[22]

Gove further suggested that, since the housewife's role was 'invisible' and 'unstructured', it was likely that she would be able to 'put things off, to let things slide, in sum – to perform poorly. The lack of structure and visibility allows her to brood over her troubles and her distress may thus feed upon itself.'[23] He claimed that, since a woman was likely to be restricted to a single societal role, 'she typically has no major alternative source of gratification.'[24] These statements are entirely inconsistent with the evidence provided by the oral history sample where, on the whole, women tended to find the flexibility inherent in the role advantageous. As has been shown, they also regularly participated in other activities outside the home. Gove concluded that the housewife's role was one of 'low prestige ... being a housewife does not require a great deal of skill, for virtually all women, whether educated or not seem to be capable of being at least moderately competent housewives'.[25] Conversely, the housewives interviewed for this study felt that their role was of considerable value and involved a certain amount of skill.

The most misleading aspect of Gove's work relates to the way in which he emphasized the domestic aspects of married life. Echoing the work of most feminist authors, Gove assumed that the most notable difficulties experienced by married women were related to their role as homemakers and mothers. As this chapter will illustrate, this claim is not supported by those women interviewed who experienced depression or anxiety. They rarely found serious fault with their domestic role, but often indicated that the marital relationship itself was related to the onset of psychological symptoms. Gove touched only briefly on the emotional aspects of married life, noting in one paragraph that 'women report more marital problems than men, and women tend to be less happy with their marriage'.[26] The remainder of his work focused on the 'limited and frustrating' nature of the housewife's role. Surprisingly, he also argued that women were 'less likely than men to get satisfaction out of being a parent'.[27]

Writing in Canada during the late 1970s, the medical sociologist and feminist Ruth Cooperstock undertook research into the effects of tranquillizer use in North America.[28] Her overarching warnings about the dangers of overprescribing and the medicalization of women's social problems were valid and important. She agreed with Gove that married women were more likely to receive prescriptions for psychotropic drugs than men and cited studies that purported to show that consumption patterns were strikingly similar for single men and women.[29] However, Cooperstock's central contention was that tranquillizer use in women was largely related to difficulties experienced with maintaining the given social role of wife, mother and house-worker.[30] In her exploratory investigation into tranquillizer use, Cooperstock noted that for women, continued use of these drugs was discussed 'in terms of permitting them to maintain themselves in a role or roles which they found difficult or intolerable without the drug'.[31] Interestingly, while the role of 'home-worker' was emphasized by the author, the majority of Cooperstock's examples featured women who had experienced marital difficulties or other traumatic circumstances. One woman was married to an alcoholic. Another spoke of her ungrateful, abusive husband and her gruelling attempts at infertility treatment, recalling that she had 'nine pregnancies and four live children in four and a half years'.[32] One woman hinted at marital discord by acknowledging that 'long term help came via attendance at marriage counselling'.[33] Others cited by Cooperstock had experienced divorce or the death of a spouse. There is certainly an undercurrent of discontent in some of the case studies cited and this is perhaps understandable given the changing social climate of the 1970s. However, the factors leading to mental illness still appear to have had less to do with the 'traditional' domestic role and more to do with dysfunctional relationships and traumatic life experiences.

As is often the case with research of this type, the statistics provided by Cooperstock were also ambiguous. She claimed that *continued* use of tranquillizers was usually a drug solution to an emotional problem. However, 'the *initial* reasons for use varied widely', with 53 per cent of those interviewed citing a somatic problem. A number of these conditions were listed in her footnotes: 'degenerative discs, lupus erythematosus, ulcerative colitis, atrial fibrillation etc.'.[34] It is certainly not clear that the onset of these conditions was related in any way to the traditional domestic role. Cooperstock also briefly drew attention to the mixed drugs that contained psychotherapeutic agents as an additional element. She acknowledged that these were not included in her statistics and thus that 'it is impossible to know how the inclusion of the "hidden" psychotropic drug would affect these tables and particularly how they would distribute between the sexes'.[35] This is an important consideration, since, as the final chapter of this book will illustrate, these 'combo-drugs' were aggressively marketed throughout the period and were more commonly directed towards the 'businessman'. The brand 'Nactisol', for example, contained 'poldine methylsulphate' for ulcer control and 'butabarbitol', a barbiturate sedative, for the relief of associated anxiety and tension.[36]

The important study *Social Origins of Depression: A Study of Psychiatric Disorder in Women,* authored by the sociologists George Brown and Tirril Harris (1978) indicated that working class women were much more likely to succumb to depression. They argued unequivocally that social factors caused psychiatric illness and suggested that working-class women experienced 'more severe life events' and greater difficulties with finance and housing.[37] They were also less likely to benefit from an 'intimate tie' – a close confidant or spouse – which was viewed as a protective factor. However, this study could not claim to provide a representative analysis of depression since men were deliberately excluded from the research. Brown and Harris based the design of their study upon the somewhat sweeping assumption that 'women probably suffer from depression more often than men' and that they were also more likely to be at home, and thus available for interview during the day.[38] They therefore omitted any consideration of social factors that might cause depression in men and since men were less likely to discuss symptoms or seek medical help, their original premise that 'women were more likely to suffer from depression' is perhaps questionable.

Joan Busfield has rightly drawn attention to the pitfalls associated with the data analysis of psychiatric conditions. She contends that there can be no universal generalization that women are more prone to mental illness than men; there can be no true notion of prevalence since diagnostic categories vary so greatly.[39] In addition to this, she points to the biases associated with the cultural acceptability of certain symptoms. Patient statistics, she argues, usually tell us more about mental health services and the particular way in which any one category is being constructed and measured than about patterns of mental illness in a community.[40] It is indeed also impossible to tell how many symptoms go unreported and undiagnosed. Marilyn Johnson, in her response to Gove's article concurred, arguing that 'the reported difference in mental health of married and unmarried women is one example of how it may be misleading to generalize about the mental health status of all women'.[41] Johnson criticized Gove's definition of mental illness, which she argued, excluded personality disorders and cases of substance abuse – effectively groups that consist, in large part, of males.[42]

As Ludmilla Jordanova has noted, it would perhaps be more productive to move away from academic inquiry that has so often produced one-sided assumptions about power and oppression.[43] Women's mental health may well be related to men, children and family structure; however, we must re-evaluate accounts that brand women as emotional in order that male experts gain 'control'.[44] Furthermore, as Foucault observed, power is not always 'repressive', but can also be 'enabling'. The oral testimonies later in this chapter will illustrate that new discourses surrounding the origins and treatment of mental symptoms often allowed women to cultivate new ways of empowering themselves, enabling them to begin new lives and distance themselves from unsatisfactory relationships.

The remainder of this chapter will assess the experience of those women interviewed who endured minor psychiatric disorders. The oral testimonies are supported by letters written by women published in the most popular women's magazines. The remit of this study is not to offer a medical opinion about the causes of mental illness; nor is it possible to retrospectively diagnose the women who spoke about their condition. Although the research does provide strong anecdotal evidence to suggest that situational factors greatly influenced the onset of anxiety or depression it is not possible to rule out a biological cause or genetic predisposition to mental illness. It is also feasible that, as Scheff proposed over forty years ago, these women were reacting in some way to their 'diagnosis' and that the meaning they attached to their experience was heavily influenced by society's ideas about mental illness.

Although this chapter attempts to provide a more nuanced appraisal of domestic experience, it is very clear that, although the social and economic structures of society during the period were often advantageous to women during marriage, the reverse was true in separation and divorce. Beveridge's breadwinner model left women economically vulnerable and socially ostracized when the marital relationship became untenable. It is therefore suggested here that where social factors were implicated in illness, it was the ongoing difficulties associated with marital discord and the material disadvantages following divorce that were the more probable cause of mental symptoms. Indeed, it appears that satisfactory personal relationships with all members of the immediate family were ultimately the key to a sense of well-being and the ability to cope during adverse circumstances.

The responses that follow have been organized around the two most prominent themes that emerged from the interviews: marital discord (which was cited most frequently as having a negative impact on mental health), and trauma during childhood or adolescence. These themes were nonetheless by no means mutually exclusive. Although several respondents located one major set of circumstances as the cause of their problems, they also implied that other aspects of their lives as children could be included as contributory factors. Interviewees were questioned about their understanding of psychiatric symptoms and they were then asked whether or not they were afflicted by nervous or emotional conditions. They were questioned in detail about their own particular coping mechanisms and any treatment that they sought for their symptoms. Approximately half of the total number of respondents interviewed for this project identified themselves as sufferers of anxiety and/or depression. The majority of these sought medical advice about their disorder; however, only a minority of consultations resulted in treatment with psychotropic medications.

Experience of Marital Discord

Although it was argued in Chapter 3 that many women were content in their role as wives and mothers, a sizeable number, while not dissatisfied with their domestic role, experienced marriages that were unhappy. These women made a direct link between their distressing situation and the onset of psychiatric symptoms. Eileen Bailey, for example, 'always wanted to be married with a family' but indicated early on in the interview that she had 'married the wrong man'.[45] Eileen was aged twenty-one when she married in 1943. She had three daughters and remained married for twenty-five years, finally divorcing her husband following years of his philandering. Her husband's affairs were with women from the local tennis club where they were both members and she recalled that 'It was awful to feel that you couldn't trust him ... and I knew that other people knew and were probably talking about it. And that doesn't make you feel very good.'[46]

At the time, Eileen was not aware of the clinical terms anxiety or depression; but she remembered things 'getting on top of her' sometimes. This she described as 'just a feeling':

> I'd go and see my doctor who knew. And he'd say: 'Oh you've got the old trouble again?' ... When I went to see him it was because I felt 'I can't cope any longer'. I don't think he gave me anything. But just to talk to someone was nice.[47]

Eileen maintained that, at this time, counselling was not an official option for treatment; however, she happened to be personally acquainted with the psychiatrist at her local hospital who invited her to come and talk to him: 'I did go and talk to him now and again, and he was helpful. I felt I was talking to somebody that really understood.'[48] This appeared to be a particularly valuable source of support since she felt that it was seen as inappropriate to discuss such intimate matters with others: 'You didn't open your heart up. But people knew – you kept it to yourself as much as you could.'[49] Eileen remembered that, despite the financial hardship she experienced following her divorce, the 'feelings' soon disappeared: 'They had been caused by the situation and by the time I'd left him, I felt much better.'[50]

Jean Hill, who was married in 1957, had believed that her marriage was happy and solid. She had a 'good' husband who shared most of the household tasks and also participated regularly in childcare. However, after thirty-three years of marriage, without warning, he announced that he wanted a divorce:

> He decided he wanted to go away. Only there was somebody else ... and the things that he told me – that he'd been unhappy since day one. He destroyed every memory that I had, every memory completely. And you think to yourself: 'what has he really been thinking all these years?'[51]

Jean's symptoms emerged much later than Eileen's, during the 1980s. However, like Eileen, she directly associated them with her distressing circumstances. Jean was eventually persuaded to visit a clinical psychologist and recalled the benefits of talking to someone who could reflect objectively on her problems; something that was not widely available to patients during the 1950s and 1960s: 'She was very good. Because I talked, but I also wrote. I wrote all sorts of things down ... and I just used to give her this folder with all this writing in and she'd say: "Tell me about that ..."'[52] During the course of the interview, Jean revealed that although she had two healthy children, she had suffered the trauma of delivering two stillborn children, one in 1957 and another in 1959. No psychological help or support system existed to help her through these stillbirths, and in retrospect, Jean felt that she had never recovered from the sadness. This was duly compounded by the divorce from her husband. The psychologist enabled Jean to talk openly for the first time about both sets of circumstances:

> I often wonder you know – all that was pushed back because I was able to have another baby ... and it was talking to her, all about the babies, all came out ... I thought [my husband] was having a nervous breakdown because he was working so hard. So for a whole month I wasn't really aware of what was really happening. I was angry for the children and when I went to see the clinical psychologist I suppose the anger did come out then ... You can't make this person love you again, so you are completely out of control.[53]

Jean was interviewed together with two friends, Anne and Rose, and all three women agreed that it was not seen as 'the done thing' to discuss marital problems with others. Anne Shepherd maintained that: 'If you were having trouble in your marriage, you didn't go talking to anyone about it. You know, you suffered on your own.'[54] Jean concurred:

> I would go as far as to use the word 'ashamed', because you viewed yourself as a failure. You were unaware that other people – you thought all their marriages were wonderful, unless you saw something obviously sticking out like a sore thumb. But everybody was having a 'lovely' marriage, so, if you had any problems at all, you didn't tell anybody.[55]

Nora Kelly was twenty-eight when she married in 1961. She emigrated to Australia with her husband soon after they were married, in order for him to commence a university post there. Not only did Nora feel isolated so far away from her family, but following the birth of her first child she decided she had made a mistake in marrying her husband. He was relocated again to America shortly after the birth of their son and Nora made what she felt to be a courageous decision, to return to England alone as a single-parent:

> I was actually depressed by the time I'd left my ex-husband because he was an awful person ... I was with [him] for about six weeks after we arrived in America and then I said 'I want to leave you'. And I would just burst into tears all the time. And I wonder if then it was the baby blues, that we hadn't sort of acknowledged at that time – although it was pretty difficult living with the ex-husband, half the time not speaking.[56]

Nora traced the origins of her long battle with mental illness back to the distressing experience of unhappy marriage. However, she also mentioned problems that had affected her family when she was a child. Her father had suffered from depression in later life which made him very difficult to live with. Nora recalled having 'a sense of guilt' about her father because she 'stopped loving him' when she was really young: 'He used to get really bad tempered. But that could have been anxiety and I didn't realize – he used to get really irritable.'[57]

Back in England, Nora enrolled at teacher-training college and attempted to juggle single-motherhood with her studies. She talked at length about her experience of obsessive behaviour and depression:

> When I started college I was getting anxiety, and I knew I was depressed ... I'd be going off to college and think 'have I got my key?' And I did geography as a main, and I would think 'oh we're going on a coach, I might be sick on the coach' and all this sort of thing.[58]

These symptoms plagued Nora for many years. She received various psychopharmacological remedies from her general practitioner which she felt helped to alleviate the worst of her symptoms and to keep her calm dealing with a class

114   *Desperate Housewives, Neuroses and the Domestic Environment, 1945–1970*

of small children. However, she spoke movingly about the effect her illness had on her son:

> When I was sent out for school practice, I wouldn't get home before Julian and he used to get home by bus. And he said: 'I'd always go and look to see if the suitcases were gone'. He always thought I wasn't coming home. I think that's really awful really ... And I can remember walking along the beach ... and I just thought: 'I want to throw myself into the sea, I want to die' and I just thought: 'I can't leave Julian on his own to go through life with people saying his mother committed suicide'.[59]

Nora was not offered any counselling for her problems. However, she felt lucky to have a doctor who was very understanding. She was prescribed tranquillizers and she felt that, for his time, the doctor was 'very good'.[60] After approximately six months, Nora decided to reduce her intake of tablets, but her emotional state did not improve until she reached her late forties:

> I just weaned myself off them. I didn't really do any follow-up because that was a bus journey the other way and I would have had to take Julian with me – or have a day off college, and it just – never seemed to have the time to do it.[61]

Despite such difficult circumstances, it is striking that these women were still able to express joy about their role as mothers. Nora, for example, remembered happy times with her son:

> Probably the best memories – just that I was absolutely smitten with Julian, it was brilliant, despite the other problems. I got fascinated with child-development and thought it was absolutely wonderful.[62]

Throughout the 1960s, women's magazines were littered with correspondence from women in similar situations to those of Eileen, Jean and Nora. Problem pages first appeared in magazines at the beginning of the twentieth-century in response to changing family patterns. As women were increasingly unable to depend upon the support of wider kin, many women began to seek advice on family matters from their favourite magazines. During the 1950s and 1960s most articles and problem pages promoted the importance of the traditional family structure and there were frequent explicit references made to the distress caused by unhappy marriage. Mary Grant, the well-known agony aunt in *Woman's Own* magazine, regularly featured letters from women in these circumstances. In one such letter entitled 'My nerves are wrecked', a woman wrote: 'my husband has left me several times for other women, but has always come back to me ... My nerves are almost wrecked with worry and anguish.'[63] Another, writing in to the equally popular Evelyn Home's page in *Woman*, declared that she had found it difficult to recover from the breakdown of her relationship 'the memory of happy times and kindly words never leaves me ... the strain is terrible'.[64] Others wrote in with dilemmas relating to whether or not they should remain in an unhappy marriage. The advice given by agony aunts reflected the acceptable prevailing social conventions, and was usually to remain married if at all possible and seek advice from the National Marriage Guidance Council. However, those who were suffering from nervous disorders as a result of such circumstances were often advised to visit their doctor. The following response was typical:

> The tension from which you are suffering shows in your writing. I do beg you to go and see your doctor – there are many reliefs for nervous tension these days, but the best is learning to relax oneself.[65]

Following the introduction of the National Health Service, women's magazines also began to include doctor's diary sections. These fostered common-sense attitudes to common health problems and provided advice about ailments that did not require medical intervention. During the late 1950s, 'experts' writing in women's magazines usually posited psychotherapeutic remedies for nervous disorders. Citing fictitious characters to illustrate a different topic each week, Dr Roderick Wimpole in *Woman's Own*, for example, reconstructed different consultations with patients. The majority of conditions discussed were organic illnesses; however, occasional reference was made to nervous disorders. These were usually described as 'nervous exhaustion' or 'anxiety and nervous tension'. The fictitious characters were by no means always married housewives and were just as likely to be unmarried working women. In an edition printed in 1955, for example, 'Miss T', prone to hypochondria, visits the surgery feeling exhausted and suffering from headaches and palpitations. The diagnosis is 'nervous exhaustion', caused by 'mental conflict', and Dr Wimpole suggests that this may have occurred for various reasons:

> 'Sometimes the trouble is due to a lack of emotional outlet – a desire to love, and be loved, which, under the circumstances is frustrated. Or it may be because the patient is in the wrong kind of job ... another kind of trouble is a feeling of guilt or resentment – often quite subconscious.' Miss T thought for a while. 'Doctor, I really do understand what you mean and I know you are right. In fact, I have a problem that for years has made me unhappy. May I tell you about it?'[66]

Increasingly through the 1960s there are subtle references made to the use of pharmacological remedies reflecting the introduction of new psychotropic medications. 'Young Mrs W' for example, newly married and working long hours, was prescribed a 'sedative' for 'feeling jittery' and unexplained weight loss. Dr Wimple asserted: 'That should calm you down and help you to sleep properly ... then there's a medicine which I should like you to take which should improve your appetite'.[67] By 1968 explicit reference was being made to 'depression' as a

116 *Desperate Housewives, Neuroses and the Domestic Environment, 1945–1970*

distinct clinical entity. Post-menopausal 'Mrs T' for example, visits the surgery having lost all interest in the things going on around her:

> Although I love my family, I am not in the mood to enjoy being with them the way I used to. I feel so low in the morning, it's usually the worst time – I usually feel a bit more cheerful in the evening ... I am so tired all the time.

The doctor's advice marked a clear shift in diagnosis and treatment:

> You have told me the typical story of one form of depression, which is clearly the cause of your fatigue ... nowadays, we recognize it as a physical illness every bit as real as acute appendicitis. Fortunately, it is just as responsive to treatment as any other bodily complaint ... we know that it will respond rapidly to present-day treatment ... you must take the tablets I will prescribe, absolutely regularly for as long as is necessary.[68]

Major articles devoted to psychological problems in the periodical press were rare until the late 1960s. Until then, the advice was analogous to that put forward in 'doctor's diaries'. References to new chemical treatments for emotional distress were not obvious in publications directed at a mass audience. Warnings about the dangers associated with the new psychopharmaceuticals usually came in books from individuals with an academic or professional background or a specific interest in the field of medicine and health. Doris Grant, for example, a champion of fresh, natural ingredients in food, wrote two books during wartime emphasizing the importance of a balanced diet.[69] In her book *Housewives Beware*, published in 1958, Grant included a critique of modern drug therapy and a section on the increased sale of tranquillizing drugs in the United States. Fearful of the consequences of such a trend in Britain, Grant contended that the new drugs not only caused physical dangers but also emotional, moral and philosophical dangers.

It was not until the late 1960s that articles about mental illness began to appear in women's magazines. A frequent contributor to the debate was Dr Claire Weeks, an Australian physician who worked for a period at the University College Hospital in London and who became a pioneer of self-help in psychiatry. She provided advice in magazines from her book *Self Help for Your Nerves*, published in 1963. In an article entitled 'You and Your Nerves', published in *Woman's Own* in 1968, Weeks promoted a common-sense approach and explained the symptoms of panic and anxiety, describing them as 'sensitization' – an exaggerated response to normal situations.[70] She rejected psychoanalytical theories and contended that the cause of nervous illness was 'usually far more simple than many suppose, and not something that requires probing into the patient's subconscious or long-forgotten past'.[71] She defined a nervous breakdown as 'a major interruption in the body's efficient functioning as a result of emotional and mental exhaustion – usually brought on and maintained by fear'.[72] Weeks then subcategorized 'nervous

Not Something You Talk About   117

breakdown' into two groups. The first was labelled as 'anxiety neurosis' which, she maintained, caused minor problems and 'the inability to cope with normal responsibilities'.[73] The second category was deemed to be more serious and was caused by 'an overwhelming problem [where] continuous tension causes physical sensations that become more and more fear inspiring'.[74] Depression was not recognized as a separate clinical entity, but as a 'phase' of nervous breakdown.[75] The same treatment principles applied to both categories of breakdown and were largely seen to be dependent upon the patient's ability to accept unpleasant sensations, safe in the knowledge that the symptoms were harmless. Weeks offered private consultations with patients and provided them with a tape or long-play record, to enable them to continue reinforcing the self-help advice at home. In her literature, she listed a variety of possible situational causes for nervous conditions, including the loss of a loved one and the fear of being alone. While marital discord was not mentioned explicitly, sexual problems, fear and guilt featured in her list. In each case, she contended, 'fear' was the culprit.[76]

While advocating practical self-help on the one hand, Weeks did not decry the use of psychotropic medications where necessary. Indeed, she noted that there had been significant adverse publicity surrounding the use of sedative drugs; however, she maintained that these drugs had a legitimate place in medical treatment. In some instances, she argued, 'sleep' had restorative powers and prescribed sedatives were sometimes recommended.[77] These views were increasingly reflected during the late 1960s in editorial contributions to women's magazines. An article entitled 'Emotional Stress: Signs and Symptoms', for example, appeared in *Woman's Own* in April 1968, advocating new chemical treatments for mental illness. The central message in this article was that psychological disorders were diagnosable and treatable. The author, Ruth Martin, appealed for awareness of early symptoms, in much the same way that one would practice preventable medicine relating to physical illness. It is notable that direct reference was made to new methods of treatment:

> The illnesses displaying these symptoms can be treated and very often in the sufferer's own home ... new drugs have revolutionized treatment and family doctors look after patients who would once have spent long periods in hospital.[78]

Certainly, by 1970, the use of psychotropic medications had become an increasingly familiar topic of discussion in the popular press. An article on depression in *Woman's Own* in 1970, for example, noted that it was thought to be 'a possible forerunner of more serious mental conditions'. However, it reminded readers that such symptoms could now 'be marvellously dealt with by various powerful drugs – taken under careful medical supervision'.[79] The debate nevertheless continued to reflect a mix of environmental and biological theories.

118   *Desperate Housewives, Neuroses and the Domestic Environment, 1945–1970*

Although they were increasingly recommended for use in primary care and in psychiatric outpatient clinics, in the popular press women rarely articulated their experiences of taking the new tranquillizers and antidepressants. It is now broadly accepted that many patients were overprescribed these drugs and that, later during the 1970s, chemical dependency to the benzodiazepines became a significant problem. Nevertheless, as Chapter 6 will illustrate, gender representations in drug advertising did not simply depict women most commonly as the patient, and prescribing patterns were complex. Jonathan Metzl, in his book *Prozac on the Couch* (2003) suggests that, despite the ways in which new drugs appeared to support the case for 'biological' psychiatry, representations of psychotropic medications in the United States continued to reproduce all the cultural and social baggage associated with psychoanalytical paradigms. Consequently, he maintains that the drugs were prescribed to women who rejected their maternal duties and who thus, 'spread a pathology that was damaging to men'.[80] However, there is little evidence from this oral history project to suggest that during the 1950s and 1960s medication was used to reinforce Freudian notions, that a woman's desire to leave the home was a 'deep illness'.[81] Conversely, some of the women interviewed for this project argued that, although it was often accepted that the use of psychotropic medications did not provide a permanent solution to the problem, such treatment gave them clarity of thought and an opportunity to assess their life circumstances with a view to change.

Ann Coles, for example, became pregnant while studying for her A Levels and married 'not very happily' at eighteen. Raised in an orthodox Catholic family, she then went on to have five children in quick succession:

> I was nearly nineteen when my daughter was born. I then had a baby every year, for four years – and then there was a gap of less than three years before the fifth one was born … I hadn't wanted to get married – I hadn't wanted to get pregnant at that point, and with hindsight, I was depressed. I was pregnant nearly the whole time … You know, I felt like for certainly most of the sixties I was just surviving, I was just getting by.[82]

Not only did Ann have deep regrets about the way in which she became a parent and the lack of control over her fertility, but she also encountered serious difficulties with her husband who developed psychiatric illness himself:

> He had a personality disorder. And that was part of the problem that brought me to the end of my wits … As the years went by, this obsessive behaviour became more compulsive and he would get into cleaning, and he'd be on his hands and knees with a tooth brush, cleaning between the tiles. He would redo things I'd already done, so if I'd taken a brush and swept the kitchen, he would then take it and do it again … You know, he would take the money from his purse and polish his pennies with Duraglitz. He was really running into trouble. And no one recognized this, so there wasn't any help.[83]

Not Something You Talk About

When Ann's youngest child was two she received a visit from her health visitor that she recalled as a turning point in her life: '[The health visitor] recognized that I was depressed and advised me to see my doctor, which I did. And he prescribed antidepressants. And it was when the antidepressants kicked in that I packed my bags and left.'[84] Ann described the way in which she felt these drugs enabled her to break free from her circumstances:

> I slept and slept and slept. I must have been sleeping twenty hours in every twenty-four. And then after a few weeks I became absolutely enraged ... whereas before, when my husband was being unreasonable and difficult, I would control my response – I couldn't control my response. And I remember being like a banshee, being quite unbalanced, screaming at him ... and you know, it was at that point that I found the wherewithal – it helped me to see through what was stopping me leaving ... I recognized he was ill, therefore I couldn't leave. So having seen through that, as a result of the antidepressants, I think probably within about a month of starting [them], I left with the children ... It sort of freed me up in terms of being able to recognize what was keeping me in this situation. And I think, having taken control, and leaving, I was into a new life.[85]

Ann acknowledged that she had been prone to short periods of depression since, largely she felt due to what her doctor had recently diagnosed as seasonal affective disorder.[86] However, she maintained that her problems had little to do with motherhood and domestic life. Instead she related them directly to the difficulties in her marriage and the consequences of being unable to control her fertility:

> I've never had a planned pregnancy. We were practising Catholics and I suppose the Pope was always sitting on the bottom of the bed. It took me a long time to rebel ... much later I remarried, and if we had had more children I would have done it very differently. It would have been done very much by choice and I think I would have savoured the experience. There was no savouring the experience, there was only surviving it, and that was to do with my particular circumstances.[87]

Ann Coles was not the only woman interviewed to experience a husband with nervous symptoms. Barbara Rogers noted that her husband had experienced 'a bout of nervous dyspepsia when something had gone wrong at work'. She also recalled that a close friend's husband had suffered 'a breakdown' as a result of pressure at work.[88] Barbara Vicary too felt that her husband was the one to succumb to 'nerves' and 'strain'. Having moved from America to live in London with her English husband, Barbara spoke of the way in which he coped with pressure:

> He was starting a company under Wilson's government. It was terrible. We had a garbage disposal strike – the garbage out in London in front of the nicest buildings. We had an electric strike ... My husband had a regular strong drink. We didn't keep a 'bar' or anything, so he would just keep it in the larder. [He] took Valium, and I was very worried about it. And he would take more because of stressful times, and I was worried about the drinking and the Valium.[89]

Barbara remembered that she had suffered regularly from migraine headaches. She related these to 'stress', but said that she had always wondered about the possibility of a hormonal cause. She felt that the pressures she encountered were not connected to her domestic role and she asserted on more than one occasion that she thought it was important for mothers to stay at home with their children. However, later in the interview Barbara revealed that she had experienced marital difficulties and ultimately divorced:

> I married someone in my class at university, exactly my age, and I don't happen to think that men and women mature in quite the same way. And I think he changed quite a bit. He developed as quite a good businessman but not much else. So I had to fill in with all the love and affection in the family ... We began to live very separate lives, and they were very full, and they overlapped as long as the children were there.[90]

After twenty-seven years of marriage, Barbara was finally divorced from her husband. She received notably inequitable treatment as recently as 1980 and recalled that it was 'quite horrifying ... and I was very naive about it, I went to a lawyer that my husband got for me, and he didn't give me very much financially – instead of giving me half. And all that was very hard.'[91]

Many of the women who were happily married also presented anecdotal evidence about friends or relatives who experienced 'nervous breakdown' as a result of unsatisfactory relationships. Betty Sanderson, for example, while never aware of feeling depressed or anxious herself, pointed out that she had had a close friend who became 'very nervy'; but that this was 'because she discovered her husband was philandering and her marriage was actually starting to break up at this point. I was aware that she was becoming on the point of a nervous breakdown really. But I knew the reason why.'[92]

Margaret Windsor agreed: 'I mean the old terminology was "nervous breakdown" – and that was usually connected with relationship breakdown.'[93] Margaret was interviewed with her friend Doris who was able to relate this to circumstances in her own family. She noted that her Aunt Geraldine had 'terrible nerves', but qualified this by confirming that 'her husband left her with Pearl as a little girl ... I think it was Andrew leaving her'.[94] In a similar way, Eileen Roberts remembered a woman she knew at her playgroup:

> One mum, her husband, he was a teacher, but he got involved with a student and she had a breakdown. He didn't go off, but he was having an affair with this young girl. The boy was in my playgroup and the father – while she was in the mental hospital – about six to eight weeks I think, he used to drop him off in the morning and I'd look after him until he could pick him up in the evening.[95]

Interestingly, although some women experienced a breakdown under these difficult circumstances, others coped without serious difficulties. This was usually because they were able to draw comfort from a network of close family who supported them. Of course, this was also seen largely as an exception to the rule, since many families ostracized women following the breakdown of a marriage. Rose Courtenay married in 1957 in Glasgow and had two children. However, she instigated a divorce after many unhappy years. She maintained that 'it was very much frowned upon. There were people who just didn't speak to you in the street ... everyone frowned upon the fact that you were leaving home – because I left home ... I wasn't happy. I took the children with me.'[96] Rose's father had been killed in the war; nevertheless, she recalled tremendous family support from her mother, aunt and grandmother:

> You can imagine how hard it was to go up to your mother and say you want to have a divorce. It was horrendous. But I was lucky, my family were very good ... And when the children went to school I had my aunts there to look after the kids until I got home from work. So I was very lucky, I had all that support.[97]

Asked whether or not she ever experienced nerves or depression as a result of this pressure, Rose said that no, she had not – she had simply been 'relieved' that the marriage had ended: 'You get through it. You get through it. I can remember it as being a very unhappy time ... it was quite fraught. But fortunately everything worked out well and we did alright you know.' Rose eventually married again and she described her second partner as 'a lovely husband ... just a different person.'[98]

Rebecca Heane, also 'survived' many years of unhappy marriage. Her husband had proved to be 'mean with money, jealous and possessive'. Rebecca 'made the best of a bad job' and always knew she would leave when the children were older. She finally left after twenty-three years of marriage and firmly contended that her strength of character was due to a supportive family network:

> I went home to father, who welcomed me with open arms. Many women would have been defeated by the way my ex-husband treated me. But looking back, I think I had very high self-esteem, due to my parents' love for me. And I refused to be put down.[99]

These testimonies indicate that women encountered significant emotional trauma and economic inequality if their marital relationship broke down. Women frequently experienced financial hardship following divorce – a situation that did not change in law until the passing of the Matrimonial Proceedings and Property Act in 1970 and the subsequent Matrimonial Causes Act in 1973.[100] In practice, the situation did not fundamentally change until much later. Nevertheless, it would appear that, despite adverse circumstances, many women were still able to find contentment and satisfaction in their role as mothers and homemakers. It is certainly true that, in many cases, symptoms of anxiety and depression disappeared following the end of an unhappy marriage.

Adverse Experience during Childhood or Adolescence

Not all respondents diagnosed with anxiety or depressive disorders were able to trace the cause to their own marriages. However, a notable number maintained that their parents' relationship had had a marked influence on them in later life. During a period when divorce was largely unobtainable and certainly seen as unacceptable, it is not surprising that a percentage of the women interviewed witnessed difficult or tense relationships between their parents. Others recalled significant incidents or traumatic experiences that were to affect them later in adulthood. A small number of interviewees remarked that they were influenced by their own relationship with their parents. Many of these women began to experience symptoms long before they became housewives, often while they were still living at home.

Frances Wilson, for example, experienced a 'breakdown' by the time she took her A Levels. To Frances, there were clear and straightforward reasons for this:

> I was a scholarship pupil at a direct grant school ... it was an absolute revelation, but I was unhappy because I had to conceal my home background. At one point, we were homeless and living in a homeless hostel ... so self-esteem was low by the time I left school. I'd collapsed by the time A Levels came, and had a nervous breakdown ... we were living in this one room and my parents were terribly unhappy, and I think what happened to me ... was a perfectly natural normal response to incredible stress ... living in one room with my parents constantly quarrelling.[101]

Frances's narrative was one of resilience and a long struggle with minor mental conditions, culminating much later with the diagnosis of depression. However, she asserted early on in the interview that 'I can explain why, and it had nothing to do with domesticity'.[102] Following her marriage in 1960, Frances recalled a strained relationship with her new mother-in-law which, in addition to the dysfunctional relationship with her own mother, ultimately reinforced her sense of low self-esteem. She was initially optimistic about becoming a member of a new family. However, her hopes were soon thwarted: '[My mother-in-law] looked at me and said "I shall say this only once. I never wanted you two to marry, but when I found out it was what John wanted, I worked for it"'.[103] Difficulties with the extended family affected Frances deeply. Her mother-in-law was indifferent to the grandchildren and favoured her nephews and nieces. Frances also experienced a miscarriage and both sets of parents appeared unsympathetic to her ordeal. She remembered one particularly distressing period, living with her in-laws as a temporary measure:

> It was the very worst time of my married life. She actually told me I was a bad mother. When we moved in December, it was the three-day week – power cuts. I sat in the dark with the children, no central heating ... and I went into depression ... Her cruelty to me was unspeakable. And to my children. Absolutely awful.[104]

Frances was ultimately able to overcome her problems by immersing herself in other activities. She joined the Townswomen's Guild and later, the National Housewives' Register. Despite her difficulties, when asked how she felt about domesticity and her role as a mother, she contended:

> Domesticity suited me very well. I was content with that. And of course the children just made it so super. Family life was good. I have to say that although I'd had very poor parenting myself, from somewhere or other I'd got a good idea of what I wanted. And although nobody had told me that shouting was bad for self-esteem, in here [pointing to her head] I knew it was. And I never shouted at them. I never said shut up to them.[105]

This approach, she argued, paid dividends as her boys grew up, and with some emotion she recalled one particular conversation with her son:

> Michael went into social work. And he phoned me up about one in the morning. He'd been on a wonderful training day, and I sat on the stairs in my nightie. He said he was enthused by what he'd learned. 'Unconditional positive regard' he said, 'I realize I've had that from day one'. And I wept and thought, how wonderful that he thinks that.[106]

Judith Morgan was another interviewee to state that her upbringing and events from her childhood had affected her emotional security in later life. Judith's parents were both in the teaching profession and she felt that undue pressure was put upon her to succeed:

> They certainly exerted a lot of pressure. My father particularly. He would check up and almost trip you up to make sure you were fulfilling everything... Even when I was very successful and done all sorts of things, he never, ever acknowledged it.[107]

Judith maintained that her mother's desire for academic achievement also had a negative effect on her:

> I always felt she was a bit before her time. My friend's mothers didn't go out to work ... and I learned by her mistakes ... I felt I couldn't divide my time up – not that I couldn't – I didn't want to. So it certainly made me very aware when I had children of my own. She never actually had time for us.[108]

Judith developed symptoms of anxiety during her adult life; however, she firmly believed that this was due to the fact that her mother had always been anxious and overprotective. She believed that these traits were consequently projected onto them as children:

> I am convinced, having had psychiatric help, that it actually has rubbed off – that you know, you're not born with fear; it's something that you learn. I think when somebody's constantly putting that in your face, then you are going to pick it up at some point ... And funnily enough, a lot of the fears diminished after her death – as if she had sort of held me for many years.[109]

Judith's mother was agitated and apprehensive about all aspects of life and was prone to making telephone calls expressing concern about normal daily events:

> I travelled endlessly when I was teaching, and it worried her. I would get endless phone calls where she would say 'do you have to go there? The weather's not very good – can you not go?' That was very difficult to come to terms with because it filtered into your existence the whole time.[110]

Her mother's anxiety is interesting in itself since, to Judith, there appeared to be no obvious cause. She maintained that it had little to do with an unfulfilling domestic life since her role as a teacher was the central focus in her life. Moreover, it was unrelated to her career as the symptoms continued into old-age. However, during the interview it became clear that Judith's parents had experienced difficulties in their marriage:

> It was very volatile. Very, very volatile. My father drank quite a lot in the early stages of the marriage which my mother wasn't happy about. And he became belligerent and aggressive. And so there were times when he used to hit her about. And I remember this as a young child, and being very upset by the fact that there was this sort of unease all the time. And he was going to leave, but he never did – so there was this unrest. And they bickered and quarrelled and fought until their dying day. We were just brought up on that which is not nice ... I often used to think 'why don't they get divorced?' You know, 'surely it must be easier than all this agro?' But I don't think it was done. I didn't know any of their generation or anyone within the family who got divorced.[111]

A number of the women interviewed suggested that traumatic experiences had affected them and their families. Eve Raddon recalled that her grandmother's sister had suffered 'a bit of a breakdown'; however, she was sure that this was due to a bomb landing on her house during the war. She also remembered a colleague at work being prescribed tranquillizers; in this instance the person's husband had committed suicide, and thus, Eve emphasized that breakdown was usually due to 'something extraordinary'.[112] Eileen Roberts, who was raised during the war in London, not only remembered harrowing events, but also remarked that the strain had badly affected relationships within her family:

> My father, because of the war, became very religious ... he became very strict – Baptist. I wasn't evacuated. My father wouldn't let me go to be evacuated, because of this religious thing – we went into the air-raid shelter, and then he decided that no, we weren't going to do that. If we were going to get killed, we were going to get killed and that was that. So we slept in the house all the time – right through the blitz ... you just don't get over anything like that really.[113]

Eileen spoke about how the war had affected her father's psychological health. His behaviour became erratic and normal family activities were suddenly banned: 'We weren't allowed to go to the pictures; he threw my mother's make-up away;

he used to read the bible to us every night – a complete change'.[114] It is notable that she also remembered her mother and father shouting a lot at each other, and this she found 'distressing'. Eileen also thought it possible that her family were predisposed to depressive disorders, and looking back felt that she had 'probably always suffered from depression – but it wasn't acknowledged you see. Nobody talked about it, there was little understanding of these conditions ... I mean Dad was a depressive. I just think it's familial and that's the way you are.'[115]

Although Eileen was married to a general practitioner, she did not confide in him. She ultimately took matters into her own hands by searching for medical literature on depression and anxiety in her husband's surgery. She found an article that helped her understand her symptoms:

> I was depressed enough to be frightened to go out. I had to stay in. I didn't tell anyone – nobody noticed you see. My husband wasn't aware of this, I just kept quiet ... In some ways being married to a doctor is difficult ... I think my expectation of him was that he would be aware and I don't think he was – his training didn't allow for it.[116]

In Eileen's case, the onset of anxiety and depression were clearly unrelated to domestic life since she remembered feeling unwell before marriage and children:

> I was like this when we lived in Luton, when I was travelling up to London – I couldn't keep awake, and I'd get into the office and I'd start typing, and I'd go into the cloakroom and I'd sit down and go to sleep.[117]

Eileen noted on several occasions that she had always planned to have a large family and she emphasized 'very strongly' that, in her opinion, mothers should remain at home with their children at least until they reach school age.

Conclusion

This chapter has suggested that previous studies of women and the home have disproportionately emphasized the negative aspects of housework and mothering. In so doing, they have often failed to engage directly with the recollections of women who experienced domestic life for themselves. As these oral histories indicate, women broadly understood their illnesses as having been influenced by trauma and marital breakdown – and in some cases by a familial tendency to depression. The various aspects of the homemaker's role are of course inextricably linked, and it is difficult to say for sure that the tedium associated with the job itself did not in turn affect a wife's relationship with her husband. However, the responses put forward by the women in this project were unequivocal; deep discontent was not evident in relation to the daily tasks of child-rearing and homemaking. In many ways, Harris and Brown echoed these findings in their study of depression when they argued that 'a woman who has a confiding relationship, particularly with a husband has much less chance of developing depression'.[118] They also pointed out that a woman's social milieu and the broader social context is critical because 'it influences the way in which she *thinks* about the world and thus the extent of [her] hopelessness'.[119] This may help explain why the responses of women who were housewives in the 1950s and 1960s differed significantly from those who married in the 1970s, when expectations for 'personal fulfilment' began to rise.

Critics of oral history have long questioned the nature of memory and might suggest that these women's recollections about domestic life are unrealistic and idealistic. However, as Paul Thompson has authoritatively maintained throughout his career in oral history, 'every source derived from human perception is subjective, but only the oral source allows us to challenge that subjectivity – to unpick the layers of memory, dig back into its darkness'.[120] Thompson has also argued that, in many ways a recording is more reliable than a purely written record, because all the exact words are used as they were spoken, and added to this might be 'nuances of uncertainty, humour or pretence'.[121] Indeed, experience from this project has shown that during an interview process that lasts several hours, inconsistencies and bias can be unmasked by addressing the same subject matter repeatedly at various stages. Thompson has also observed that, in later life, the last stage of memory development is characterized by a sudden emergence of memories and a desire to remember. Crucially, at this stage, he maintains that there appears to be 'a diminished concern with fitting the story to the social norms of the audience'.[122] In any case, the women interviewed for this investigation were not claiming that housework and childcare were problem-free; on the contrary, at times they found life at home tiresome and frustrating. However, they still saw it as worthwhile and much of it as enjoyable. Many saw the world of work outside the home as having greater drawbacks. By and large, most women took a pragmatic approach and acknowledged that there were positive and negative aspects to both roles.

Finally, it has been suggested here that general awareness and overt discussion of psychological conditions was not widespread in popular media until the late 1960s. This was indeed reflected in the oral testimonies, where the women interviewed confirmed that one did not usually discuss personal problems with others – nor did they openly discuss psychological symptoms. Katherine Stead maintained that:

> You didn't admit to 'stress' quite honestly. You just – I was going to say the old thing 'pull yourself together', and get on with it. If people were struggling, then it wasn't apparent to all and sundry. You never admit you can't cope ... and if you're strong, you keep going.[123]

When articles did begin to appear in the popular press, they were presented in an informative and factual format. New psychotropic drugs were included in treat-

Not Something You Talk About

ment advice as part of a possible combination of therapies which also included psychotherapy and practical advice on dealing with symptoms. However, it would seem that the primary objective of such articles was to raise consciousness and overcome stigma. This is exemplified in an article by Ruth Martin in 1970 in *Woman's Own* entitled 'Not Something You Talk About', in which Martin reassured readers that although statistics tended to suggest a rise in mental illness, the reality was that diagnostic techniques had greatly improved, so that more people were willing to recognize and treat psychological symptoms. A whole range of conditions could now be helped 'by drugs developed in the 1950s'; however, psychotherapy was also recommended in order that 'a patient is given a chance to talk about her symptoms, her anxieties and stresses and to come to terms with them'. All these things, she claimed, 'have done much to help break down the barriers between the mentally ill and the apparently well'.[124] Although there were few articles devoted explicitly to nervous disorder until the late 1960s, evidence from the letters section of women's magazines suggested that women were experiencing a whole range of nervous symptoms. Significantly, these appeared to be related to marital breakdown and not domesticity. An unnamed 'consultant in psychological medicine' at St Thomas's Hospital in London remarked in an article in the *Times* in 1970 that:

> Sometimes the root of the trouble stems from the attitude of a husband to his wife, or vice versa. There have been times when one has had to tell a husband: 'your wife's illness is only an outward symptom. But I think you may have been the cause.'[125]

The following chapter examines representations of anxiety and depression through the analysis of advertising of pharmaceutical drugs in medical journals and over-the-counter remedies in the popular press. As a corollary of the claim that domesticity caused mental symptoms in women, authors such as Cooperstock and Gove also claimed that, in an attempt to suppress them in a role within which they were unhappy, doctors prescribed psychoactive drugs to women more frequently than men. It has thus been argued that women were overrepresented in promotional material for psychotropic medicines.[126] Chapter 6 assesses this claim and provides a close examination of advertisements for a wide range of psychotropic medications. It is suggested that, although a degree of stereotyping was evident in promotional images, in an attempt to expand their market share, pharmaceutical companies in fact directed medications for nervous disorders at a wide range of individuals, including men, children and the elderly.

6 FOR LADIES IN DISTRESS: REPRESENTATIONS OF ANXIETY AND DEPRESSION IN THE MEDICAL AND POPULAR PRESS

> Both the public and the medical profession are the targets of the pharmaceutical industry's marketing policies. The industry has created an increasing supply of new products both for the ethical and over-the-counter markets; the public and the doctors keep up the demand.
>
> Karen Dunnell and Ann Cartwright,
> *Medicine Takers, Prescribers and Hoarders* (1972)

In 1975, public health sociologist Gerry Stimson drew attention to the importance of the images produced in the advertising of psychopharmaceutical drugs in medical journals, and claimed that the individuals used in such depictions portrayed 'the typical person who has the illness'.[1] He then went on to suggest that, not only did women appear in pictures more often than men, but that the images reflected 'a limited view of a woman's role ... women are shown as dependent – the victims of circumstances'.[2] This argument has been developed by a number of authors since the 1970s. Ruth Cooperstock, for example, argued that physicians' perceptions of female patients were, at least in part, influenced by pharmaceutical advertising and its 'pejorative attitudes' toward women.[3] Ludmilla Jordanova, while making the case for a move away from accounts of women and mental illness that emphasize their subordination and oppression, still maintained that drugs for psychiatric conditions were 'advertised with a clear sexual association with women'.[4] Writing more recently in the United States, Jonathan Metzl has produced a close analysis of representations of psychotropic medications in sources from American print culture from 1950.[5] The central contention of his work is that the new psychotropic drugs developed during the 1950s were constructed as a treatment for the symptoms of American culture that was facing a fundamental change in gender roles. The notion that mankind was destabilized by the 'uncivilized' presence of women, he argues, proved an enormously popular conceptual weapon, and as a result, white, middle-class women were consistently scripted into the role of the patient. A woman's ambition was viewed as a symptom of mental illness to be treated with

– 129 –

pharmacological preparations. Thus: 'housewives of the 1950s and feminists of the 1970s ... all became mothers when they took medication'.[6]

These authors rightly draw attention to the manner in which the medical model of mental illness has disregarded external factors that may intelligibly account for the onset of, or exacerbate psychiatric symptoms. As Stimson notes, 'where the patient has problems that can only, according to the advertisement, be solved by taking a tranquillizer/antidepressant: social problems remain unresolved'.[7] However, it is argued in this chapter that previous analyses have placed too much emphasis on images of women in medical advertising. While Metzl might be correct in his observation that psychopharmaceuticals functioned 'within a notion of gender that normalizes married women, men doctors and other requisite components of a heterosexual symbolic order',[8] in Britain it does not necessarily follow that 'there was a marriage of mothers and medication'.[9] The following analysis will illustrate how pharmaceutical companies targeted a diverse range of individuals from within a set of culturally acceptable social roles, largely because this was a pragmatic marketing strategy. Ultimately, as Melville and Johnson have pointed out, 'advertising sells drugs in the same way that it sells everything else'.[10]

This chapter is divided into two broad sections. The first provides a brief history of pharmacy and the regulatory framework that developed from the mid-1800s as a result of concerns about the widespread supply and use of addictive substances. It then considers the strategies employed by psychopharmaceutical manufacturers in order to market their products during the late 1950s and the 1960s. It is argued that, while some stereotyping existed, there is little evidence to suggest that women were a deliberate target in advertising images. By emphasizing sexual stereotyping, historians have previously underplayed the ways in which such companies purposefully intended to capture not only a wide range of conditions, but also individuals of both sexes and of all ages.

The second strand to this chapter provides an analysis of advertising in the women's periodical press for over-the-counter medications associated with 'nerves' and fatigue. Previous debates have lacked this dimension and there are important parallels to be drawn between the advertising of prescription drugs and those intended for self-medication. While these advertisements were in magazines intended for a female audience, the messages they communicated about their products did not uniformly suggest that housewives and mothers were predisposed to nervous conditions. Indeed, similar advertisements appeared in national newspapers for identical products directed at men. Furthermore, throughout the 1960s, promotional material suggested that women should purchase these products not only for themselves, but also for their husbands and other members of their families. Thus, manufacturers began to target a wide range of individuals and make increasingly expansive claims about the value of their products.

The Background to Pharmacological Regulation

During the late nineteenth century, the legislative framework surrounding the intake of medicinal substances developed largely in relation to the regulation of the supply and sale of poisons. Before this time, opium and other drugs were on open sale and in regular use. As Stuart Anderson notes:

> Laudanum was to be found in most homes as an essential standby ... it was commonly used as an infant soother ... and its deliberate use to produce death, either by suicide or murder, was well known.[11]

Not only were these potent, addictive substances widely in use, but other remedies were also taken regularly in line with the 'therapeutic framework' that existed at that time, namely 'the notion that the body was in constant dynamic relation with its environment ... equilibrium was associated with health, imbalance with disease'. As a result, 'enormous quantities of medicines were consumed in order to maintain or re-establish health'.[12] Indeed, the Canadian physician William Osler (1849–1919) who became Regius professor of medicine at the University of Oxford, often described as the greatest teacher of medicine, is said to have remarked at the end of the nineteenth century that 'one of the most characteristic features of human beings, compared with other animals, lies in their propensity to self-medicate'.[13]

The 1868 Pharmacy and Poisons Act attempted to provide a safeguard to the general public against the supply of poisons and gave the Pharmaceutical Society the power to determine which substances should be regulated and who should be authorized to sell them.[14] These powers were then extended by the 1908 Pharmacy Act, which required that the purchaser of opiates should be known to the seller and that an entry of the sale be made in the Poisons Register.[15] However, it was not until fears emerged surrounding the illicit use of drugs in the army during the First World War that concern shifted to the misuse of addictive substances. The Dangerous Drugs Act 1920 implemented the regulations that had been ratified by the 1912 Opium Convention at The Hague. Under this legislation, the trade and consumption of addictive drugs were limited to 'medicinal and legitimate uses'.[16] As Anderson observes, this Act had significant ramifications for the pharmaceutical profession since '[it] marked the beginning of the displacement of a pharmaceutical system of regulation ... by a medical system of control through the writing of prescriptions'.[17] The sale of regulated drugs (morphine, cocaine and heroin) was, in future, to be restricted to medical practitioners and to pharmacists acting on a doctor's written prescription.[18] Other drugs such as digitalis and the barbiturate compounds were subsequently included in the Act. However, legislation surrounding other therapeutic treatments such as insulin and antigens remained focused upon the manufacture and supply to the public. This situation

132 *Desperate Housewives, Neuroses and the Domestic Environment, 1945–1970*

was to change following the discovery of penicillin which, it was recognized, was 'capable of causing danger to the health of the community if used without proper safeguards'.[19] Three consecutive Acts passed during the 1940s and 1950s brought the supply of other therapeutic substances under regulatory control and thus, their supply was limited to the public, permitted only by medical practitioners or from pharmacies on the authority of a doctor's prescription.[20] Finally, the Medicines Act 1968 brought all previous legislation together.[21]

Prescribing laws are central to the work of David Healy, historian of psychopharmacology. He argues that:

> The significance of the contemporary position is that this process has become much more regulated and structured that it ever was before, and our automatic access to available compounds has been curtailed. An increasingly large industrial enterprise has geared itself up to supply our needs and, in the process, this enterprise has commandeered the science that can be extracted from our attempts to regulate our internal balance.[22]

Healy is not critical of all aspects of regulation; however, he suggests that the component of law that restricts access to psychotropic medications disempowers the individual,[23] largely because 'the "system" operates at almost every turn to frustrate an individual's access to the information they need to make the decisions that they – and no one else – should be making about their life'.[24] Ultimately, Healy also raises important questions about the ways in which the financial interests of pharmaceutical companies have influenced medical science.

One of the primary means of influence utilized by pharmaceutical manufacturers was undoubtedly the use of advertising in the medical press. Legislation relating to the advertising of medicines was initially enacted as a result of misleading claims put forward by manufacturers of proprietary medicines. In 1914, a House of Commons Select Committee on Patent Medicines was assigned the task of investigating the regulation of medicines, and the subsequent Food and Drugs Act 1938 made it illegal for a person to sell a drug labelled in such a way that it falsely described the drug, or that was in any way calculated to mislead as to its nature, substance or quality.[25] These regulations were ultimately extended in 1941 with the passing of the Pharmacy and Medicines Act 1941, which also ensured that manufacturers were required to disclose the composition of drugs.[26] Although legislation developed in relation to patent medicines, the advertising of prescription drugs in professional journals also prompted a heated debate among physicians and pharmaceutical manufacturers. In 1959 concerns were raised about the ethics of advertising in a leading article in the *BMJ* and drug companies were urged to utilize the marketplace responsibly.[27] By 1962, the controversy had escalated and regular references to irresponsible sales techniques appeared in the correspondence section of the journal.[28] One article commented specifically on the mistrust of the motives of the drug industry;[29] another noted the 'profound influence of adverts on prescribing' and served to remind pharmaceutical companies of their ethical responsibilities.[30] These concerns had been elevated by the thalidomide tragedy. Advertisements for Distaval (brand name for thalidomide) were still in print as late as November 1961, only one month before the drug was withdrawn. The tragic irony about these advertisements was that the image depicted a small child holding an open medicine bottle, with the message that Distival was not only 'highly effective' but 'outstandingly safe'.[31]

Letters appeared regularly in the *BMJ* during the 1960s from general practitioners who disapproved of the proliferation of promotional material sent to their surgeries. The following letter was typical:

> In a recent number of an excellent medical journal, the following pictorial themes all basically irrelevant to the product advertised, were displayed in advertisements to catch my eye: human faces expressing pain or relief; children, either in pain or playing with toys; children's toys; fluffy rabbits; cartoon characters; seascapes, depicting calm or storms; family groups; barristers; dogs; dolls; egg whisks; fortune tellers; potters at the wheel; queues at bus stops; smoking chimneys; sword-swallowers and taxi-drivers. I suspect that most general practitioners, like myself, get their knowledge of new drugs from the exchange of conversation and ideas with colleagues, from advice and lectures from specialists and from their reading of medical journals ... Who exactly is this childish nonsense intended to impress?[32]

This often prompted angry responses from business executives defending their products and services. The Managing Director of the 'Medical Mailing Company' retorted that most doctors were not opposed to receiving promotional literature. He concluded: 'what an unenlightened lot we'd be without it – for one thing, professional journals would cease to exist'.[33] The Managing Director of another marketing company maintained that, while constructive criticism should be welcomed, it must not be forgotten that many of the advertised drugs had transformed lives:

> Tranquilizers, for example, have, without question, had a profoundly beneficent effect in the treatment of disturbed patients ... the remarkable fact is that so very few [adverts] offend, while the great majority perform the indispensable function of keeping the doctor abreast of a multitude of important developments ... [Doctors] are under no obligation to read the material prepared for them, with such care and, for the most part, responsibility.[34]

The debate continued with increasing intensity throughout the 1960s. One hospital physician noted in 1966 that he had collected all 301 circulars received during the previous year; 79 per cent were from drug companies, and 47 per cent of these were from psychotropic drug manufacturers. The sheer 'weight' of this promotional literature, he remarked, 'totalled twenty-eight pounds'.[35] In addition to his disapproval of the volume of material received, this physician was equally unimpressed with the quality of information provided:

> I received twenty-one similar postcards advertising the same phenothiazine [anti-depressant] ... an announcement for a new anti-depressant gave no reference to the nature of the product ... essential details about the possible toxicity were often lacking

134   *Desperate Housewives, Neuroses and the Domestic Environment, 1945–1970*

or ambiguously phrased [and] extravagant claims were frequently based upon the results of small and uncontrolled investigations.[36]

A study of prescribing patterns in psychotropic drugs published in 1971 raised further concerns about the volume of promotional material aimed at physicians. Reporting on the 1965 Ministry of Health Committee of Enquiry into the relationship of the pharmaceutical industry with the NHS, the study stated that nine out of ten of the general practitioners consulted considered they received too much promotional literature and one in four said they wanted 'no literature' at all. The committee also noted that some sales representatives did not have sufficient knowledge of their company's products and that some pharmaceutical manufacturers were failing 'to measure up to their responsibility of informing doctors adequately about new (and existing) preparations'.[37]

Pharmaceutical advertisements form the basis of Jonathan Metzl's study *Prozac on the Couch*. He argues that print adverts for psychopharmaceuticals are 'unique because of their history of representing women patients in particular ways'.[38] To Metzl, the adverts articulated 'mainstream concerns about feminist protests. That is, the ads reflected the threat that these protests seemed to pose to marriage, maternity, femininity and normality.'[39] He suggests that historians have been wrong to assume that the new chemical treatments for mental disorders prompted a paradigm shift from 'mother-blaming' psychoanalytical notions, towards objective, biological explanations. Instead, he argues that pervasive Freudian messages were still evident in biological discourse.[40] However, the following section of this chapter will suggest that sources in British print culture do not support this contention.

Psycho-Pharmaceutical Advertising in the British Medical Press

Although it is certainly true that the proliferation of advertising during the 1960s produced numerous images of women, they should not be seen in isolation. Due consideration should be taken as to their relation to other advertisements for the same product, and for other products in a similar range. In Jonathan Metzl's opening chapter, he utilizes a classic image of what he describes as 'a threatening "feminist" woman'.[41] The advertisement, for Valium (diazepam), depicts an enlarged facial image of a woman with 'psychic tension', clenching her teeth in an alarming, menacing manner. Central to Metzl's reading of this advertisement is the foregrounding of the use of a woman – a 'visually threatening woman' who is 'tamed centripetally, by Valium'.[42] The advertisement in Figure 6.1 for Largactil (chlorpromazine), released in the *BMJ* in 1961, might be read in a similar way. The woman featured could be viewed as non-compliant, rejecting her maternal role and disinterested in her child and her surroundings. Largactil in this instance might plausibly restore the woman's interest in her domestic role and thus, enable her to resume her place in the appropriate social order. In this reading, the imagery of a middle-class housewife implies that her psychotic designs on a better life are pathogenic.[43]

Figure 6.1: Largactil, *BMJ,* 1 April 1961 Reproduced with the permission of Sanofi Aventis Pharma Ltd and the Health Library, Peninsula Medical School, Exeter.

However, with this and many of the advertisements that feature in previous histories, close textual analysis of the technical information and recommended indications reveals a different story. Largactil, first discovered in 1952, was eventually to become a specific treatment for schizophrenia; however, during the 1950s it was reported to be useful for almost every psychiatric condition.[44] Certainly, this advertisement claims that it was of 'outstanding value in a wide variety of conditions, including: anxiety and tension states; intractable pain; nausea, vomiting and hiccup; pruritus; hyperpyrexia; convulsive and dyskinetic conditions'. Most importantly, the phrase 'your next patient may need Largactil' implies that any number of patients waiting in the general practitioner's surgery might have benefited from the use of this drug. As Healy notes, the European trade name of 'Largactil' meant exactly that – 'large action'.[45] The sequence of images that followed through the 1960s indicated that the manufacturers of Largactil intended to target not only women, but a diverse range of individuals in order to sell their product effectively. Figure 6.2, for example, illustrates how the drug was described as 'highly versatile and established for use in: general medicine; psychiatry; geriatrics; paediatrics; anaesthesia; neurology and obstetrics'.[46] Significantly, this versatility was reflected in the imagery as the depictions include those of a man and a woman, but also an infant, a small child and an elderly person. These individuals were portrayed with the semblance of normality; thus, the advertisement aimed to establish a link between the drug and the 'ordinary' person.

In 1964, May and Baker produced an advertisement promoting Largactil specifically for improving the quality of life beyond middle-age.[47] The imagery utilized by the advertisers on this occasion was taken from the Ancient Aztecs depicting the stage of life of an ancient Mexican suffering from a variety of 'grumbling pains'. In the accompanying text, there were no specific suggested indications for either physical or psychological symptoms. Instead, the advertisement made the vague claim that Largactil was suitable for countering 'the querulousness of old-age' and the image evoked somewhat ominous connotations of a cantankerous elderly person, mollified by the tranquillizing effects of the drug. The following year, Largactil was advertised as recommended specifically for use in the treatment of alcohol withdrawal, in particular for reducing restlessness, aggression, nausea and vomiting, while aiding sleep and 'improving the patient's ability to cooperate in his treatment'.[48] In the same year, its manufacturers continued with the 'broad-spectrum' theme which they developed in an advert that appeared in the *BMJ* bearing the slogan 'In the seven ages of man Largactil plays many parts'.[49] Once again, individuals from infancy to old-age appear in the illustration (shown in Figure 6.3). The lack of technical information given about the drug perhaps gives weight to the claim made by contemporary physicians; that essential details about dosage and toxicity were often lacking or ambiguously phrased.

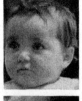

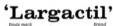

Figure 6.2: Largactil, *BMJ*, 27 July 1963. Reproduced with the permission of Sanofi Aventis Pharma Ltd and the Wellcome Library, London.

xiv 24 April 1965   ADVERTISEMENT   BRITISH MEDICAL JOURNAL

In the

seven ages of man

'LARGACTIL'

plays many parts

AN **M&B** BRAND MEDICAL PRODUCT

trade mark

Detailed information is available on request
MAY & BAKER LTD
DAGENHAM · ESSEX

Figure 6.3: Largactil, *BMJ,* 24 April 1965. Reproduced with the permission of Sanofi Aventis Pharma Ltd and the Wellcome Library, London.

For Ladies in Distress 139

Largactil was not the only drug that claimed to be effective for the treatment of a wide range of symptoms in a variety of patients. In 1964, Eli Lilly marketed a tricyclic antidepressant, nortriptyline, in a similar way. Using brand names Aventyl and Allegron, the company used promotional literature to draw upon increasing tensions that existed within the medical profession relating to the difficulties associated with the diagnosis of anxiety and depression. In an advertisement for Aventyl that appeared in professional journals in 1964, Eli Lilly suggested that 'patients don't always fit neatly into diagnostic categories. They may suffer diverse symptoms such as depression, agitation, loss of appetite and tension fatigue.' However, the great strength of Aventyl was that 'its beneficial actions range widely over the symptoms which plague these problem patients'.[50] Significantly, while this advertisement clearly features a woman 'feeling awful', the following month an advert appeared that was identical in every way, except that the figure on this occasion was that of a man (shown in Figure 6.4).[51] This strategy was employed by a number of other companies in an attempt to create an association with both men and women in a range of different situations. Advertisements for the benzodiazepines regularly used this format and a pair of adverts appeared during May 1965, one featuring a photograph of a women; the other a man. In the case of the woman, the manufacturers, Roche, claimed that Valium helped her 'to enjoy her family'; whereas the man is helped 'to enjoy his work'. *Both*, 'formerly nervous and tense', after treatment are 'better able to meet and solve [their] daily problems'.[52]

Although the man and woman who featured in the Valium adverts were both clearly depicted in stereotypical roles, this was not to say that women were always represented at home or in a maternal role. Some manufacturers chose to portray them in a professional environment. This was one of a variety of approaches employed by William Warner, makers of the MAOI antidepressant Nardil. In one example, their promotional material featured a female music teacher, nervously perched by her piano looking anxious. The advert explains: 'Once a promising soloist', but now teaches music 'to increasingly few pupils'. This patient was now 'a frequent visitor to the surgery' and her career appears to have been threatened by 'endogenous depression', for which Nardil is recommended.[53]

Certainly, historians who have chosen to focus on female imagery have underplayed the portrayal of men in pharmaceutical advertising. Melville and Johnson, while providing an insightful and thought-provoking argument about the deleterious effects of our obsession with mass medication, nevertheless still made a direct connection with women and psychopharmaceuticals. Their analysis of promotional literature was as follows:

> One advertisement shows a young, attractive, affluent woman with clean children and material goods and other symbols of the things that are considered necessary and desirable to her. But acute anxiety and emotional turmoil seethe behind the chic exterior. The cause of this lamentable state of affairs may well be her apparent total inability to choose decisively one of the eight brands of cereal on offer to her. One ad of this type is captioned 'Now she can cope ...' She has taken Stelazine to help her through the maze of the supermarket.[54]

"Doctor, I feel awful"

Once he might have been diagnosed as "anxiety state". Today, you know he might be a depressive, but it doesn't seem as simple as all that. The truth of the matter is that patients don't always fit neatly into diagnostic categories. They may suffer from such diverse symptoms as depression, agitation, loss of appetite and tension-fatigue at the same time.

The great strength of 'Aventyl' is that its beneficial actions range widely over the symptoms which plague these problem patients. 'Aventyl' is not merely an anti-depressant, nor is it a combination of drugs. It is a *single substance* which relieves a constellation of mental and emotional symptoms embracing depression, anxiety and their effects on awareness and mood.

'Aventyl' is not a monoamine oxidase inhibitor, and no serious side-effects have been reported at the recommended dosage.

'AVENTYL' lightens the troubled mind
Nortriptyline

'Pulvules' of 10 mg. and 25 mg. Liquid: 10 mg. in each 5 ml., in bottles of 120 and 480 ml.
Full information will be sent on request.

ELI LILLY AND COMPANY LIMITED   BASINGSTOKE   ENGLAND

Figure 6.4: Aventyl, *BMJ*, 26 September 1964. Reproduced with the permission of Eli Lilly and Co. and the Wellcome Library, London.

For Ladies in Distress 141

In their somewhat cynical assessment of the situation, Melville and Johnson concluded that:

> We have all experienced the labyrinth problem of finding what we want in the supermarket, and no doubt felt near the brink of schizophrenia when confronted by a multiplicity of breakfast cereals; but is this tenuous connection sufficient to justify persuading the medical profession to prescribe powerful anti-psychotic drugs to harassed housewives?[55]

However, a more accurate evaluation of the advertising for this particular drug would reveal how men often featured prominently in such representations. An example is given in Figure 6.5, where a low-spirited man is pictured on a park bench, described as 'tired, irritable, often apathetic, unable to concentrate and lacking all will to cope'. The copy text further suggests that 'he is typical of the emotionally disturbed patient who will respond rapidly to Stelazine therapy'. The practitioner is reassured: 'Stelazine puts him back in the right frame of mind'.[56]

While some manufacturers continued to market their products for use in the treatment of a variety of anxiety-related and depressive disorders, some were compelled to seek a change in direction and to reduce the range of recommended indications. The tricyclics and the monoamine oxidase inhibitors (MAOIs) were two types of antidepressant drug discovered during the late 1950s. Healy notes that, as was the case with so many psychotropic medications, the 'antidepressive' characteristic of these compounds was discovered by chance and thus, he argues, 'what was discovered was not just a drug, but a disorder that the drug treated'.[57] Initially, both the MAOIs and the tricyclics were packaged for use in depression and anxiety. However, by the end of the 1960s, the tricyclics had become largely associated with 'major' or 'endogenous' depression, while, on the other hand, the MAOIs became the preferred option for what became known as either 'atypical' or 'neurotic' depression. The stimulus for this shift in association has been set out clearly in Healy's *The Antidepressant Era*. He illustrates how a Medical Research Council (MRC) trial in 1965 compared the effects of the MAOI compound phenelzine (sold in Britain as Nardil) with the tricyclic compound imipramine (sold as Tofranil). Their benefits were evaluated in comparison with a placebo and ECT treatment. While the tricyclics proved quite effective in the treatment of straightforward, 'major' depression, phenelzine appeared to be no more useful than the placebo.[58] Healy argues that this left manufacturers of MAOIs with a considerable marketing problem:

> Despite the MRC study, many clinicians were convinced that the compounds worked – if they didn't work for straightforward depression, they must work for atypical depression … subsequently, a variety of atypical forms of depression were proposed by various authorities … Where typical depressions showed a loss of sleep and appetite, [atypical] depressions had increased appetite and sleep … The idea that there might also be forms of depression manifesting as anxiety or phobic states, uncomplicated by personality difficulties was also canvassed.[59]

Figure 6.5: Stelazine, *BMJ*, 11 September 1965. Reproduced with the permission of GlaxoSmithKline UK Ltd and the Wellcome Library, London.

Consequently, a profile was constructed for the MAOIs in terms of their effects on anxiety-related states and a corresponding impression developed in the late 1960s that tricyclic antidepressants were only effective for endogenous depression.[60]

Healy argues that these concepts flourished during the 1960s and 1970s 'at least in part because it was in the interests of certain companies for them to survive'.[61] He also suggests that 'ensuring [their] survival lay in advertising campaigns that presented images of phobic or otherwise neurotic depressions responding to MAOIs'.[62] Indeed, the new classification of 'neurotic depression' was visibly promoted in literature produced by William Warner, manufacturers of Nardil, following the research trial in 1965. Previous advertisements had clearly stated that Nardil would resolve 'endogenous depression'. In other adverts, such as the example in Figure 6.6, William Warner suggested that it was also suitable for the treatment of 'anxiety overlaying depression'.[63] However, later in the decade, the term 'endogenous depression' disappeared from promotional material, leaving Nardil as suitable only for the atypical or neurotic category of depressive illness. The manufacturers achieved this association by introducing the inventive concept of the 'Previous Good Personality' patient – often simply referred to as the 'PGP' patient. Such individuals, it was argued, were likely to have had no previous history of psychiatric symptoms and were thus not typical of those patients who experienced classic chronic anxiety. This diagnosis can be seen in the advert reproduced in Figure 6.7 in which the woman is described as 'of previously good personality' – the type of patient who rarely visited the surgery. The diagnosis in this case is described clearly as atypical or neurotic depression.[64]

This strategy was not devised solely by William Warner pharmaceuticals. Clinicians, including William Sargant and Peter Dally, had suggested previously that the MAOI group of compounds might be useful in the treatment of certain anxiety states.[65] Nevertheless, Healy maintains that 'no form of atypical depression with a specific response to MAOIs was ever substantiated'.[66] The manufacturers of drugs such as Nardil were perhaps able to exploit the confusion surrounding contemporary debates about anxiety and depression, each carving their own niche in the market. As Sargant and Dally themselves observed: 'endogenous, reactive or atypical depressions and anxiety states do overlap and cannot always be distinguished with certainty ... it may be that there is no basic distinction between them'.[67] What is crucial about these debates for the purpose of the argument presented here is that neither women nor men were deliberately singled out in the advertising of these drugs. As is evident in the illustrations, both appeared with regularity and were depicted in a variety of situations. While it is true that some women were featured at home, men were also frequently depicted as depressed and neurotic. As Andrea Tone has recently shown in her study of American advertising, the surest path to profits was to position the drugs as suitable for all.[68] Healy refers to this as 'the marketing of psychiatric disorders', and reminds us that 'drug companies are businesses. This leads to a need for intense marketing [which] has all the characteristics of any other marketing enterprise, from automobiles to washing machines.'[69]

Figure 6.6: Advertisement, *BMJ*, 2 September 1961. Reproduced with the permission of Pfizer Ltd and the Health Library, Peninsula Medical School, Exeter.

Figure 6.7: Advertisement, *BMJ*, 12 March 1966. Reproduced with the permission of Pfizer Ltd and the Wellcome Library, London.

146   *Desperate Housewives, Neuroses and the Domestic Environment, 1945–1970*

Manufacturers chose to depict human images in their advertisements as only one of a variety of promotional strategies. The reproduction of outlandish and extreme imagery was another device used frequently in an attempt to appeal visually to prescribing physicians. Harvey pharmaceuticals also manufactured the drug Atarax, an antihistamine preparation with sedative properties. Once again, this drug was recommended for use in emotional disturbance in childhood, anxiety in adults and agitation and excitement in the elderly. One somewhat alarming advert for Atarax released in 1963 featured a close-up of a shotgun alongside a caption that stated: 'It needs just a touch to set me off, doctor'.[70] The slogan 'Atarax helps take anxiety out of general practice' indicated that it was possibly the busy practice, and not the patient, that was encumbered by the 'increase' in minor mental symptoms. Equally striking was the image of a large cabbage in an advertisement for Equanil (brand of meprobamate) in 1963. This drug, first discovered in 1955, was the first 'non-barbiturate sedative' and was thus classified as a minor tranquillizer in order that it could be distinguished from the more potent antipsychotic compounds.[71] The manufacturers, John Wyeth, drew upon the notion of 'minor' tranquillizers in their advertising campaign for this drug which posed a cryptic question: 'What has Equanil to do with a cabbage? The answer is nothing. And neither has your patient if you prescribe Equanil.' The drug company in this instance claimed that if 'potent antidepressants are prescribed for mild anxiety and tension, there is a tendency for them to be over-sedated and become mere cabbages'.[72] There is a certain irony in William Warner's use of a cabbage to illustrate their advert for a psychotropic drug, given that feminists from the 1970s onwards frequently alleged that the stultification of domestic chores and mothering were likely to induce a 'cabbage-like effect' on a woman's brain. Yet, in this instance, there is clearly no association with gender and psychiatric disorder. Drug manufacturers Sandoz also went to inordinate lengths to promote their antipsychotic compound thioridazine (Melleril) for use in 'Senile Agitation'. Advertisers in this instance used a photograph of an aged tortoise, supplemented by a quote from King Lear, 'The oldest hath borne most', in order to firmly anchor the association between Melleril and its use in elderly patients with confusion and anxiety.[73]

While some advertisers chose illustrations that symbolized neurotic or depressive illness prior to treatment, an alternative strategy was to utilize a design that reflected peace and tranquility – the 'after-effects' of psychotropic medication. Sandoz, in another promotional campaign for the drug Melleril, illustrated their advert with a peaceful-looking landscape alongside the caption 'Mirror-Calm ... in mental and emotional disturbance'.[74] A similar image was reproduced by Wyeth who also promoted Equanil for insomnia, on this occasion assisted by an extract from William Wordsworth's poem *To Sleep*.[75] Other manufacturers produced abstract illustrations with geometrically styled forms and darkened clouds. This strategy was taken up by the pharmaceutical firm Geigy in their adverts for the drug Tofranil, a trycyclic antidepressant, and it was typical of many others produced in this style.[76]

As the decade progressed, there was a proliferation of advertisements for the new benzodiazepine compounds, first available on the market in 1960.[77] Initially hailed as 'extremely safe and effective', these compounds provided serious competition to the barbiturate sedatives which had developed a negative reputation in relation to their potential for dependence and the risk of fatality in overdose.[78] This later led to campaigns to replace the barbiturates with the benzodiazepines.[79] Roche, manufacturers of Librium, exploited the bad press surrounding barbiturate sedatives and produced an advertisement that suggested that all medical techniques and treatments would eventually become outdated, with the implicit assumption that Librium was at the cutting edge of psychopharmaceutical treatment. They released an advert in 1965 which featured a picture of a cupping set, now outmoded and relegated to the museum. The message from Roche in the text makes the claim: 'That's the way with medicine, the old is constantly being replaced by the new....since the introduction of Librium, earlier forms of therapy take second place'.[80] Manufacturers of barbiturate compounds were thus faced with having to defend the benefits of their products and find a place for them in an increasingly competitive market. This defensive tone was evident in advertising campaigns during the 1960s, where, by necessity, the 'safety margin' of one brand was often emphasized over another. Abbott Laboratories, makers of Nembutal, a brand of pentobarbitone for example, released an advert in which they stated that: 'the dosage required is only about half that of many other barbiturates. With less drug to be inactivated, there's a wider margin of safety'.[81] To this end, some drugs were promoted specifically as being 'non-barbiturate', as is evident in the advertisement for the sedative Tricloryl (brand name of triclofos) in 1965. Glaxo promoted this drug as having 'a number of outstanding advantages for promoting sleep and daytime sedation', notably that it was 'free from the tendency to cause hangover'.[82]

Although the barbiturates came to be less commonly used as an independent treatment for psychiatric disorders, they often appeared in compounds containing other agents that were prescribed for conditions that were potentially aggravated by anxiety. These drugs are important because they are often excluded from analyses of gender, psychopharmaceutical advertising and prescribing. Indeed, Ruth Cooperstock conceded that it was impossible to know how the inclusion of the 'hidden' psychotropics would affect her analysis of sex differences in psychotropic drug use.[83] These drugs were promoted widely in Britain during the 1960s and notably, the images often point to use in male patients – usually in relation to gastritis and duodenal ulcers. The drug Pro-Banthine was a good example of these 'mixed' compound preparations. It contained, a tranquillizing agent, Dartalan (thiopropazate dihydrochloride) and was formulated for use in the treatment of ulcers 'where anxiety plays a part'.[84] In a similar way, Nactisol, featured in Figure 6.8, combined an ulcer drug with the barbiturate butabarbitol for use 'where anxiety complicates ulcer management'.[85] Anxiety was often also implicated in disorders of appetite. A range of psychotropic drugs were included in preparations both to stimulate and suppress appetite, with specific reference to worry and anxiety. Beplete, manufactured by Wyeth for instance, contained a combination of phenobarbitone 'to offset irritability ... and that edgy feeling' and a vitamin B complex to stimulate appetite. However, nervousness was also implicated in weight gain. Riker Laboratories, who produced a drug called Durophet-M, shown in Figure 6.9, claimed that 'Anxiety and similar emotional factors lie at the root of most overeating problems'. The caption in the advertisement explicitly asks the question 'How much does worry weigh?' Durophet-M was a classic 'combo drug' that contained both a stimulant and a tranquillizer. The promotional literature claimed that a 'calmative' would counter the underlying emotional factors that motivated the compulsive eater'.[86]

Although the majority of advertisements mentioned one or more symptoms related to anxiety, worry or depression, the manufacturers of the benzodiazepine range were the first to explicitly draw upon the notion of 'stress' as a marketing tool. As has been noted previously, developments within a number of intellectual disciplines, including, physiology, psychology and psychosomatic medicine, coalesced during the 1950s and 1960s to provide 'fertile ground' for a renewed interest in the basic premise that 'stressful life-events can be harmful'.[87] The pharmaceutical company Roche, drew directly upon this idea in the images they released for Valium and Librium during 1963. One pair of advertisements featured, firstly, a woman in the supermarket and, secondly, a man in the office, both of whom it is claimed, are 'prisoners of the society of stress'. Valium was thus indicated definitively for the alleviation of symptoms caused by the pressures of life – the implication being that the stresses inherent in modern life exceeded those experienced previously.[88] Another advertisement for the benzodiazepine Librium featured a pair of hands clenched tightly around a handkerchief alongside an emotive caption 'How do you help a pair of white knuckles?' The answer of course, lay with Librium which, it was claimed, relieved the anxiety and physical symptoms created by 'stress'.[89] Hence, the benzodiazepine brands became imbued with symbolic meaning; in this instance as a panacea for the stresses of hectic, modern life.

For Ladies in Distress 149

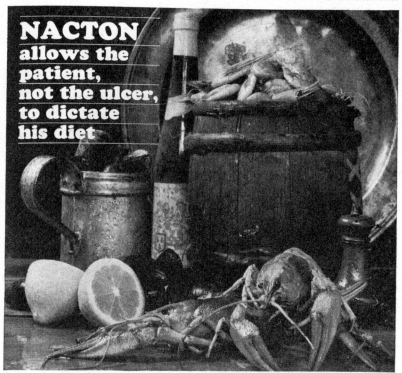

One man's meat (or fish!)...
Are delectable foods barred to your ulcer patients?
Once control is established with NACTON, more pleasures of the table can be enjoyed.
How does NACTON achieve this control?
☐ It halves gastric secretion of acid
☐ and reduces gastric and intestinal spasm.
With this established, the patient can:
  choose his own food
  gain prolonged relief from pain
  get a good night's rest
  do away with milk and cream diets
  reduce or eliminate antacid consumption
  lead a normal life.

NACTISOL—
where anxiety complicates ulcer management

NACTISOL combines the advantages of NACTON with butabarbital, a mild sedative which provides relief from anxiety and tension.

Each Nacton tablet contains 2mg. poldine methylsulphate B.P.

 NACTON* and NACTISOL* are products of British research at
Beecham Research Laboratories
Brentford, England.   Telephone: ISLeworth 4111

*regd.

Figure 6.8: Nactisol, *BMJ*, 4 December 1965. Reproduced with the permission of GlaxoSmithKline UK Ltd and the Wellcome Library, London.

Figure 6.9: Durophet, *BMJ*, 16 April 1966. Reproduced with the permission of 3M UK Ltd and the Wellcome Library, London.

For Ladies in Distress 151

As has been well documented, these drugs became increasingly popular and widely prescribed. A wide-scale chemical tranquillization of anxiety ensued.[90] Increasingly, other manufacturers began to produce representations of the modern world as pressurized and 'stressful'. In 1966, Wyeth promoted their brand of benzodiazepine, oxazepam (marketed as Serenid), as 'prompt and effective in the control of all the symptoms of stress', namely, tension, irritability, lethargy, insomnia and headache.[91] In a similar way, Allen and Hanburys claimed that 'as society becomes progressively more complex, the problem of emotional disturbance grows steadily more acute'. This company claimed that, in the treatment of emotional disorder, a drug for one symptom often aggravated another. Their answer was a drug called Triptafen which combined an antidepressant, amitriptyline hydrochloride, and an antipsychotic, perphenazine.[92] Advertisements also appeared in *The Chemist and Druggist* for preparations that purported to ease the symptoms of nervous anxiety resulting from the demands of modern life. Relaxa-Tabs, which contained the antihistamine mepyramine, were marketed to ease worry, fear and anxiety caused by 'the pressures of modern life', and Neuro Phosphates, which featured a picture of weary-looking businessmen on a train, claimed to be the 'ideal tonic' for the chronically overworked.[93]

In 1962, the Health Secretary, Enoch Powell, reported in parliament that prescriptions for tranquillizers had escalated considerably during the twelvemonth period 1960–1. The cost to the NHS had risen from £1.6 million to £2.4 million.[94] The cost of Meprobamate prescriptions alone totalled £320,000 in 1961.[95] These figures appeared to indicate a rise in emotional disorders. However, a parallel debate existed in the medical press that questioned the notion of 'stress' in modern society and the concomitant rise in neuroses. A consultant psychiatrist from the Royal Hampshire County Hospital wrote a number of articles in the *BMJ* during the late 1950s and early 1960s which provided a critique of the modern notion of stress. In one such article, Dr I. Atkin remarked that many of the hardships in life had been reduced due to the implementation of the welfare state and an unprecedented rise in the standard of living:

> It is not clear why crossing the ocean comfortably by aeroplane in a few hours should be more stressful than being sea-sick on a schooner which may roll and pitch for several weeks; or why traveling in an express train should be worse for the nerves than being rattled in a horse-drawn chaise ... with the added chance of being waylaid by a highwayman.[96]

He maintained that tranquillizers were not necessarily required for minor distress, since their primary use was to assuage symptoms leaving the social origins of emotional disorders untouched. Atkin was concerned that problems and conflicts were increasingly being 'obscured in a thick cloud of chemically induced tranquility' at enormous cost to the NHS.[97] In a later article, he reminded physicians that:

152   *Desperate Housewives, Neuroses and the Domestic Environment, 1945–1970*

> Stresses centering around food, shelter, disease, life, sex and prestige have in fact existed in every era; and in privileged countries, with greater security and more opportunities for individual development, such stresses are becoming less rather than more pathogenic.[98]

He added that the 'faster tempo of modern life' had been used through the generations to explain a supposed increase in mental abnormalities, pointing out that Max Nordau, physician and social critic, had described the 'vertigo and whirl of our frenzied life' in 1895.[99] Atkin concluded that:

> We frequently hear that the intensity and struggle of life in the modern era are potent causes of mental disease. Probably more morbific is a narrow and restricted life ... in many occupations, the weekly hours of work have been reduced from forty-eight to forty and this has created quite a new problem – that of longer periods of leisure – for which adequate social programmes have not been planned. The increasing frequency with which the phrase 'stress diseases' is being used has given the word 'stress' an excessively weighted pathogenic association. It has become fashionable to prescribe tranquilizers right and left to subdue what are in fact normal reactions to ordinary living – worries and anxieties, alternating hopes and fears, irritabilities and vexations that we must all undergo if we are to play a full, active, enthusiastic role as members of society.[100]

Metzl states that representations in American print culture during the 1950s and 1960s implied that the patients in need of tranquillizers were predominantly women who threatened to keep their wartime jobs and neglect their duties in nuclear households.[101] The images, he argues, were testimony to the ways in which 'psycho-pharmaceuticals were shaped by the very psychoanalysis the biological psychiatry disavowed'.[102] There is thus a clear disparity between the findings presented here and Metzl's analysis in the United States. There are several possible explanations as to why these findings differ. Firstly, the discrepancies might be due to the selection of advertisements and the range of products included in the analysis. Many of the images of women portrayed in the British medical press could perhaps be analysed from a feminist perspective. Reviewed in isolation from the other advertisements that include men and other subjects, the pictures could certainly be seen as denigrating to women. However, it is also likely that the story differs across continents. In post-war America, psychiatry was dominated by psychoanalysis, and Metzl observes that it enjoyed 'near hegemonic influence'.[103] Conversely, as Porter notes, psychoanalysis spread rather slowly to Britain.[104] It is well known that, with the rise of the Nazi party in Germany, many psychoanalysts migrated to the United States. Whereas in Europe after the war psychiatrists were broadly based in asylums and psychiatric hospitals, in the United States private practice dominated. As Healy notes, 'The new analysis that emerged in America after the war was to make the idea that everybody needed treatment a public health issue: the way to right the world's wrongs was not just to treat mental illness but to re-sculpt personalities to promote mental health'.[105] Thus, it may be the case that the 'wide acceptance of the central analytic notion that psychiatric symptoms were the result of early-life experiences with moth- ers'[106] was less influential in British marketing strategies.

Metzl has also omitted from his analysis those drugs that contained 'hid- den' psychotropics and were often directed deliberately at men. Indeed, it is not clear from his text whether or not men featured in advertisements in any capac- ity other than as physicians. Finally, at various stages in his work, Metzl alludes to the important influence of wider social, economic and political forces that combined to explain why psychotropic medicines became imbued with 'gender tensions'. However, he acknowledges a number of times that the remit of his work was not to examine these factors.[107] As a result, the role of commerce and the aggressive marketing of medications are perhaps underplayed. These strategies are central to our understanding of developments within psychopharmacology during a period within which expectations of 'happiness', both materially and emotionally, rose exponentially. The evidence presented here indeed suggests that the new psychotropic medications encouraged the pursuance of calm and tranquility in both male and female individuals of all ages.

Advertising for Over-the-Counter Medicines in the Popular Press

There were distinct differences between the marketing strategies of psychophar- maceutical prescription drugs and over-the-counter medicines for wide-scale public consumption. In the first instance, manufacturers of prescribed drugs were directing sales literature at medical professionals, and as such, their aim was to tap into existing concerns relevant to physicians diagnosing and treating psychological disorder. Their advertisements largely focused on the complexities inherent in recognizing ill-defined and vague symptoms and aiding physicians in finding the appropriate treatment during what was usually a brief patient consultation. However, a sales psychology designed to attract the attention of the ordinary consumer was applied to the advertising of tonics and other sub- stances recommended for nervous disorders. As this section will illustrate, these products were not directed solely at women. While the majority of products promoted in women's magazines depicted images and portrayed scenarios that were relevant to women, advertisements appeared for identical products in the daily press that featured men in alternative settings. Furthermore, as women were identified as the 'new consumer', companies increasingly persuaded them to purchase products for home-medication for other members of their family.[108]

In her comprehensive history of the women's periodical press, Cynthia White has shown how editorial autonomy was undermined during the 1950s

154 *Desperate Housewives, Neuroses and the Domestic Environment, 1945–1970*

by intense pressure from advertisers who were becoming aware of the vast new potential purchasing power of women of all ages:

> Before the war, money had been short while goods were plentiful. After it, people had money to spend but the shops were empty. Now, for the first time, production matched spending power, and manufacturers and consumers were eager to make contact through the medium of advertising. Women especially, after a long period during which they had been able to buy only essential commodities (and those in limited quantities), wanted information about the new products flooding onto the market. They were ready to be persuaded to buy, and the advertisement columns of the women's magazines were their fire-side shop windows.[109]

Following a period of austerity immediately after the war, in terms of gross domestic product the British economy grew at a rate of 2.8 per cent per annum during the years 1951–73. This exceeded the long-run growth rates experienced both before the First World War and in the interwar years. The era was further characterized by low unemployment and low inflation.[110] The average male employed in manufacturing saw his weekly earnings rise from £7.30 in 1950 to £41.52 in 1973.[111] As a result of economic expansion and higher incomes, more goods and services became available to more people. White notes that these changes had a significant impact on the existing class system:

> An important effect of the general increase in purchasing power was the closing of the gap between classes in patterns of spending ... many superficial class differences were thereby eliminated, and tastes were leveled upwards as a result of mass production which brought high quality and good design within reach of the mass of the population. [This] together with the growth of a state system of education helped to produce a greater similarity in the attitudes, interests and modes of life between the different social strata.[112]

Given that more married women were also working up until the birth of their first child, many households began to enjoy greater disposable income and were able to spend it on new consumer durables and leisure time. Circulations of women's magazines also grew considerably during the period. One publication, *Woman*, saw enduring success with its sales which grew from 750,000 in the late 1930s to 3.5 million by the late 1950s.[113]

The growth of advertising in women's magazines began during the last three decades of the nineteenth century. Technological developments in papermaking and printing resulted in an upturn in productivity and the ensuing costs compelled manufacturers to attract advertising revenue.[114] However, this did not always sit comfortably with editorial teams who began to lose autonomy in relation to the content of their magazines. Indeed, in 1938, the Political and Economic Planning *Report on the British Press* 'found disturbing evidence that newspapers had begun both to suppress minor items likely to be disadvantageous to advertisers, and to discourage the airing of issues that might cause publicity unfavourable to them'.[115] From the 1950s, The British Code of Advertising attempted to protect against manufacturers making fraudulent claims about their products; however, it could do little to protect against the exploitation of emotions and fears by the methods employed by the new 'psychological sell'. White argued that during the 1950s 'the vast increase in advertising brought rich profits which soon attracted the attention of the giant publishing corporations'.[116] Writing in 1970, she asserted that 'women's magazines are today run according to strict business methods and are answerable to cost-accountants. Their primary aim is to attract the maximum amount of advertising which is the source of their profits.'[117]

Given that the post-war period saw a reinforcement of traditional gender roles, advertisers began to underline the image of the ideal wife and exploit it as the ideal selling device. White noted that increasing use was being made of what she described as 'depth' techniques where manufacturers attempted to exploit a woman's concern to do her best for her family.[118] Brand names emerged imbued with symbolic meaning that resonated with the beliefs and values of post-war women. Vance Packard explored this new and insidious selling technique in his influential text *The Hidden Persuaders*, first published in 1957.[119] Although this work was largely a study of American advertising, Packard illustrated how these methods became extraordinarily effective and were soon exported all over the world. He was able to show how 'motivational analysts' were employed during the 1950s to conduct psychoanalytical studies into what prompted consumers in their purchases:

> Motivation research seek[s] to learn what motivates people in making choices. It employs techniques designed to reach the unconscious or subconscious mind, because preferences generally are determined by factors of which the individual is not conscious ... actually in the buying situation, the consumer generally acts emotionally and compulsively, unconsciously reacting to the images and designs which in the subconscious are associated with the product.[120]

The individual most famed for his work on motivational research was Dr Ernest Dichter (1907–91). Born in Vienna, Dichter moved to the United States and in 1946 set up the Institute for Motivational Research in Croton-on-Hudson, New York. His organization conducted studies on merchandising and he employed psychologists, sociologists and anthropologists to investigate consumer responses to advertising appeals.[121] Packard argued that the use of psychological techniques such as those espoused by Dichter became widespread from the 1950s:

> Thus it was that merchandisers of many different products began developing a startling new view of their prospective customers. People's subsurface desires, needs and drives were probed in order to find their points of vulnerability ... once these points of vulnerability were isolated, the psychological hooks were fashioned and baited and placed deep in the merchandising sea for unwary customers.[122]

Manufacturers also began to explore the manipulation of fears and anxieties and play on concerns such as smelling bad, the dangers of being overweight and tooth decay.[123] These techniques were bolstered by other factors that made selling easier. The growth of supermarket stores, for example, helped to boost sales of all manner of products as customers were able to serve themselves for the first time.[124] The incidence of impulse buying increased as manufacturers began to package their products in attractive, brightly coloured packaging. Packard claimed that by the mid-1950s, merchandisers of many different products were being urged by psychological counsellors to become 'merchants of discontent' and further to create new or insatiable demands for their products.[125]

Dichter was also well known to publishers and was called upon as an advisor for the restyling of the Canadian magazine *Chateleine* and the American monthly *Family Circle*. In 1964 he was commissioned by the publishers of the British magazine *Woman's Own* to prepare a report on its performance and requirements in the future. One of the things he suggested was that women could no longer be classified by age, since age no longer presupposed a particular stage in the 'family cycle'.[126] Instead, he argued, women needed to be grouped according to their outlook, experience and activities. Many of his recommendations went on to influence the editorial boards of other publications and 'soon, the mass weeklies and monthlies alike were given a new, modern look to strengthen their visual appeal and improve their image'.[127]

While the subject matter of the majority of advertisements harmonized with articles about household care, mothering and fashion, following the introduction of the NHS there was also heightened interest in medical topics. Advertisers were quick to exploit this new and profitable marketing opportunity. Packard observed that psychological sales techniques were used in the promotion of medicines. For example, motivational analysts identified the two groups of people most likely to buy painkillers: firstly, anxiety-ridden hypochondriacs who were prone to exaggerate aches and pains; and secondly, aggressive, self-reliant types who scorned doctors and preferred to self-medicate.[128] The women's periodical press afforded to manufacturers the opportunity of communicating with target groups about personal and medical problems in a quiet, personal way. As a consequence, an array of promotional advertisements appeared for medicinal and health-related products, a sizeable number of which were related in some way to nervous disorders.

Before 1960, references to 'nerves' and anxiety were usually related in some way to traditional discourses about women and menstruation. The makers of Dr Cassells tablets, for example, suggested that if a woman felt 'run-down and nervy', it might well be due to 'iron deficiency'.[129] This, it was claimed, was likely to result in tiredness, depression and low energy levels. While there is no explicit use of the word menstruation, the advertisement claimed that 'women suffer

For Ladies in Distress 157

more ... as so many demands are made on their blood supply'. Dr Cassells tablets contained iron, calcium phosphorus and vitamin B and they claimed to restore a woman back to 'happy, smiling health again'. The manufacturers of Iron Jelloids, also drew upon this notion in their advertisements which suggested that iron supplements were 'something most women need'. Once again the text alluded to the problems of menstruation:

> From those exciting, emotional days when she first becomes a woman, when she stops being a child and grapples with the problems of adolescence ... from those days on through womanhood and motherhood, every woman needs iron.[130]

Other manufacturers drew upon associations with the medical and scientific communities to add weight to the claims made in their advertisements. The makers of a well-known tonic, Phosferine, for example, claimed that 'medical research shows that between fifteen and twenty in every hundred people are over-anxious'. They went on to suggest that Phosferine promoted 'a healthier function of the gastric nerves, which leads to a better appetite and restful sleep'.[131] The manufacturers of Sanatogen went one stage further and provided an illustration of 'nerve cells' under the heading 'Your nerves may make you worry'. The strapline read: 'Ramifications of nerve fibres in the grey matter of the brain' and the recommendation was that supplements of protein and phosphorous were sometimes necessary in order to maintain healthy nerve cells.[132] In this instance, Sanatogen appeared to carry a medical seal of approval as the manufacturers claimed that 'Sanatogen is fully recommended by the medical profession and widely used by doctors here and abroad'. In many ways analogous to advertisements for prescribed psychopharmaceuticals, the manufacturers included details of a wide range of conditions caused by 'nerves', including depression, sleeplessness, lack of energy and irritability.

Although promotional material published in the women's periodical press was evidently intended to reach a female audience, a range of 'tonic' products were widely advertised in daily newspapers and these were clearly directed at men. In 1956, the manufacturers of Sanatogen produced an advertisement in *The Times* that was similar in format to the one that featured in *Woman's Own*. It also featured an illustration of 'nerve fibres' and indicated clearly on this occasion that men too were prone to experience nervous exhaustion as a result of a deficiency of 'essential nutrients'.[133] Another example was Supavite vitamin tablets, manufactured by Angier Chemical Company in London. An advert for this product reproduced in *The Times* in 1954, featured the slogan 'Asleep in the train again?' and, correspondingly, a businessman was pictured asleep, slumped over his newspaper. The company suggested that a 'vast number of people' suffered from persistent tiredness, and even claimed that short-temperedness and lassitude in a man was likely to spoil, not only his health, but the lives of his family, friends and colleagues at work.[134] The stimulation of energy and vitality also appeared as a recurring theme in advertisements for a product called DCL Yeast Tablets, which contained Vitamin B1. The consumption of these supplements, it was claimed, would result in 'vigorous health ... snap-action vitality ... power and poise!'[135]

As with the advertisements for dual-action hidden psychotropic preparations, manufacturers of over-the-counter remedies also drew a correlation between anxiety and stomach acidity. Once again, these were directly marketed at the businessman and often featured illustrations confirming the link between the tension of a high-pressure job and dyspepsia. The makers of Meggeson's Bismuth Dyspepsia Tablets, regularly produced advertisements that pictured executive businessmen. One advert explicitly asked the question 'Is nervous tension the cause of your indigestion?' Underneath the image of a well-dressed man at work, it is noted in the text that 'anxiety affects the glands that secrete digestive juices in the stomach [and that] many "nervy", busy people suffer from dyspepsia.'[136]

Some advertisers in the women's periodical press took the notion of tiredness and lethargy to the extreme, and before long a wide range of products claimed to offer symptomatic relief. The makers of the popular drink Lucozade developed the concept of the 'tiredness peak' which was employed in a sequence of advertisements in 1960, and used to describe the symptoms of low blood glucose. The fictional-style drama sequence shown in Figure 6.10, featured a woman who was running into marital difficulties as her tiredness and lack of enthusiasm began to create tension in the relationship. Following a week of treatment with Lucozade, the woman appears restored to her usual strength, to the great relief of her husband.[137] Other products too, suggested that the symptoms of lethargy and listlessness were connected in some way to the smooth running of the digestive system. In an advert for the laxative Bile Beans, for example, an animated woman appears next to the catchphrase 'She doesn't let constipation get her down – do you?'[138] Designed to 'restore regularity', this preparation claimed to clear skin and eyes and unwanted waste matter, since 'bowels that are sluggish ... upset your whole system'. The advertisement ended with the slogan 'Bile Beans today make you brighter tomorrow'. The makers of Nimble Bread even declared that eating their new, lighter loaf would promote 'energy' and 'love of life'. Their advert drew visual parallels with the advert for Bile Beans and featured a woman jumping in the air who was 'full of go'. It went on to assure readers that 'if you want to feel on top of things, fit and active all the day – change to Nimble now'.[139] As Packard had previously observed, advertisers increasingly began to invoke hidden fears and anxieties related to personal hygiene. In 1955, the manufacturers of MUM deodorant suggested that 'keyed up nerves mean danger to freshness'.[140] In this instance, a young woman is pictured at work sitting at her typewriter, bearing a fraught expression as her boss approaches. The copy text invites an association between anxiety about body odour and confidence, ultimately providing the assurance that 'Mum Lotion keeps you nice to be near'.

Figure 6.10: Lucozade, *Woman's Own*, 25 June 1960. Reproduced with the permission of GlaxoSmithKline UK Ltd and the British Library, London.

160   *Desperate Housewives, Neuroses and the Domestic Environment, 1945–1970*

Figure 6.11: Horlicks, *Woman's Weekly*, 30 September 1961. Reproduced with the permission of GlaxoSmithKline UK Ltd and the British Library, London.

For Ladies in Distress 161

Many of these themes endured through the first half of the 1960s. The makers of Horlicks, for example, emulated the marketing tool used by the makers of Lucozade and produced their own imaginative sequence-drama. This company developed the ingenious notion of 'night starvation' and suggested that it was a likely cause of tiredness and irritability.[141] In the advertisement shown in Figure 6.11, a farmer's wife is pictured experiencing difficulties in her personal life and is unable to keep up with ongoing daily demands. Having discovered Horlicks, she is not only able to attend to her work with a renewed sense of energy, but her husband appears relieved to find his wife back to her 'old self again'. The suggestion was thus that Horlicks not only aided the treatment of fatigue, but also opened up possibilities for a whole new way of life.

Other chemical companies continued to promote the benefits of supplementing the diet with iron. Dr William's Pink Pills (first manufactured in the United States in the late nineteenth century as Dr William's Pink Pills for Pale People), claimed to cure headaches, listlessness, poor complexion and 'nerviness'.[142] However, these tablets were not directed exclusively at women, but instead they were advertised for use in anyone who experienced such symptoms. The correlation between digestion and nervous irritability also continued into the 1960s with products such as Bengers which claimed to 'aid digestion and promote nourishment'. This wheat-based drink was described as 'predigested' and contained two substances found naturally in the body that were known to break down protein and starch – trypsin and amylase. Bengers claimed to provide the helping hand in 'major crises' where 'nervous irritability [could] explode into an emotional storm'. The advertisers in this instance used the familiar technique of personal endorsement, where a customer shared her experience of the product and explained how it helped her cope when she found herself 'embroiled in a personal crisis'.[143]

Simultaneously, manufacturers of products previously indicated for conditions unrelated to nervous disorder began to include 'nerves' in their list of recommended uses. The makers of Anadin painkillers, for example, devised the concept of the 'Tense Nervous Headache', which became a well-known catchphrase for over a decade.[144] Not only did these tablets claim to soothe nerves, relax tautness and relieve pain, but they also purported to 'throw off depression'. Throughout the 1960s, the manufacturers expanded the range of illnesses that were likely to respond to Anadin. By 1967, it was promoted for use with influenza and feverish colds. Nevertheless, the tablets still claimed to 'lift depression' that resulted from flu-like illness.[145] Trevor Millum in his study of advertising in women's magazines argued that, in the world of cures and preventatives, Anadin was marketed directly at women. This, he claimed, was because 'headaches prevent, among other things, the woman attending to dealing with the children and doing the ironing'. They are thus 'the deadliest enemy of the wife and mother in the carrying out of her duty'.[146] However, these images suggest that it was more likely that the makers of Anadin identified a wide range of possible consumers for their product and recommended it for an increasing number of conditions.

162 *Desperate Housewives, Neuroses and the Domestic Environment, 1945–1970*

In 1962, the manufacturers of the malted-chocolate drink, Bournvita, released a series of advertisements that perhaps reflected the increasing anxiety about prescribed tranquillizing drugs. A variety of family members were pictured at home in consecutive adverts, looking 'relaxed', drinking cups of Bournvita. However, there was a more sinister undertone to these adverts. In each edition, the 'relaxed' family member was placed alongside the silhouette of a figure taking tablets with a glass of water. The adverts warned that it was not wise to 'take things – artificial things' to aid relaxation. What was really needed was 'nourishment'.[147] The obvious message was that the drink Bournvita was a nourishing and warming way to relax and promote sleep. However, the implicit message was one of warning: that the increasing use of tranquillizing drugs should be treated with suspicion and be discouraged. Thus, while the major pharmaceutical companies were taking advantage of new biological notions of mental illness in order to market their chemical cures for neuroses, manufacturers of patent medicines and tonics conversely promoted their products as 'safe' alternatives. The Bournvita adverts are also good examples of the ways in which manufacturers attempted to influence the buying decisions of British women who increasingly had the benefit of a disposable income. In these advertisements, as in many others, the message was that readers should be buying these products, not necessarily for themselves, but for other members of their family. As guardian of her family, the housewife was called upon to care for them. It is notable that, simultaneously, during the first half of the 1960s, promotional material for tonics and other remedies for 'nerves' all but disappeared in from national newspapers. It is therefore possible that advertisers found it more profitable to market products at a female readership, since women were more likely to be persuaded to buy products for home medication by the whole family.

During the late 1960s there was also a proliferation of advertisements for 'tonic wines'. These were 'nutritional' or 'tonic' beverages that contained an amalgamation of substances such as quinine, glycero-phosphates and extracts of coca leaves, in a base of British ruby wine.[148] Chemists and grocery stores required a wine license to sell these products. Tiredness and lethargy continued to be the predominant theme in adverts for the top-sellers: Buckfast Tonic Wine, Hall's Wine, Wincarnis Wine and Sanagtogen Tonic Wine. However, the advertisements for Sanatogen were illuminating, since they were the first to explicitly draw on notions that were being promoted by second-wave feminists such as Betty Friedan. The adverts, shown in Figures 6.12 and 6.13, resonate with Freidan's idea that there was a 'strange stirring' of discontent among middle-class suburban housewives.[149] In Figure 6.12, the scene portrayed depicts a typical, middle-class suburban driveway. A well-dressed businessman is pictured leaving for work; the silhouette of his wife is a dark, figure in the foreground. The message in the copy text is that:

> It's alright for him! He goes off in the morning – and you can see he's anticipating the bustle, the life his day will bring. Problems to sort out, people to talk to, have a joke with. Lunch with his friends. Then back to his work, absorbed and interested ... But all you have is an empty house. And the same dull round of household tasks. There are times when the thought of it takes the heart out of you.[150]

Figure 6.12: Advertisement, *Woman's Realm*, 24 September 1966. Reproduced with the permission of Constellation Europe Ltd and the British Library, London.

164 *Desperate Housewives, Neuroses and the Domestic Environment, 1945–1970*

Figure 6.13: Advertisement, *Woman*, 18 February 1967. Reproduced with the permission of Constellation Europe Ltd and the British Library, London.

For Ladies in Distress 165

The advert in Figure 6.13 is produced in a similar style and the eye is drawn to the picture of a woman, slumped in a chair. Beneath, the message in large, bold font reads: 'Kids are murder'. It continues:

> You always seem to be screaming at them. Nagging and bullying ... It wears you out. And your husband wonders what's wrong with you! It's on days when you feel like this that 'Sanatogen' Tonic Wine is such a help. It makes life so much more bearable for you – and them.[151]

Since advertisements were an important indicator of changes in society, it is notable that, even in the late 1960s, depictions like those in the Sanatogen promotions were in the minority. Mostly, advertisers empathized with mothers and housewives, and suggested that their products would help ease the strains of family life. The advert for Wincarnis wine for example, implied that, while being a housewife and mother was hard work, with the help of this product it could still be great fun.[152] Indeed, some manufacturers even produced depictions of a 'new' kind of woman – independent, with an income and leisure time of her own. In contrast to the image portrayed by Sanatogen, the advert for Complan shown in Figure 6.14, featured a woman looking carefree and relaxed, enjoying a sightseeing trip to London. The message in the text suggested that, given the pressure and pace of modern life, some women might be tempted to skip meals or 'make-do' with quick snacks, and thus experience a loss of vitality. However, it was claimed that Complan – the complete meal in a cup – used as a meal replacement or supplement, would ensure that any woman could reclaim their 'vim and vigour'.[153] Certainly, the majority of products were not directed solely at women. As a marketing strategy, this would arguably have restricted sales potential. Some manufacturers actually provided a list of a wide range of individuals who might potentially benefit from their products. Pro-Plus tablets, for example, contained caffeine to aid 'intellectual alertness' and 'enhance sparkle'. Although they appeared in a woman's magazine, these tablets were explicitly recommended for 'businessmen, housewives, TV stars, students, sportsmen, office workers, holidaymakers and manual workers'.[154] The list of recommended uses was equally diverse.

It is difficult to gauge the impact of these advertisements upon consumers. Among the women interviewed for this project, only a small number recalled using tonic medicines. These women remembered that products such as Sanagtogen and Wincarnis Wine were usually taken as nutritional supplements after illness or childbirth. From the evidence available, opinion among the general public was divided. One investigation among Mass Observation's national panel undertaken some years earlier in 1944 revealed that 'seven people out of ten were in some way opposed to the present position of patent medicines'.[155] The report stated that:

> Some feel that further restrictions should be imposed on the sale of patent medicines. These feelings are based on the belief that commercial interests should not be allowed to profit out of illness, that these medicines make exaggerated claims, that they are habit-forming and that they prevent people from seeking a doctor's advice in the early stages of illness.[156]

166 *Desperate Housewives, Neuroses and the Domestic Environment, 1945–1970*

Figure 6.14: Complan, *Woman*, 11 February 1967. Reproduced with the permission of GlaxoSmithKline UK Ltd and The British Library, London.

For Ladies in Distress 167

However, it was noted that in this instance 'the survey was made among a more than averagely informed and thoughtful section of the community' and that other smaller surveys had indicated greater numbers were indifferent or partially in favour of these medications.[157] Indeed, another survey published later in 1953 reporting on the newly established NHS included a survey of 'home cures' and 'the chemist'.[158] Within this report, patent medicines were roughly divided into two groups. One group, labelled the 'psychosomatic' group, included remedies such as tonics, vitamins, laxatives and analgesics – medicines that could be loosely associated with 'semi-nervous ailments'. The other group included medicines that were used for other conditions such as cold or influenza mixtures and antiseptics. Of those interviewed, 48 per cent 'bought one of the "psychosomatic" group of medicines on their last visit to the chemist', whereas, only 27 per cent had made a purchase from the second group. It was noted that the chemist's market for patent medicines was composed 'disproportionately of women'.[159] However, it is not clear whether women were buying these items for self-medication or on behalf of other family members. Ultimately, the report concluded that 'the chemist's shop offers people a type of medical independence; with its help they can try, at least, to dose away their ailments'.[160]

Conclusion

This chapter has shown that advertising both in the medical and popular press provides little evidence to support the popular conceptualization of the 'neurotic' housewife. Men and women of all ages featured in advertisements and medications were not recommended exclusively for anxiety and depression, but also for a wide range of other conditions. The messages conveyed in promotional literature were designed to resonate with the values and concerns of the intended audience. Thus, the techniques employed by psychopharmaceutical manufacturers differed from those used by companies who produced patent medicines. Large psychopharmaceutical companies were required to address the concerns of busy medical practitioners who were dealing with a range of symptoms that were often obscure and puzzling. However, as Packard remarked, advertisers had to tread cautiously in this pursuit since motivational research undertaken by Dichter in the United States found that some doctors felt threatened by the growth of factory-compounded medicines, and were resentful of drug ads that relegated the doctor to the position of a pill dispenser rather than a chief diagnostician and healer. 'The shrewd drug-house' Dr Dichter counselled 'will ... not go over the doctor's head to the public. Instead it will seek to reinforce the doctor's self-image as the all-powerful healer'.[161]

It is perhaps a measure of the success of biochemical theories of mental illness that by 1970, the British Medical Association's publication *Today's Drugs* confidently recommended pharmacological preparations for the majority of psychiatric conditions.[162] This advice stood in contrast to that provided in the 1964 edition, which stated that 'evidence about the biochemical and neurophysiological events is still insufficient to classify depressions reliably', and further that, professional opinions about the use of drugs 'varied greatly'.[163] By 1970, psychiatrists argued that endogenous depression was easily identifiable and treatable with tricyclic medication. The 'neurotic' category of the illness was now clearly associated with personality types and the approved treatment was with a combined dose of benzodiazepine tranquillizer and MAOI. For the treatment of anxiety, now labelled 'psychoneurosis', benzodiazepine compounds were recommended; however, barbiturate drugs were still seen as useful with the proviso that care should be taken to avoid addiction and tolerance. In addition to this, hypnotic sedatives were recommended for insomnia, amphetamines were seen as advantageous for use in 'neurotic states', phenothiazines (such as Phenergan) were endorsed for use in children, and the tricyclic antidepressants were listed as an appropriate treatment for nocturnal enuresis. The only category of affective order viewed as less responsive to chemical treatment was 'reactive depression' caused by a 'reaction to environmental stresses'. General measures of 'encouragement' and 'possibly a holiday' were recommended to ameliorate symptoms associated with this condition, although tranquillizers were still a considered option.[164] Thus, psychopharmaceutical preparations were evidently seen, by an expanding number of professionals, as appropriate for use in a growing number of psychiatric conditions.

Manufacturers of products for self-medication also began to make increasingly expansive claims about their products. Throughout the 1960s, tonics and supplements were imbued with symbolic meaning, because the advertising industry soon realized that consumers 'buy a product, not per se, but as the bearer of a description of benefits'.[165] Thus, customers were persuaded to buy medicinal preparations, not just for symptomatic relief of their condition, but often because it was inferred that the product would transform their lives in some other way. These companies utilized an increasingly sophisticated set of persuasive techniques to attract interest in their products. Pictorial images were designed to be memorable and hold attention, while written messages were increasingly characterized by catchy slogans in striking, bold typefaces. Advertisers also made use of personal narratives and anecdotal evidence which were a powerful tactic of persuasion. Throughout the decade, advertising for over-the-counter preparations drew upon a range of shifting contemporary concerns, from female menstruation to new anxieties about the pressures of modern life.

By the close of the 1960s, manufacturers of tonic preparations began to shift their emphasis yet again in an attempt to create new and original needs and desires in their potential customers. The majority of articles and editorials continued to focus on the topics of homemaking and relationships. However, advertisers soon became aware of a new direction which offered profitable opportunities: the affiliation of health with beauty. An array of cosmetic haircare products and articles appeared as manufacturers of tonic products began to suggest that anxiety and irritability might damage your looks. An advert for Phillips Tonic Yeast appeared in 1969, for example, and the manufacturers of this product claimed that 'worry, strain and anxiety play such havoc with the way you look'. Phillips Tonic Yeast claimed to be 'better than a beauty treatment', since 'life's best beauty treatment is a healthy body and a calm mind'. The preparation also drew on the undercurrent of fear surrounding prescribed psychotropic medication and promised to provide a 'drug-free way to new vitality'.[166]

As Katherine Ott has perceptibly noted in her social history of tuberculosis, the 'meaning' of any disease evolves from the interaction of many things, including people, technology, medical doctrine and state affairs. 'Illness', she argues, 'is as dependent upon the palpable human experience of it, as it is upon impersonal physiology and pathology'.[167] This book has explored a range of factors that influenced both medical and popular understandings of anxiety and depression during the post-war period. It has suggested that, although men and women were usually depicted in traditional roles, gender was only one aspect of a more complex picture that included the medicalization of emotional problems, developments in medical science, the financial motives of pharmaceutical companies and, perhaps most importantly, the broader political and social context of the period. Many of these aspects have previously been eclipsed by accounts that have implied straightforwardly that domesticity made women ill and that doctors and pharmaceutical companies conspired to medicate women back into the home.

CONCLUSION

This book has taken as its starting point the popular twentieth-century image of the 'desperate housewife'. It has traced the origins of an association between minor mental illness and domesticity and has suggested that, since the 1970s, ideas about this association have been dominated by theories formulated by feminist academics. However, the testimonies provided by the women interviewed for this project in fact suggest that, while not always easy, domestic life provided many married women with a role that they valued and, in many cases, enjoyed. It is of course possible that post-war social commentators, politicians and religious leaders saw it as politically expedient to construct the breadwinner model of the family as 'natural' and 'normal', and to return women to their 'place' in the home. Neither is it assumed here that there is universally something 'proper' or 'desirable' about the traditional family unit. It is nevertheless argued here that middle-class housewives did not uniformly evaluate their living arrangements as oppressive. Feminist accounts have sought to exclude the possibility that some women wanted to remain at home. As Katie Roiphe has noted, feminists are in danger of creating 'their own rigid orthodoxy' – the movement that once promised women a voice is now being used to tell them what they ought to say and think.[1]

The previous chapters have illustrated how, during the 1950s and 1960s, as notions of mental illness expanded to include less serious symptoms, minor mental illness was in fact constructed in a number of different ways. On the one hand, neuropsychiatrists stressed the importance of biological factors and put forward the notion that illness was likely to be caused by chemical or genetic abnormality. It is easy to see why these ideas gained ground. The discovery of new drugs that were capable of altering mood and mind appeared to provide timely corroboration to neuroscientific theories of brain chemistry, at the same time providing welcome respectability to psychiatrists and their speciality. On the other hand, physicians who aligned themselves with behavioural therapy formulated an equally persuasive construction of illness that emphasized environmental factors. These theories were dominated by the principle that childhood experience, family life and interpersonal relationships could affect psychological well-being. Such ideas fitted comfortably within the social climate, where, following the loss and dislocation of war, the quality of the home environment was cited among commentators as a critical factor in emotional and physical health.[2] Finally, as the 1960s progressed, notions of depression and anxiety were increasingly driven by preoccupations with the possible links between the pressures of daily life and disease. Although these ideas were not new, they attained renewed significance during the 1960s following the work of early twentieth-century stress researchers such as Selye, Cannon and Wolff who were interested in exploring possible links between stress and disease.

In an attempt to exploit all marketing avenues, pharmaceutical companies produced advertising material that drew variously upon a wide range of ideas about mental illness. Many of the compounds appealed to neuropsychiatrists because they claimed to act specifically on neurotransmitters in the brain. However, pharmaceutical companies claimed that some drugs (the tranquillizing agents in particular) were suitable for the relief of a constellation of symptoms, irrespective of their cause. Through the 1960s, the manufacturers of these compounds increasingly exploited the idea that the pressures of daily life could trigger illness. Medicines that were developed for over-the-counter purchase were also marketed for 'nervous irritability' in imaginative ways. By the 1970s, manufacturers of an expansive range of products claimed that their remedies offered solutions to a multitude of symptoms related to nervousness, including tiredness, headaches, constipation, indigestion and perspiration.

If, as this book has indicated, there is little evidence to suggest that women were deliberately targeted in the prescribing of psychotropic medicine, it would be fair to ask why the overmedicated housewife captured the public imagination in such a way. Part of the answer must lie in statistics that routinely suggested the sex ratio of psychotropic drugs prescribed was at least two to one female to male. These statistics emerged at a significant time for the feminist movement which was promoting awareness of genuine inequality and injustice towards women, and the figures indicated a correlation between rising cases of psychiatric disorder and the 'experience' of being a woman. This was perhaps broadly correct, since the women from this study spoke of a range of social, political and economic hardships and discriminatory practices that caused emotional distress. However, these wider discontents were duly conflated with the specific idea that the homemaker's role was intrinsically damaging to women. Many of the second-wave feminists in fact argued explicitly that radical change to the nuclear family itself was necessary for gender equality.[3] In the United States, where the popular depiction was more powerful, Andrea Tone has shown how 'the realization that stay-at-home moms – sentimentalized symbols of wholesome family values – were the biggest users of tranquilizers' caused significant disquiet in popular consciousness.[4] 'The feminization of tranquilizers', she argues, 'precipitated a sensationalistic media campaign that dramatized the pathology of the

Conclusion 173

overmedicated woman'.[5] This was duly exacerbated by a number of high profile cases of addiction, such as the American First Lady Betty Ford, and later, the accumulating evidence that all manner of prescription drugs could be dangerous.[6] Tone also acknowledges that, as was the case in Britain, researchers were debating the reasons why women appeared in American statistics with such regularity. Reflecting the findings in Britain, some noted that women simply visited their primary care practitioner more often and were more open to discussions about everyday health during regular visits with children. Others suggested that the stereotype of the emotive woman 'enabled women to discuss psychological problems with doctors more freely than men did'.[7] Ultimately, as Tone reminds us, the stereotype of the overmedicated housewife 'ignored contemporary and historical realities', by overlooking the thousands of 'career' women who were addicted to tranquillizers, and by glossing over a long history of male use.[8]

The statistical representation of psychiatric disorder certainly concealed a more complex picture. Physicians in Britian indeed acknowledged that it was very difficult to draw any firm conclusions from studies of psychiatric morbidity. Such investigations depended upon a wide range of variables such as the size of the sample, diagnostic classifications, indices of morbidity, the system of sampling, the methods of recording data and the attitudes of health professionals towards mental illness.[9] Most importantly, these studies were usually based upon patients who attended their GP. These were a self-selected group whose attitudes and expectations may have differed from those who did not attend and yet suffered from symptoms.[10] Health practitioners and policymakers have indeed recently acknowledged that men are less likely to seek medical help for emotional disorders and more likely to present with physical symptoms in primary care.[11] Although women featured more regularly in statistics for the use of psychotropic drugs, it is impossible to know how many men experienced symptoms but failed to seek medical help. It is certainly likely that men were less aware of psychological problems, and correspondingly less likely than women to recognize them. In contrast to women, men would not have acquired information from magazine articles and they were also less commonly exposed to social gatherings where such matters might be discussed. It is also probable that they would not have confided in close friends about personal matters. Thus, it might be that gendered aspects of mental illness are as much bound up with 'masculinity' as with 'femininity'.[12]

In 1972, Dunnell and Cartwright undertook a research project into 'medicine-taking behaviour' in Britain.[13] They noted that the production of pharmaceutical preparations had increased by 67 per cent between 1963 and 1968 and argued that 'the industry ha[d] created an increasing supply of new products both for the ethical and over-the-counter markets'.[14] One of the aims of their project was to explore how personal characteristics and attitudes influenced

174   *Desperate Housewives, Neuroses and the Domestic Environment, 1945–1970*

decisions about seeking medical advice and treatment. Dunnell and Cartwright noted that, in recent years, certified sickness absences had also increased and that less serious illness was more frequently regarded as justification for absence from work. The Office of Health Economics had deduced from official statistics that there had been a 'change in threshold levels at which an illness is translated into a spell of sickness absence'.[15] It was argued that there had also been a change in the level at which treatment was felt to be appropriate, which had led to a corresponding increase in the consumption of medicines. During interviews, Dunnell and Cartwright also noted that women generally reported more symptoms than men and that they purchased greater quantities of home remedies. However, the research pointed explicitly to a number of factors that might explain this. Firstly, the authors argued that 'women did not take more medicines just because they had more symptoms; they were simply more likely to take medicines for their symptoms'.[16] They added that 'one possible explanation might be that women generally take responsibility for the family shopping. They will therefore be exposed to displays and advertising in shops [which] may make them more likely to buy over-the-counter medicines for their symptoms.' One further important observation was that women were also responsible for stocking the home medicine-cabinet, and therefore, 'medicines may be more readily available to women and they may more often be made aware of them'.[17] Nancy Tomes has recently shown how, during the mid-twentieth century, a similar situation existed in the United States, where women became the target for a new style of health promotion that equated good health with the wise choice and use of an increasing array of product lines 'from food and toothpaste to household cleaners and over-the-counter drugs'.[18]

With specific reference to psychotropic medicines, Dunnell and Cartwright noted that the number of prescriptions written for sedatives and antidepressants had risen sharply over the six-year period under examination. The authors concluded that this was in part due to successful advertising campaigns, but they also reiterated that there had been a general 'lowering of the threshold at which illness was perceived at all'.[19] They were keen to emphasize that more people recognized psychological symptoms and the general public felt increasingly that depression, sleeplessness and 'personal problems' now fell 'within the doctor's province'.[20] The authors' discussion highlighted a growing awareness of, and concern about, sleeplessness and irritability among individuals.

From the sources examined by Dunnell and Cartwright, no clear correlation emerged between women's experience of domesticity and nervous disorder. Similarly, the evidence put forward in this book from the oral history, medical editorials and case studies suggests that women who experienced psychological symptoms did not locate the cause of their problems in their role as homemakers. Although women who joined the National Housewives' Register were openly in support of equality for women and promoted greater opportunities in education

Conclusion   175

and employment, they also recognized the value of homemaking and mothering. Many of them were keen to emphasize that everyone has 'problems' and that being occasionally 'bored' with one's role was in no way synonymous with the 'dislike' of it.[21] Most women devised imaginative solutions when faced with feelings of isolation and joined organizations or groups that fostered friendship and intellectual stimulation. In 1963, Mary Stott, the woman's editor of the *Guardian* expressed her concern about 'the myth of the whining graduate housewife' that was taking root. She asserted that her page was 'not inundated with letters from discontented young mothers wailing that their education was wasted and that their intellects were withering while they [were] tied to the kitchen sink'. On the contrary, she confirmed that the majority of those who wrote in expressed pleasure about the company of children who were often described 'as a source of constant interest, surprise and amusement'.[22] Indeed, Brenda Prys Jones, the second National Organiser of the Register affirmed in a letter to the *Guardian* that 'a woman who describes her problems is not necessarily "moaning"', and she warned sociologists and critics alike that women writing to the organization did not express discontent with family life.[23]

Cynthia White has pointed out that, during the early and middle decades of the twentieth century, the vast majority of women were not moved by ideologies that suggested alternative long-term goals and that the changes fostered by the women's movement were too narrowly channelled to influence more than a relatively small number of women. This was manifest in the range of articles and editorials in women's magazines which remained focused on the traditional domestic role. Interestingly, White argued that ultimately millions of women themselves favoured this traditional formula: 'the values and priorities projected reflected those held by women themselves'.[24] Indeed, following the Second World War, publishers of *Woman* attempted to introduce a new range of 'progressive journalistic articles with a social conscience'; however, they soon returned to their traditional format because sales of the magazine dropped by 30 per cent.[25] Mary Grieve, editor of *Woman*, affirmed that:

> In holding the interest week after week of almost every second woman in the country, it was inevitable that *Woman* should concentrate on those interests which are generally held, rather than on minority interests ... there are fewer women strongly drawn to subjects like equal pay and racial problems than to practical skills; personal relationships and increased self-confidence.[26]

White ultimately concluded that, in Britain:

> The formula laid down more than half a century ago, when a woman's sphere was far narrower than it is today, has endured, despite attempts to modify it. The fact that it has withstood the emancipation of women; two world wars and the social upheavals following them; the growth of affluence and multilateral social change; indicates that the majority of women find in it certain ingredients which satisfy their deepest needs.[27]

176 *Desperate Housewives, Neuroses and the Domestic Environment, 1945–1970*

Attempts to upgrade the intellectual level of magazines were more successful in the United States where articles appealed to women who were under greater pressure to gain a college degree and become involved in community affairs. This is reflected in the testimonies of the two women from the United States who were interviewed for this project. Both remarked that American women were expected to gain a degree, although they were keen to emphasize that this was seen as grounding for the ultimate role of traditional wife and mother. Indeed, Coontz has revealed greater levels of discontent in her study of American housewives. It is likely that this was partly because women were exposed to new intellectual ideas at university, where British women were not. However, there are other possible reasons for such contrasts. Firstly, although American women were greatly affected by the loss of service personnel during the war, British women's perception of family life was clearly framed by the impact of homeland bombing. As the oral testimonies and contributions to Mass Observation illustrate, this instilled in them a sense of the sanctity of human life and an even stronger sense of indebtedness for having survived the war at all. That so many homes were destroyed also intensified the feeling that 'a home of one's own' was something to be valued and appreciated. Secondly, the introduction of the welfare state in Britain brought with it many new advantages in health and social security. The ideals of the breadwinner family that underpinned it must therefore have been seen as something worth supporting. Finally, Coontz notes that Freudian theories of 'penis envy' were endlessly recycled in the media in 1950s America, providing, she argues, 'the ideological bulwark of the sexual counter-revolution'.[28] As this book has shown, these ideas were less influential in Britain, and as Metzl's work suggests, this might also explain the divergence of trends in pharmaceutical advertising between Britain and the United States.

In Britain, the broad message communicated to women did not change until the early 1970s. Deirdre McCloskey observes that an ideological change then occurred:

> In short, rising life expectancies and falling size of families left millions of British women with labour on their hands . . . the labour force participation of British women aged 25–34 (the prime years for having pre-school children) rose from 29.5 per cent in 1961 to 38.4 per cent in 1971 to 48.6 per cent in 1981.[29]

These changes were mediated in part through magazine articles that both reflected and reinforced a sense of change among women. Whereas leading editorials had previously reinforced the values of full-time motherhood, by the early 1970s, articles extolled the advantages of working outside the home. Many of them called upon women to help fill the labour shortage in Britain, and they were written with emotive language and led by striking titles. One article published in *Woman's Own*, for example, asked 'Are you a Housewife? A mother of school-age children? You are the most wanted women in Britain!'[30] The editor of this 'special investigation' claimed that readers at home were experiencing 'niggling pangs of boredom' and that the contact with others gained from work was now essential: 'Even if you've read every magazine ... you can't be sure what people really are wearing, doing and talking about. Women can "cabbage" at home and it is only when they return to work that they realize just how much they're out of the swing of things.'[31] Women writing about childcare now argued that young children did not need the undivided attention of their mothers twenty-four hours a day. Claire Rayner, for example, nurse and childcare author, argued that although a child needed 'mothering', he or she need not get it exclusively from the mother – a substitute mother figure would suffice.[32] Some 'experts' even indicated that boring wives were the cause of marriage breakdown. The 'Kelly Looks at Life' column in *Woman's Own* suggested that wives who became 'depressed' or 'a bit mousy' should look for a job and independence. Kelly drew attention to this problem because she felt 'it may have a message for other married women who, although not on the verge of divorce, may worry in secret because they feel that their husbands meet younger and more attractive women at work.'[33] Other articles indicated that there had been a sizeable shift towards a consumer-orientated society. Women spoke of raising their standard of living and being able to purchase their own homes and new cars.[34] Faced with these constant and all-pervasive messages portrayed in the media, it is possible that some women who were previously content with full-time motherhood began to question the value of their role at home.

The changes that took place during the 1970s marked a trend that continued throughout the last quarter of the twentieth century and into the twenty-first century. The employment rates of women rose from 51 per cent in 1984 to 70 per cent in 2003. The difference in rates of employment between men and women has narrowed from 19 per cent in 1984 to 10 per cent in 2003, confirming the now-established pattern of the two-income family.[35] Unsurprisingly, the debate about the desirability of working mothers persists and many of the current arguments reflect the sentiments put forward by post-war women.

In 2005, an article by the novelist Lucy Cavendish, entitled 'Breaking the Last Taboo', sparked a heated debate in the *Daily Mail*.[36] Cavendish, despite having been encouraged by her mother to gain an education and a career, had opted for life as a full-time mother and homemaker and she argued that being successful – beating men at their own game – now seemed so unfulfilling: it was 'more fun to have freedom: the freedom to be at home'.[37] A series of articles followed over the following months and impassioned readers wrote in with personal perspectives on both sides of the argument.[38] A month later, the television presenter Lowri Turner added to the furore in an article caustically entitled 'A Plague on You Smug, Stay-at-Home Mums'.[39] Turner claimed that, as a working mother,

178 *Desperate Housewives, Neuroses and the Domestic Environment, 1945–1970*

she too was trying to do the best for her children. However, she asserted that she was also actively 'contributing to life' and was therefore able to 'function intellectually' in a way that full-time mothers could not.

Recent academic contributions to the debate have also shifted. Professor of education policy James Tooley, for example, has suggested that society (and education policy specifically) has been shaped by feminist politics of the 1970s and 1980s. Although he fully supports women achieving in careers, he argues that there is an alternative route – celebrating the differences between men and women. This, he claims, would assign to women who wish to choose motherhood and family life, the value they deserve.[40] Clinical psychologist Daphne De Marneffe also addresses these concerns.[41] She advocates a midpoint between traditional and feminist ideologies and proposes that paid employment is not the only path to freedom and happiness, arguing ultimately that many women desire to be with their children. These ideas could perhaps be seen within the context of what has recently been described as the 'post-feminist' era, in which second-wave feminism has come to be seen as less relevant to the concerns of twenty-first-century women.[42]

The economist Alison Wolf has also drawn attention to the wider social consequences of a generation of working mothers. Although she acknowledged the many positive changes to women's lives, Wolf argues that the new generation of 'go-getting women' has diverted talent away from the caring professions and, most importantly, has prevented women from volunteering for charity work.[43] Indeed, one sixty-nine-year-old woman writing in to the *Daily Mail* noted that the younger generation of women do not have time to help with good causes:

> There was a network of women like me who did charitable work and I think we did make a difference. I'm very proud of the work we did then and the sense of togetherness it fostered. I did prisoners' wives once a week, meals on wheels twice a week and then helped various elderly neighbours . . . I felt as if the state had helped me a great deal with my university grant, and that it was up to me to put something back into society. All my friends did charity work too. It was fun and we took it in turns to look after each other's children.[44]

The same woman argued that her life as a housewife and mother had been easier than that of her daughter who now 'lives with the constant need to earn money to fuel her lifestyle'. There was thus an inference from many of the contributors to this debate that in recent years, working mothers were the ones to succumb to 'stress' and depression. One woman admitted that, the pursuit of two holidays a year, two cars and private education for their children, had resulted in a fifty-hour working week and 'little time to look after the family'.[45] The possible dangers associated with this lifestyle have recently been highlighted by the psychologist Oliver James in his book *Affluenza*, in which he argues that the

Conclusion 179

English-speaking Western world is obsessed with consumerism, appearance and celebrity – a phenomenon he refers to as 'selfish capitalism' – which is making us vulnerable to depression, anxiety and addiction.[46]

Within medicine, the biochemical model of mental illness still dominates and a new, but no less controversial, generation of antidepressant drugs, the selective serotonin reuptake inhibitors (such as Prozac) have taken centre stage in the treatment of affective disorders. However, it is interesting that despite this, suburban life retains its pathogenic overtones. The early twenty-first century has seen the release of a new cluster of films which focus upon the misery of suburbia. However, in these more recent productions, the suburban husband is often the character most deeply affected by the stifling restrictions of modern life. *American Beauty* (1999), directed by Sam Mendes, starring Kevin Spacey and Annette Benning was perhaps the first and most memorable of these examples. This film's overarching theme is of the shallowness of American middle-class suburbia. However, it is Lester Burnham who has the mid-life crisis. His status-seeking, materialistic wife Carolyn is the main wage-earner, leaving Lester feeling inadequate and expendable. He is sexually frustrated and utterly miserable, and the film reflects many of the concerns about men and masculinity that emerged on both sides of the Atlantic during the last years of the twentieth century. In the 'post-feminist' world, as the British psychiatrist Anthony Clare wrote in 2000, 'the whole issue of men – the point of them, their purpose ... is a matter for public debate. Serious commentators declare that men are redundant, that women do not need them and that children would be better off without them.'[47]

Ultimately, when Lester Burnham begins to break free from the suffocating constraints of conventional married family life, his world (that appears so perfect on the surface) begins to unravel. In *American Beauty*, as in many of these films, the alternative to conformity is always worse – anarchic and disturbing. Burnham ends up dead, murdered by his neighbour; although, in the opening voiceover of the film, he had already noted that suburban life, 'in a way', had left him 'dead already'. *American Beauty* is not the only film to portray this new breed of man, eclipsed by his post-feminist, career-orientated wife. *Little Children* (2006), based upon the novel by Tom Perrotta, also features a suburban house-husband (Patrick Wilson) who has repeatedly failed to pass his state bar exams, while his controlling wife excels as a television documentary-maker. His co-star and lover (Kate Winslett) tolerates an equally loveless marriage and both 'hunger for an alternative'.

Although a number of these films are set in modern times; other directors have attempted to revive the post-war period. *Far From Heaven*, released in 2002, starring Julianne Moore and Dennis Quaid, explores themes of 'difference' on a number of levels: race, class and sexuality. Moore's character Cathleen is married to a homosexual who has tried to suppress a lifetime of desires for other men. The film examines her struggle, as she discovers the truth and attempts to hold her conventional, suburban world together. However, it is Quaid's character Frank's difficulties in trying to overcome his homosexuality, viewed uncompromisingly as 'sickness', that are most captivating. On the one hand, Mr and Mrs 'Magnatech' live the American Dream – they have the suburban house, the big car and material items. Yet on the other hand, these things serve only as camouflage for the isolation, hypocrisy and destructiveness of suburban living. The most recent, and perhaps the most dystopian portrayal of post-war values, is the film *Revolutionary Road* (2008). Kate Winslett is again cast as wife and mother, only this time the film is set in the 1950s. She yearns to run from the 'hopeless emptiness' of the suburban home, with its 'simple clean lines and good lawns'. Notably, it is her husband Frank (Leonardo Di Caprio) who tolerates his monotonous, unsatisfying job in order to provide for his family, and the film is as much about his journey trying to reconcile a need for passion and excitement with the demands of supporting a family financially.

Betty Friedan's bored housewives, it would seem, have retreated into the past. Although some inequality arguably still exists, most women can at least aspire to higher education and a career. Yet recent figures show that one in four Britons will experience mental illness and that mixed anxiety and depression is the most common mental disorder in Britain. Some might argue that the pharmacological revolution of the 1950s has therefore done little to reduce the large numbers of people affected with depression and anxiety. But perhaps Oliver James might have a point in suggesting that the consumer society (that accelerated with such energy during the 1950s) has resulted in our placing a high value on money and possessions, leaving us vulnerable to disappointment and distress. We are, he argues, destined for disaster if we conflate what we 'want' with what we really 'need'. The 'needs' he identifies are those that are built upon emotional and physical security; among them are a need to feel part of a community and to be valued and effective in our chosen tasks.[48] What strikes me is how closely these needs reflect those identified by many of the women who have featured in this book. I have tried to avoid making my own judgements about what really made women 'happy'; a pursuit which has previously seemed destined to uncover narratives of victimization and oppression. My endeavour instead has been to try and understand the needs, beliefs and values of mothers and wives who lived in another era, under greatly different circumstances to my own. Although these beliefs and values are undoubtedly culturally and historically specific; as a historian, a woman and a mother, I have learned much from women of the 1950s.

APPENDIX

Biographical Details of Respondents*

Name	Year of Birth	Marriage	Children
Betty Sanderson	1929	1955	1956, 1957, 1962
Margaret Lincoln	1930	1951	*Adopted 2 children in 1964
Chris Richards	1927	1949	*Two children during the 1950s
Jean Hill	1933	1955	1958, 1961 and two stillborn 1957 and 1959
Anne Shepherd	1938	1960	No children
Rose Courtenay	1938	1957	1958 and 1962
Nora Kelly	1936	1961	1963 and 1976
Christine Calderwood	1937	1960	*Two children during the 1960s
Barbara Vicary	1931 in the US	1953	1956 and 1959
Val Parker	1935	1955	1958 and 1962
Judith Morgan	1943	1971	*Two children during the 1970s
Ann Coles	1944	1962	1963, 1964, 1965, 1966, 1969
Christine Stead	1937	1958	1959, 1961, 1963, 1964, 1968
Eileen Roberts	1929	1949	1952, 1955, 1958, 1959, 1961
Gwen Collins	1919	1940	1942, 1946, 1948
Margaret Windsor	1933	1953	1956, 1959
Doris Carter	1915	1945	1951
Diane Braithwaite	1937 in the US	1962	1965 1967
Frances Wilson	1938	1960	1965, 1968
Kath Greenham	1927	1946	1950, 1953, 1957
Faith Lawson	1945	1967	No children
Jane Davy	1950	1969	1976, 1981
Edna Goodridge	1925	1950	1954, 1956
Barbara Rogers	1940	1962	*Four children during the 1960s
Rebecca Heane	1923	1942	*Four children between 1944 and 1951
Mary Hayes	*	1960	*Two children during the 1960s
Eileen Bailey	1922	1943	*Three children between 1945 and 1955
Joan Talbot	1937	1957	1958, 1960
Eve Raddon	1934	1958	1960, 1964, 1967

* In certain cases, information has been withheld to protect respondents' anonymity. Pseudonyms have been used in all cases. A number of respondents sent written testimonies prior to/in addition to interview. A further six women wrote with memories of domesticity during the 1950s and 1960s.

– 181 –

NOTES

Introduction

1. J. Giles, *The Parlour and the Suburb: Domestic Identities, Class, Femininity and Modernity* (Oxford: Berg, 2004), p. 162. See also: L. Johnson and J. Lloyd, *Sentenced to Everyday Life: Feminism and the Housewife* (Oxford: Berg, 2004); and J. Meyerowitz, 'Beyond the Feminine Mystique: A Reassessment of Post-War Mass Culture', in J. Meyerowitz (ed.), *Not June Cleaver: Women and Gender in Post-War America, 1945–1960* (Philadelphia, PA: Temple University Press, 1994).

2. S. Coontz, *A Strange Stirring: The Feminine Mystique and American Women at the Dawn of the 1960s* (New York: Basic Books, 2011).

3. J. Busfield, *Men, Women and Madness: Understanding Gender and Mental Disorder* (Basingstoke: Palgrave Macmillan, 1996), p. 14.

4. See B. Jerman, *The Lively Minded Women: The First Twenty Years of the National Housewives' Register* (London: Heinemann, 1981).

5. Pseudonyms have been used throughout and in certain cases, information (such as date of birth) has been withheld to further protect respondents' identity.

6. J. Bornat and H. Diamond, 'Women's History and Oral History: Developments and Debates', *Women's History Review*, 16 (2007), pp. 19–39, on p. 19.

7. K. Fisher, 'Oral History and the History of Medicine', in M. Jackson (ed.), *The Oxford Handbook of the History of Medicine* (Oxford: Oxford University Press, 2011), pp. 598–616, on p. 601.

8. P. Summerfield, 'Intersubjectivities in Oral History', in T. Cosslett, C. Lury and P. Summerfield (eds), *Feminism and Autobiography: Text, Theories, Methods* (London: Routledge, 2000), pp. 91–106.

9. P. Summerfield, *Reconstructing Women's Wartime Lives: Discourse and Subjectivity in Oral Histories of the Second World War* (Manchester: Manchester University Press, 1998), p. 11.

10. A. Green, 'Individual Remembering and "Collective Memory"', *Oral History*, 32 (2004), pp. 35–44, on p. 42.

11. Ibid., p.39.

12. Ibid.

13. Ibid., p. 35.

14. D. Sheridan, *Wartime Women: A Mass Observation Anthology, the Experiences of Women at War* (London: Mandarin, 1991), p. 4.

15. Ibid.

184 *Notes to pages 5–9*

16. P. Summerfield, 'Mass Observation: Social Research or Social Movement?', *Journal of Contemporary History*, 20 (1985), pp. 439–52, on p. 440.
17. Sheridan, *Wartime Women*, p. 5.
18. Summerfield, 'Mass Observation', p. 441.
19. M. Pugh, *State and Society: A Social and Political History of Britain 1870–1997* (London: Arnold, 1999), p. 279.
20. Ibid.
21. M. Pugh, *Women and the Women's Movement in Britain 1914–1999*, 2nd edn (Basingstoke: Macmillan, 2000), p. 291.
22. Ibid., p. 290.
23. M. Francis, 'Leisure and Popular Culture', in I. Zweiniger-Bargielowska (ed.), *Women in Twentieth-Century Britain* (Harlow: Pearson, 2001), pp. 229–43 on p. 234.
24. Ibid., p. 235.
25. M. Abrams, 'The Home-Centred Society', *Listener*, 26 November 1959, pp. 914–15.
26. Ibid., p. 915.
27. Ibid.
28. Ibid.
29. C. White, *The Women's Periodical Press in Britain 1946–1976: The Royal Commission on the Press* (London: HMSO, 1977), p. 1.
30. Pugh, *Women and the Women's Movement in Britain*, p. 291.
31. Ibid., p. 292.
32. Women from the upper/professional/middle and clerical classes tended to read *Woman* and *Woman's Own*, while those from working-class skilled and unskilled groups preferred *Woman's Realm* and *Woman's Weekly*. See T. Millum, *Images of Woman: Advertising in Women's Magazines* (London: Chatto Windus, 1975), p. 105; and C. White, *Women's Magazines 1693–1968* (London: Michael Joseph, 1970), p. 217.
33. White, *Women's Magazines 1693–1968*, pp. 96–97.
34. Ibid., p. 126.
35. Ibid., p. 98.
36. Ibid., p. 279.
37. J. Winship, *Inside Women's Magazines* (London: Pandora, 1987), p. 18.
38. White, *Women's Magazines*, p. 140.
39. K. Ott, *Fevered Lives: Tuberculosis in American Culture since 1870* (Cambridge, MA: Harvard University Press, 1996), p. 4.
40. C. M. Callahan and G. E. Berrios, *Reinventing Depression: A History of the Treatment of Depression in Primary Care, 1940–2004* (Oxford: Oxford University Press 2005), p. 94.
41. See M. Thomson, *Psychological Subjects: Identity, Culture and Health in Twentieth Century Britain* (Oxford: Oxford University Press 2006).
42. E. Millar, 'Twentieth Century British Clinical Psychology and Psychiatry', in H. Freeman and G. E. Berrios (eds), *150 Years of British Psychiatry, Vol. II: The Aftermath* (London: Athlone, 1996), pp. 156–68, on p. 161.
43. Ibid., p. 163.
44. M. Micale, *Hysterical Men: The Hidden History of Male Nervous Illness* (Cambridge, MA: Harvard University Press, 2008), p. xiv.
45. Ibid.
46. See in particular: P. Chesler, *Women and Madness* (New York: Avon Books, 1972).

Notes to pages 11–14

1 Reflections on the Desperate Housewife

1. B. Friedan, *The Feminine Mystique* (London: Penguin, [1963] 1992), p. 16.
2. C. P. Gilman, *The Yellow Wallpaper* (New York: The Feminist Press, [1892] 1996), p. 14.
3. M. T. Orne, 'Foreword', in D. W. Middlebrook, *Anne Sexton: A Biography* (Boston, MA: Houghton Mifflin Co., 1991), p. xiii.
4. Giles, *The Parlour and the Suburb*, p. 162.
5. See for example D. Horowitz, *Betty Friedan and the Making of the Feminine Mystique: The American Left, the Cold War and Modern Feminism* (Amherst, MA: University of Massachusetts Press, 2000).
6. Giles, *The Parlour and the Suburb*, p. 148.
7. Friedan, *The Feminine Mystique*, p. 88.
8. Ibid.
9. Ibid., p. 89.
10. C. Beaumont, 'The Women's Movement, Politics and Citizenship, 1918–1950s', in Zweiniger-Bargielowska (ed.), *Women in Twentieth Century Britain*, pp. 262–77, on p. 266.
11. Ibid., p. 267.
12. For a full account of these organizations and their aims see: Pugh, *Women and the Women's Movement in Britain*.
13. J. Giles, *Women, Identity and Private Life in Britain, 1900–50* (Basingstoke: Macmillan, 1995), p. 7.
14. S. Thornton, 'Second-Wave Feminism', in S. Gamble (ed.), *The Routledge Companion to Feminism and Postfeminism*, 2nd edn (London: Routledge, 2004), pp. 29–42, on p. 30.
15. Ibid. A full account of the development of second-wave feminism in the United States and Britain can be found in ibid.
16. A claim now contested in: Horowitz, *Betty Friedan and the Making of the Feminine Mystique.*
17. Friedan, *The Feminine Mystique*, p. 214.
18. M. Clapson, *Suburban Century: Social Change and Urban Growth in England and the USA* (Oxford: Berg, 2003), p. 1.
19. Ibid., p. 52. Clapson discusses national and regional variations between the United States and Britain.
20. Friedan, *The Feminine Mystique*, pp. 219–20.
21. Ibid., p. 18.
22. G. Greer, *The Female Eunuch* (London: Flamingo, 1999 [1970]), p. 307.
23. J. Sutherland, *Reading the Decades: Fifty Years of the Nation's Bestselling Books* (London: BBC, 2002), pp. 61, 110.
24. Coontz, *A Strange Stirring*, p. xv.
25. M. Jackson, '"Home Sweet Home": Historical Perspectives on Health and the Home', in M. Jackson (ed.), *Health and the Modern Home* (New York: Routledge, 2007), pp. 1–17, on p. 3.
26. See R. Hayward, 'Desperate Housewives and Model Amoebae: The Invention of Suburban Neurosis in Inter-War Britain', in Jackson (ed.), *Health, and the Modern Home*, pp. 42–62.
27. S. Taylor, 'The Suburban Neurosis', *Lancet*, 26 March 1938, pp. 759–61.
28. Ibid., p. 761.
29. Ibid.

186   *Notes to pages 14–20*

30. P. Bartrip, *Mirror of Medicine: A History of the British Medical Journal* (Oxford: BMJ and Clarendon Press, 1990), p. 11.
31. See Hayward, 'Desperate Housewives'.
32. Ibid.
33. Ibid.
34. E. H. Hare and G. K. Shaw, *Mental Health on a New Housing Estate: A Comparative Study of Health in Two Districts of Croydon* (London: Oxford University Press, 1965).
35. Ibid., pp. 60, 62.
36. Friedan, *The Feminine Mystique*, pp. 32, 33.
37. Ibid., p. 320.
38. See H. Gavron, *The Captive Wife* (London: Routledge and Kegan Paul, 1966). For a study on working class neighbourhoods, see M. Young and P. Willmott, *Family and Kinship in East London* (Harmondsworth: Penguin, 1990 [1957]).
39. J. Hubback, *Wives Who Went to College* (London: William Heinemann, 1957), p. 83.
40. Ibid., p. 5.
41. Ibid., p. 142.
42. Ibid., p. 138.
43. V. Klein, *Britain's Married Women Workers* (London: Routledge and Kegan Paul, 1965), pp. 26, 77.
44. Ibid., p. 50.
45. A. Oakley, *Woman's Work: The Housewife Past and Present* (New York: Pantheon, 1974), p. 61. See also: A. Oakley, *Sex, Gender and Society* (Aldershot: Gower, 1989 [1972]); A. Oakley, *The Sociology of Housework* (London: Martin Robertson, 1974); A. Oakley, *From Here to Eternity: Becoming a Mother* (Oxford: Martin Robertson, 1979); and A. Oakley, *Gender on Planet Earth* (Cambridge: Polity, 2003).
46. Giles, *The Parlour and the Suburb*, p. 159.
47. Ibid., p. 155.
48. Johnson and Lloyd, *Sentenced to Everyday Life*, p. 11.
49. The Rolling Stones, 'Mother's Little Helper', 1966.
50. S. Faludi, 'Afterword', in M. French, *The Women's Room* (London: Virago, 1997 [1977]) p. 518.
51. *Times*, 10 May 1980.
52. Ibid.
53. French, *The Women's Room*, p. 26.
54. K. A. Loudermilk, *Fictional Feminism: How American Bestsellers Affect the Movement for Women's Equality* (New York: Routledge, 2004), p. 45.
55. French, *The Women's Room*, p. 67.
56. Ibid., p. 372.
57. Ibid., p. 376.
58. P. Mortimer, *The Pumpkin Eater* (London: Bloomsbury, 1995 [1962]), p. 30.
59. *The Pumpkin Eater* (1964), Columbia Pictures.
60. Ibid.
61. M. Tyrrell, 'The Politics of George Orwell (1903–1950): From Tory Anarchism to National Socialism and More Than Half Way Back', *Cultural Notes*, 36 (London: Libertarian Alliance, 1997), p. 2.
62. Ibid.
63. G. Orwell, *Coming up for Air* (1939), in *The Complete Novels* (London: Penguin, 2000), p. 435.

Notes to pages 20–6 187

64. Ibid., pp. 442–3.
65. W. H. Whyte, *The Organization Man* (New York: Doubleday Anchor, n.d. [1956]), p. 4.
66. H. Marcuse, *One-Dimensional Man* (Abingdon: Routledge Classics, 2002 [1964]), p. 11.
67. D. Riesman, N. Glazer and R. Denney, *The Lonely Crowd: A Study of the Changing American Character* (New Haven, CT: Yale University Press, 2001 [1950]), p. 6.
68. Clapson, *Suburban Century*, p. 15.
69. Ibid.
70. S. Wilson, *The Man in the Gray Flannel Suit* (London: Penguin Classics, 2005 [1955]), p. 3. Original author's italics.
71. *The Stepford Wives*, Palomar Pictures, 1974.
72. Ibid.
73. Middlebrook, *Anne Sexton*; and L. Wagner-Martin, *Sylvia Plath: A Literary Life* (Basingstoke: Palgrave MacMillan, 2003).
74. Middlebrook, *Anne Sexton*, p. xx. See also, J. Gill, *Anne Sexton's Confessional Poetics* (Gainesville, FL: University Press of Florida, 2007).
75. E. Showalter, *The Female Malady: Women, Madness and English Culture 1830–1980* (London: Virago, 2001 [1987]), p. 216.
76. Ibid., p. 213.
77. Middlebrook, *Anne Sexton*, p. 14.
78. Ibid.
79. Ibid., pp. 4, 10.
80. Ibid., p. 16.
81. Ibid., p. 59.
82. Ibid., p. 73.
83. Ibid., p. 40.
84. Ibid.
85. Ibid., p. 107.
86. Wagner-Martin, *Sylvia Plath*, p. 6.
87. Ibid., p. 15.
88. Ibid., p. 24.
89. Ibid., p. 33.
90. P. Mortimer, *About Time* (Harmondsworth: Penguin, reprint 1981), p. 74.
91. Ibid., p. 170.
92. P. Mortimer, *About Time Too*, paperback edn (London: Phoenix, 1994), p. 182.
93. Ibid., p. 74.
94. Her seventh pregnancy had ended in miscarriage.
95. Mortimer, *About Time Too*, p. 80.
96. Ibid.
97. Ibid., p. 204.
98. Ibid., p. 181.
99. Ibid., p. 209.
100. D. Callard, *The Case of Anna Kavan: A Biography* (London: Peter Owen, 1992), p. 18.
101. Ibid.
102. Ibid., p. 38.
103. Ibid., p. 77.
104. J. Reed, *A Stranger on Earth: the Life and Work of Anna Kavan* (London: Peter Owen, 2006), p. 180.

188   *Notes to pages 26–31*

105. Callard, *The Case of Anna Kavan*, p. 155.
106. Ibid., p. 20.
107. V. Glendinning, *Elizabeth Bowen* (New York: Avon, 1977), p. 23.
108. M. Ludwig, *The Price of Greatness* (New York: The Guilford Press, 1995).
109. Ibid., p. 130.
110. Reed, *A Stranger on Earth*, p. 190.
111. Middlebrook, *Anne Sexton*, p. 72.
112. Ibid., p. 173.
113. G. Ward, 'The Wibberlee Wobberlee Walk: Lowry, Hamilton, Kavan and the Addictions of 1940s Fiction', in R. Mengham and N. H. Reeve (eds), *The Fiction of the 1940s: Stories of Survival* (Basingstoke: Palgrave, 2001), pp. 26–45, on p. 26.
114. See Horowitz, *Betty Friedan and the Making of the Feminine Mystique*.
115. Ann Oakley, a guest speaker on 'Thinking Allowed', BBC Radio Four, 22 June 2005.
116. www.AnnOakley.co.uk/AOFAQs.htm.

2 The Art of Marriage

1. S. Coontz, *Marriage, a History: From Obedience to Intimacy, or How Love Conquered Marriage* (New York: Viking, 2005), p. 229.
2. M. Pugh, *State and Society*, p. 302.
3. Statistics taken from L. Stone, *Road to Divorce* (Oxford: Oxford University Press, 1990), p. 402.
4. R. Phillips, *Putting Asunder* (Cambridge: Cambridge University Press, 1988), p. 560.
5. See for example: E. Shorter, *The Making of the Modern Family* (New York: Basic Books, 1975); and L. Stone, *The Family, Sex and Marriage in England 1500–1800* (London: Weidenfield and Nicolson, 1977). For a critique, see J. R Gillis, *For Better for Worse: British Marriages 1600 to the Present* (Oxford: Oxford University Press, 1985).
6. J. R Gillis, *A World of Their Own Making: Myth, Ritual and the Quest for Family Values* (New York: Basic Books, 1996), p. 21.
7. Ibid., pp. 3, 4.
8. A. McLaren, *Twentieth Century Sexuality* (Oxford: Blackwell, 1999), p. 143.
9. See also: S. Coontz, *The Way We Never Were* (New York: Basic Books, 1992); and J. Weeks, *Sex, Politics and Society: The Regulation of Sexuality since 1800* (Harlow: Longman, 1989).
10. J. Lewis, *Women in Britain since 1945* (Oxford: Blackwell, 1992), p. 14.
11. Oakley, *Sex, Gender and Society*, p. 136.
12. Ibid., pp. 156, 7.
13. Gillis, *A World of Their Own Making*, p. 134.
14. Phillips, *Putting Asunder*, p. 355.
15. Ibid., pp. 335–7.
16. P. Summerfield, 'Women in Britain since 1945: The Companionate Marriage and the Double Burden', in J. Obelkevich and P. Catterall (eds), *Understanding Post-War British Society* (London: Routledge, 1994), pp. 58–72, on p. 159.
17. W. Beveridge, *Social Insurance and Allied Services* (London: HMSO, 1942), paras 107, 108, 110.
18. Pugh, *State and Society*, p. 261.
19. Ibid., p. 273.

20. M. Thomson, 'Before Anti-Psychiatry: "Mental Health" in Wartime Britain', in: M. Gijswijt-Hofstra and R. Porter (eds), *Cultures of Psychiatry* (Amsterdam: Editions Rodopi B.V, 1998), pp. 43–59, on p. 46.
21. Ibid, p. 47.
22. Weeks, *Sex, Politics and Society*, p. 235.
23. J. Lewis, *The End of Marriage? Individualism and Intimate Relations* (Cheltenham: Edward Elgar, 2001), p. 45.
24. Lewis, *Women in Britain since 1945*, pp. 30, 37.
25. E. Wilson, *Only Half-Way to Paradise* (London: Tavistock, 1980), p. 61.
26. Mass Observation Archive, File Report 1616, 'Some Psychological Factors in Home-Building: What Does Home Mean to You?', March 1943.
27. P. Clark, *Hope and Glory: Britain 1900–1990* (London: Penguin, 1997), p. 240.
28. Mass Observation, 'Some Psychological Factors in Home-Building'.
29. Ibid.
30. Wilson, *Only Half Way to Paradise*, p. 61.
31. Ibid., p. 71.
32. See J. Lewis, D. Clark and D. Morgan, *Whom God Hath Joined Together: The Work of Marriage Guidance* (London: Routledge, 1992).
33. Ibid., p. 46.
34. O. R. McGregor, *Divorce in England: A Centenary Study* (London: William Heinemann, 1957), p. 100.
35. A. Brayshaw, *The Stability of Marriage* (London: NMGC, 1952), pp. 6, 7.
36. Lewis et al., *Whom God hath Joined Together*, p. 39.
37. Ibid., p. 50.
38. Ibid., p. 51.
39. Ibid., p. 45.
40. Weeks, *Sex, Politics and Society*, p. 237.
41. H. Lyon, *Happy Ever After?* (London: NMGC, 1950), p. 11.
42. Ibid.
43. Ibid., p. 12.
44. Brayshaw, *The Stability of Marriage*, p. 5.
45. Lord Denning, *The Equality of Women; The Eleanor Rathbone Memorial Lecture* (Liverpool: Liverpool University Press, 1960), p. 1.
46. Ibid., pp. 12–15.
47. See for example: T. Bovet, 'Human Attitudes Towards Suffering', *Humanities*, 9 (1973), pp. 5–20.
48. T. Bovet, *A Handbook to Marriage and Marriage Guidance* (London: Longmans Green, 1958), pp. 18, 26.
49. K. Walker, *Marriage, Sex and Happiness: A Frank and Practical Guide to Harmony and Satisfaction in Conjugal Life* (London: Oldhams Books, 1963), p. 26.
50. Ibid., pp. 27, 28.
51. K. Kirk, *Marriage and Divorce* (London: Hodder and Stoughton, 1948), p. 17.
52. Ibid., p. 16.
53. Mass Observation Archive, File Report 2495, 'State of Matrimony', June 1947.
54. Ibid.
55. H. Gray, Foreword to M. Macaulay, *The Art of Marriage* (London: Delisle, [1952], 1956).
56. Macaulay, *The Art of Marriage*, p. 25.

190   *Notes to pages 36–40*

57. Wilson, *Only Half Way to Paradise*, p. 93.
58. Macaulay, *The Art of Marriage*, pp. 68, 69.
59. NMGC, *Sex Difficulties in the Wife* (London: 1958), pp. 2–4.
60. Ibid.
61. Gillis, *A World of Their Own Making*, p. 153.
62. Ibid.
63. Ibid., p. 175.
64. Oakley, *Sex, Gender and Society*, p. 134.
65. A. Dally, *Inventing Motherhood* (London: Burnett Books, 1982), pp. 92, 95.
66. Ibid., p. 97.
67. Ibid., p. 96.
68. R. Easterlin, *Birth and Fortune: the Impact of Numbers on Personal Welfare* (London: Grant Mcintyre, 1980), cited in Phillips, *Putting Asunder*, p. 618.
69. Gillis, *A World of Their Own Making*, p. 181.
70. S. Hays, *The Cultural Contradictions of Motherhood* (New Haven, CT: Yale University Press, 1996), p. 25.
71. Ibid., p. 187.
72. H. Jones, *Health and Society in Twentieth Century Britain* (London: Longman, 1994), p. 17.
73. R. Porter, *The Greatest Benefit to Mankind: A Medical History of Humanity From Antiquity to the Present* (London: Fontana, 1999), p. 640.
74. Ibid., p. 176.
75. Gillis, *A World of Their Own Making*, p. p. 191, 192.
76. B. Ehrenreich and D. English, *For Her Own Good: 150 Years of the Experts Advice to Women* (London: Pluto, 1979), p. 190.
77. See for example: Dally, *Inventing Motherhood*; Ehrenreich and English, *For Her Own Good*; Hays, *The Cultural Contradictions of Motherhood*; and C. Hardyment, *Child Care from Locke to Spock* (London: Johnathan Cape, 1983).
78. Ehrenreich and English, *For Her Own Good*, pp. 206, 207.
79. J. Bowlby, *Maternal Care and Mental Health* (Geneva: World Health Organization, 1952 [1951]), p. 13.
80. Ehrenreich and English, *For Her Own Good*, p. 207.
81. See M. Vicedo, 'The Social Nature of Mother's Tie to Her Child: John Bowlby's Theory of Attachment in Post-War America', *British Journal for the History of Science*, 44 (2011), pp. 401–26.
82. A. Holdsworth, *Out of the Doll's House: The Story of Women in the Twentieth Century* (London: BBC, 1988), p. 125.
83. This charge is laid both explicitly and implicitly in feminist literature. See for example: Dally, *Inventing Motherhood*, p. 97; Lewis, *Women in Britain since 1945*, pp. 18, 19; and J. Muncie and M. Wetherell, 'Family Policy and Political Discourse', in J. Muncie, M. Wetherell, R. Dallos and A. Cochrane (eds), *Understanding the Family* (London: Sage, 1995), pp. 40–78, in particular, p. 47.
84. D. Riley, *War in the Nursery: Theories of the Child and the Mother* (London: Virago, 1983).
85. J. Bowlby, *Child Care and the Growth of Love* (Middlesex: Pelican, 1963 [1953]), p. 47.
86. J. Bowlby, *Attachment and Loss; Volume 1, Attachment* (London: Hogarth, 1969), p. xii.
87. See for example, Bowlby, *Maternal Care and Mental Health*, pp. 85, 87.
88. Ibid., p. 88.

89. Ibid., p. 13.
90. See the website: www.eventoddlersneedfathers.com.
91. M. Rutter, 'Maternal deprivation, 1972–1978, New Findings, New Concepts, New Approaches', *Child Development*, 50 (1979), pp. 283–385.
92. See also: M. Rutter, *Maternal Deprivation Reassessed* (Baltimore: Penguin, 1972).
93. Bowlby, *Attachment Theory; Volume 1*, pp. 304, 306.
94. J. Holmes, *John Bowlby and Attachment Theory* (London: Routledge, 1993), p. 47.
95. Bowlby, *Attachment Theory; Volume 1*, p. 179.
96. J. Bowlby, *Attachment and Loss; Volume 2, Separation, Anxiety and Anger* (London: Hogarth, 1973), p. 26.
97. Lewis, *Women in Britain since 1945*, p. 77.
98. D. W. Winnicott, *The Family and Individual Development* (London: Tavistock Publications, 1965), p. 21.
99. Ibid., p. 40.
100. D. W. Winnicott, *The Child and the Family: First Relationships* (London: Tavistock Publications, 1957), pp. 5, 82.
101. Ibid., p. 141.
102. Ibid., p. 142.
103. Ehrenreich and English, *For Her Own Good*, p. 192.
104. Ibid., p. 193.
105. B. Spock and M. Morgan, *Spock on Spock: A Memoir of Growing up with the Century* (New York: Pantheon, 1989), p. 101.
106. Ibid.
107. Hays, *The Cultural Contradictions of Motherhood*, p. 49.
108. B. Spock, *Baby and Child Care*, 3rd edn (London: Bodley Head, [1955], third edition, 1973), p. 17.
109. Ibid., p. 575.
110. Ibid., pp. 575, 576.
111. Hays, *The Cultural Contradictions of Motherhood*, p. 205.
112. Ibid., p. 49.
113. Spock, *Baby and Child Care*, p. 113.
114. Ibid.
115. Pugh, *State and Society*, p. 312.
116. Ehrenreich and English, *For Her Own Good*, p. 227.
117. Cited in Ibid.
118. Spock and Morgan, *Spock on Spock*, p. 156.
119. Ibid., p. 167.
120. See: Ibid., p. 168; and T. Meier, *Dr Spock, An American Life* (London and New York: Harcourt Brace, 1998), p. 224.
121. D. Hooper and J. Roberts, *Education Today: Disordered Lives, an Interpersonal Account* (London: Longmans, 1967), p. 9.
122. Obituary, *Guardian*, 16 November 2010.
123. Hooper and Roberts, *Education Today*, pp. 32, 36.
124. Bovet, *A Handbook to Marriage*, p. 4.
125. Ibid., pp. 19–20.
126. Ibid.
127. Lyon, *Happy Ever After?* p. 17.
128. A. Reed, *The First Five Years of Marriage* (London: NMGC, 1963), p. 19.

192   *Notes to pages 46–51*

129. Ibid., pp. 39–41.
130. Ibid., pp. 44, 47.
131. Ibid., p. 43.
132. Macaulay, *The Art of Marriage*, pp. 71, 86.
133. Gillis, *A World of Their Own Making*, p. 177.
134. Ibid., p. 240.
135. Dally, *Inventing Motherhood*, p. 18.
136. Hooper and Roberts, *Education Today*, pp. 37–9.
137. Father J. A. O'Brien, *Happy Marriage: Guidance Before and After* (London: WH Allen, 1956), p. 200.

3 The Housewife's Day

1. See for example, P. Summerfield, 'Approaches to Women and Social Change in the Second World War', in B. Brivati and H. Jones (eds), *What Difference Did the War Make?* (London: Leicester University Press, 1995 edition), pp. 64–79; G. Braybon and P. Summerfield, *Out of the Cage: Women's Experience in Two World Wars* (London: Pandora, 1987); D. Riley, '"The Free Mothers": Pronatalism and Working Women in Industry at the End of the Last War in Britain', *History Workshop Journal*, 11 (1981), pp. 59–118; A. Marwick, *War and Social Change in the Twentieth Century* (London: Macmillan, 1974); and Klein, *Britain's Married Women Workers*.
2. P. Summerfield, 'Women and War in the Twentieth Century', in J. Purvis (ed.), *Women's History: Britain 1950–1945*, (London: UCL Press, 1995), pp. 307–32.
3. See Summerfield, 'Approaches to Women and Social Change in the Second World War', p. 64. Juliet Mitchell and Betty Friedan argued that while women's lives were profoundly changed for the better during the Second World War, the reverse occurred post-war. Summerfield and Riley differ in the sense they both argue that changes for women were piecemeal and temporary – thus wartime was not directly responsible for positive change.
4. H. L. Smith, *War and Social Change: British Society in the Second World War* (Manchester: Manchester University Press, 1986), p. 210.
5. Ibid.
6. Summerfield, *Reconstructing Women's Wartime Lives*, p. 7.
7. Summerfield, 'Approaches to Women and Social Change in the Second World War', p. 72.
8. Ibid.
9. Riley, 'The Free Mothers', p. 81.
10. Oakley, *Gender on Planet Earth*, p. 11.
11. Coontz, *A Strange Stirring*, p. 30.
12. A. Scales, *Legal Feminism: Activism, Lawyering and Legal Theory* (New York and London: New York University Press, 2006), p. 130.
13. Giles, *The Parlour and the Suburb*, p. 144.
14. Young and Willmott, *Family and Kinship in East London*, p. 126.
15. R. S. Lynd and H. M. Lynd, *Middletown: A Study in American Culture* (New York: Harcourt Brace, 1956 [1929]), pp. 116, 118. See also R. S. Lynd and H. M. Lynd, *Middletown in Transition* (New York: Harcourt Brace, 1937) and T. Caplow, H. M. Bahr, B. A. Chadwick, R. Hill and M. Holmes-Williamson, *Middletown Families: Fifty Years of Change and Continuity* (Minneapolis, MN: University of Minnesota Press, 1982).

16. E. Roberts, *A Woman's Place: an Oral History of Working-Class Women 1890–1940* (Oxford: Blackwell, 1984) and E. Roberts, *Women and Families: An Oral History, 1940–1970: Family, Sexuality and Social Relations in Past Times* (Oxford: Blackwell, 1995).
17. See <http://www.history.ac.uk/reviews/review/50/response>.
18. P. Willmott and M. Young, *Family and Class in a London Suburb* (London: New English Library, 1976 [1960]), p. 31.
19. M. Sanderson, 'Education and Social Mobility', in P. Johnson (ed.), *Twentieth Century Britain: Economic, Social and Cultural Change* (Harlow: Addison Wesley Longman, 1998 edition), pp. 374–91, on p. 375.
20. Ibid.
21. Ibid.
22. Jean Hill. Interviewed on 25 September 2004.
23. Kath Greenham. Interviewed on 11 April 2005.
24. Young and Willmott, *Family and Kinship in East London*, pp. 176, 177.
25. Jean Hill.
26. Christine Calderwood. Interviewed on 5 October 2004.
27. Gwen Collins. Interviewed 18 January 2005.
28. Ann Shepherd was born in Clevedon in 1938. Interviewed on 24 September 2004.
29. Gwen Collins.
30. Eileen Roberts. Interviewed on 17 January 2005. Eileen is referring to the bombing of Sandhurst Road School, Lewisham on 20 January 1943. The official number of mortalities totalled thirty-eight pupils and six teachers.
31. Giles, *The Parlour and the Suburb*, p. 161.
32. Barbara Vicary. Interviewed 14 October 2004.
33. Diane Braithwaite was born in 1937. Interviewed on 4 January 2005.
34. Barbara Vicary.
35. Diane Braithwaite.
36. Written testimony of Barbara Rogers.
37. Faith Lawson was born in 1945 and became a teacher. She married in 1967 but chose not to have children. Interviewed on 5 January 2005.
38. Ibid.
39. Jane Davy married in 1969 and had two children. Interviewed on 18 January 2005.
40. Judith Morgan was married in 1971 and had two children. Interviewed on 2 November 2004.
41. I. Zweiniger-Bargielowska, 'Housewifery', in Zweiniger-Bargielowska (ed.), *Women in Twentieth Century Britain*, pp. 149–64, on p. 151.
42. Cited in Gavron, *The Captive Wife*, p. 61.
43. Survey report 5/NHR/1/16, 1966, National Housewives' Register archives, The Women's Library, pp. 4–5.
44. Chris Richards. Interviewed on 6 September 2004.
45. Betty Sanderson was married in 1955 and had three children. Interviewed on 3 September 2004.
46. Frances Wilson was married in 1960 and had two children. Interviewed on 11 April 2005.
47. Written testimony of Barbara Rogers.
48. Mass Observation Archive, File Report 2059, 'Do the Factory Girls Want to Stay Put or Go Home?', March 1944.
49. Ibid.

194   *Notes to pages 58–65*

50. Ibid.
51. Testimony of Edie Rutherford in S. Garfield, *Our Hidden Lives: The Everyday Diaries of Forgotten Britain, 1945–1948* (London: Ebury, 2004), p. 355.
52. Jean Bills.
53. Mass Observation Archive, File Report 3150, 'Teenage Girls', August 1949.
54. Ibid.
55. Beveridge, *Social Insurance and Allied Services*, para. 110.
56. Christine Calderwood.
57. Val Parker married in 1955 and had two children. Interviewed on 2 November 2004.
58. Letters, *Woman's Realm*, 6 April 1968, p. 9.
59. Letters, *Woman's Own*, 7 May 1960, p. 7.
60. Letters, *Woman's Own*, 13 August 1960, p. 7.
61. Cited in Oakley, *Gender on Planet Earth*, p. 91.
62. Edna Goodridge. Interviewed on 4 January 2005.
63. Doris Carter. Interviewed with her daughter Jane (born in 1951) and two friends on 18 January 2005.
64. Jean Hill.
65. Written testimony of Val Parker.
66. Ann Oakley, cited in Millum, *Images of Woman*, p. 180.
67. Eileen Roberts.
68. Gwen Collins.
69. Holdsworth, *Out of the Doll's House*, p. 29.
70. Katherine Stead. Interviewed on 30 November 2004.
71. Ann Coles. Interviewed on 16 November 2004.
72. Kath Greenham.
73. Christine Calderwood.
74. Jean Hill.
75. Margaret Windsor was married in 1953 and had two children. Interviewed on 18 January 2005.
76. Mass Observation Archive, Bulletin No. 18, 'Domestic Male', June 1948.
77. Ibid.
78. Willmott and Young, *Family and Class*, p. 33.
79. D. Beyfus, *The English Marriage* (Harmondsworth: Penguin, 1971 [1968]), p. 13.
80. Val Parker.
81. Eve Raddon was born in 1944. She worked in the family business until her children were born and later trained as a teacher. Interviewed on 10 May 2005.
82. See Klein, *Britain's Married Women Workers*, p. 37.
83. Gavron, *The Captive Wife*, p. 111.
84. Denis Harley, *Woman's Own*, 16 July 1960, pp. 27–8.
85. Christine Calderwood. Alone, Christine's testimony could be seen as untypical, since she is talking about ex-pat community life. However, her experience is echoed in the accounts of the other women.
86. In later years Eileen Roberts went on to become a teacher, and the Pre-School Playgroup Association was the topic of her dissertation at university.
87. J. Faux, 'A Learning Experience for Us All', in H. Curtis and M. Sanderson (eds), *The Unsung Sixties: Memoirs of Social Innovation* (London: Whiting and Birch, 2004), pp. 381–93, on p. 385.

Notes to pages 65–72 195

88. Upon moving to a new area, Katherine later founded her own group of the National Housewives' Register.
89. Letters, 5NHR/5/3, National Housewives' Register archives, The Women's Library.
90. The Townswomen's Guild was formed when universal franchise was granted in 1928. Eva Hubback, Margery Corbett Ashby and others saw the need for an organization for women living in towns and cities which would help them manage their new found freedom. The Inner Wheel was formed in 1923 by the womenfolk of Rotarians who, for many years, had assisted Rotary with their varied humanitarian and charitable projects.
91. Mass Observation Archive, Bulletin New Series 38, 'Friends and Families', October 1950.
92. Eileen Bailey. Interviewed on 30 November 2004.
93. Gwen Collins.
94. Frances Wilson.
95. Margaret Windsor.
96. Gwen Collins.
97. Written testimony of Val Parker.
98. Katherine Stead.
99. Eileen Roberts.
100. Barbara Vicary.
101. Diane Braithwaite.
102. Ibid.
103. With the exception of Faith Lawson who chose not to have children, and Ann Shepherd who was unable to.
104. Betty Sanderson.
105. J. Bourke, *Fear: A Cultural History* (London; Virago, 2005), p. 258.
106. Joan Talbot. Interviewed on 17 January 2005.
107. Chris Richards.
108. Margaret Lincoln.
109. Ibid. Margaret continued to work for financial reasons following the adoption. However, she was always home for the children after school and stressed the importance of being at home to care for them when they were ill.
110. Ibid.
111. Gwen Collins.
112. Eileen Bailey.
113. Rose Courtenay was married in 1957 and had two children. Interviewed with Jean Bills and Ann Shepherd on 24 September 2004.
114. Frances Wilson.
115. Ibid.
116. Katherine Stead.
117. Mass Observation Archive, Bulletin New Series 44, 'Babies and Children', March 1952.
118. Christine Calderwood.
119. Katherine Stead.
120. Diane Braithwaite.
121. Mrs M. B. Laceby, Letters, *Woman's Realm*, 3 September 1966, p. 7.
122. Eve Raddon.
123. Betty Sanderson.
124. Barbara Rogers.
125. Gwen Collins.
126. Katherine Stead.

196   *Notes to pages 72–7*

127. Christine Calderwood.
128. Frances Wilson.
129. Edna Goodman.
130. G. M. Carstairs, *This Island Now: The 1962 Reith Lectures* (Middlesex: Penguin, 1963).
131. Val Parker.
132. Chris Richards.
133. Hubback, *Wives Who Went to College*, p. 156.
134. Beyfuss, *The English Marriage*, p. 152.
135. Ibid., p. 157.
136. Mass Observation Archive, Bulletin New Series 54, 'The Housewife's Day', June 1957.

4 Lightening Troubled Minds

1.   *BMJ*, 20 January 1962, p. 187.
2.   For a full account of the rise of the asylum, see A. Scull, *Museums of Madness: The Social Organization of Insanity in Nineteenth-Century England* (London: Allen Lane, 1979). See also: D. Russell, *Women, Madness and Medicine* (Cambridge: Polity, 1995).
3.   E. Shorter, cited in Callahan and Berrios, *Reinventing Depression*, pp. 87–8.
4.   G. Rivett, *From Cradle to Grave: Fifty Years of the NHS* (London: King's Fund, 1997), p. 77. For a full account of mental health services in Britain between 1744 and 1971, see K. Jones, *A History of Mental Health Services* (London: Routledge and Kegan Paul, 1972); and J. Busfield, 'Restructuring Mental Health services in Twentieth Century Britain', in Gijswijt-Hofstra and Porter (eds), *Cultures of Psychiatry*, pp. 9–28.
5.   Rivett, *From Cradle to Grave*, p. 77. For a full account of these early treatments, see E. Shorter, *A History of Psychiatry: From the Era of the Asylum to the Age of Prozac* (New York: John Wiley, 1997).
6.   Porter, *The Greatest Benefit to Mankind*, p. 520.
7.   Callahan and Berrios, *Reinventing Depression*, p. 90.
8.   Ibid., p. 92. For the effects of war on mental health and psychiatric discourse see also: P. Leese, *Shell Shock: Traumatic Neurosis and the British Soldiers of the First World War* (Basingstoke: Palgrave Macmillan, 2002); J. Bourke, 'Effeminacy, Ethnicity and the End of Trauma: The Sufferings of "Shell-Shocked" Men in Great Britain and Ireland, 1914–39', *Journal of Contemporary History*, 35 (2000), pp. 57–69; E. Leed, 'Fateful Memories: Industrialized War and Traumatic Neuroses', *Journal of Contemporary History*, 35 (2000), pp. 85–100; H. Merksey, 'Shell-Shock', in Freeman and Berrios (eds), *150 Years of British Psychiatry*, pp. 245–67; R. Cooter, 'War and Medicine', in Bynum and Porter (eds), *Companion Encyclopedia of the History of Medicine*; B. Shephard, *A War of Nerves: Soldiers and Psychiatrists 1914–1994* (London: Jonathan Cape, 2000); and E. Showalter, 'Male Hysteria', in *The Female Malady*.
9.   See M. C. Smith, *A Social History of the Minor Tranquilizers: The Quest for Small Comfort in the Age of Anxiety* (New York: Pharmaceutical Products Press, 1991).
10.   A. Scull, *Decarceration: Community Treatment and the Deviant – a Radical View* (Cambridge: Polity, 1884), pp. 85, 135.
11.   E. Shorter, *Before Prozac: The Troubled History of Mood Disorders in Psychiatry* (Oxford: Oxford University Press, 2009), p. 13.
12.   Ibid., p. 19.
13.   Ibid., p. 24.

Notes to pages 77–81

14. N. Rasmussen, *On Speed: the Many Lives of Amphetamine* (New York: New York University Press, 2008), p. 51.
15. Ibid.
16. Ibid., p. 118.
17. D. Healy, *Psychiatric Drugs Explained* (London: Churchill Livingston, 2002), p. 10.
18. D. Healy, *The Anti-Depressant Era* (Cambridge, MA: Harvard University Press, 1999), p. 45.
19. Healy, *Psychiatric Drugs Explained*, p. 10.
20. See Callahan and Berrios, *Reinventing Depression*, p. 100.
21. Ibid., p. 98.
22. D. Healy, *The Creation of Psychopharmaclogy* (Cambridge, MA: Harvard University Press, 2002), p. 101.
23. Ibid., p. 102.
24. Shorter, *A History of Psychiatry*, pp. 291, 292.
25. Callahan and Berrios, *Reinventing Depression*, p. 109.
26. Ibid., p. 106.
27. *BMJ*, 15 December 1962, p. 1624.
28. A. Tone, 'Tranquilizers on Trial: Psychopharmacology in the Age of Anxiety', in A. Tone and E. Siegel Watkins (eds), *Medicating Modern America* (New York: New York University Press, 2007), pp. 156–79, on p. 168.
29. Callahan and Berrios, *Reinventing Depression*, p. 107.
30. R. D. Laing, *The Politics of the Family and Other Essays* (London: Tavistock Publications, 1971), p. 58.
31. R. Mullan, *R D Laing: A Personal View* (London: Duckworth, 1999), p. 98.
32. Thomson, *Psychological Subjects*, p. 192.
33. Ibid., p. 194.
34. D. Armstrong, 'Madness and Coping', *Sociology of Health and Illness*, 2 (1980), pp. 293–316.
35. N. Rose, *Inventing Our Selves: Psychology, Power and Personhood* (Cambridge: Cambridge University Press, 1998), p. 72.
36. Ibid.
37. H. Dicks, *Fifty Years of the Tavistock Clinic* (London: Routledge and Kegan Paul, 1970), p. 1.
38. Ibid., p. 2.
39. Henry Dicks, cited in: Thomson, *Psychological Subjects*, p. 188.
40. T. Turner, 'James Crichton-Brown and the Anti-Psychoanalysts', in Freeman and Berrios (eds), *150 Years of Psychiatry*, pp. 144–55, on p. 145.
41. Ibid., p. 147.
42. Thomson, *Psychological Subjects*, p. 188.
43. Ibid., p. 190.
44. See: W. Cannon, *Bodily Changes in Pain, Hunger, Fear and Rage* (New York: D Appleton and Co., 1920); W. Cannon, *The Wisdom of the Body* (New York: W.W. Norton and Co., 1939); H. Selye, *The Stress of Life* (New York: McGraw-Hill, 1956) and H. Selye, *Stress in Health and Disease* (Boston, MA: Butterworth's, 1976). See also C. L. Cooper and P. Dewe, *Stress: A Brief History* (Oxford: Blackwell, 2004).
45. H. Weiner, 'The Concept of Psychosomatic Medicine', in E. R Wallace IV and J. Gach (eds), *History of Psychiatry and Medical Psychology* (New York: Springer, 2008), pp.

485–516, on p. 505. See also H. Flanders Dunbar, *Synopsis of Psychosomatic Diagnosis and Treatment* (St Louis, MO: C.V. Mosby Co., 1948).

46. Ibid., p. 504. See also F. Alexander, *Psychosomatic Medicine: Its Principles and Applications* (New York: W.W., Norton and Co., 1950).

47. H. Weiner, 'Psychosomatic Medicine and the Mind-Body Relation', in Wallace and Gach (eds), *History of Psychiatry and Medical Psychology*, pp. 781–834, on p. 799. See also J. L. Halliday, *Psychosocial Medicine: A Study of the Sick Society* (London: William Heinemann, 1948).

48. Thomson, *Psychological Subjects*, p. 252.

49. N. Kessel and M. Shepherd, 'Neurosis in Hospital and General Practice', *Journal of Mental Science* (referred to hereafter as *JMS*), 108 (1962), pp. 159–66, on p.159.

50. G. Wilkinson, 'The General Practice Research Unit at the Institute of Psychiatry', *Psychological Medicine*, 19 (1989), pp. 787–90, on p. 787. See also M. Shepherd, *Psychiatric Illness in General Practice* (Oxford: Oxford University Press, 1966).

51. Kessel and Shepherd, 'Neurosis in Hospital', p. 163.

52. 'Psychological Medicine in General Practice', *British Medical Journal*, 6 September 1958, pp. 585–90.

53. See C. A. H. Watts, *Psychiatry in General Practice* (London: J. and A. Churchill, 1952) and C. A. H. Watts, *Depressive Disorders in the Community* (Bristol: John Wright, 1966).

54. See 'Today's drugs: drugs for depression, panel discussion', *BMJ*, 28 September 1963, pp. 799–802.

55. Ibid.

56. Thomson, *Psychological Subjects*, p. 258.

57. See H. J. Eysenck and S. B. G. Eysenck, *The Personality Questionnaire* (London: Hodder and Stoughton 1975). Eysenck's theory of personality was first described in *Dimensions of Personality* (1947). He studied under Cyril Burt and became Professor of Psychology at the Institute of Psychiatry in 1955.

58. J. H. Abramson, 'The Cornell Medical Index as an Epidemiological Tool', *American Journal of Public Health, Nation's Health*, 56 (1966), pp. 287–98.

59. Ibid.

60. See M. Hamilton, 'A Rating Scale for Depression', *Journal of Neurology, Neurosurgery and Psychiatry*, 23 (1960), pp. 56–62. The rating scale is still used today.

61. L. G. Kiloh and R. F. Garside, 'The Independence of Neurotic Depression and Endogenous Depression', *British Journal of Psychiatry* (referred to hereafter as *BJP*), 109 (1963), pp. 451–63, on p. 452.

62. W. Sargant, 'Drugs in the Treatment of Depression', *BMJ*, 28 January 1961, pp. 225–7, on p. 227.

63. See E. West and P. J. Dally, 'Effects of Iproniazid in Depressive Syndromes', *BMJ*, 13 June 1959, pp. 1491–4 and P. J. Dally and P. Rohde, 'Comparison of Antidepressant Drugs in Depressive Illness', *Lancet*, 7 January 1961, pp. 18–20.

64. Sargant, 'Drugs in the Treatment of Depression'. See also W. Sargant and P. Dally, 'Treatment of Anxiety States by Antidepressant Drugs', *BMJ*, 6 January 1962, pp. 6–8.

65. E. H Hare, J. Dominian and L. Sharpe, 'Phenelzine and Dexamphetamine in Depressive Illness', *BMJ*, 6 January 1962, 9–12.

66. N. McDonaghy, A. D. Joffe and B. Murphy, 'The Independence of Neurotic and Endogenous Depression', *BJP*, 113 (1967), pp. 479–84, on p. 481.

67. Ibid., p. 482.

Notes to pages 85–93

68. C. G. Costello and M. M. Selby 'The Relationship between Sleep Patterns and Reactive and Endogenous Depressions', *BJP*, 111 (1965), pp. 497–501.
69. C. Chacon and E. T. Downham, 'Amitriptyline and Amitriptyline-with-Perphenazine in Depression – a Retrospective Study', *BJP*, 113 (1967), pp. 201–7, on p. 205.
70. A. L. Sanderson, *BMJ*, 3 March 1962, p. 642.
71. Ibid.
72. 'Psychological Medicine in General Practice', *BMJ*, 6 September 1958, pp. 585–90, on p. 587.
73. M. Shepherd, 'Research in the Field of Psychiatry', *BMJ*, 18 October 1969, pp. 161–3, on p. 162.
74. Cooper and Dewe, *Stress*, p. 40.
75. Ibid., p. 43.
76. Ibid., p. 44.
77. E. Howarth, 'Headache, Personality and Stress', *BJP*, 111 (1965), pp. 1193–7.
78. A. Ryle, 'The Whirligig of Time', *Psychiatric Bulletin*, 22 (1998), pp. 263–7, on p. 265.
79. Ibid.
80. A. Ryle and M. Hamilton, 'Neurosis in Fifty Married Couples', *JMS*, 108 (1962), pp. 265–73.
81. Ibid., p. 269.
82. Ibid., p. 271.
83. D. A., Pond, A. Ryle and M. Hamilton, 'Marriage and Neurosis in a Working-Class Population', *BJP*, 109 (1963), pp. 592–98.
84. Ibid., p. 593.
85. Ibid., p. 598.
86. Ibid., pp. 594–5.
87. A. Ryle, 'A Marital Patterns Test for Use in Psychiatric Research', *BJP*, 112 (1966), pp. 285–93, on p. 285.
88. A. Ryle, *Neurosis in the Ordinary Family* (London: Tavistock, 1967), p. 119. For further debate about the effects of childhood experience on mental health, see M. J. Abrahams and F. A. Whitlock, 'Childhood Experience and Depression', *BJP*, 115 (1969), pp. 883–8. Here the authors concluded that unsatisfactory parent-child relationships were important determinants of personality and neurotic symptom formation.
89. G. Langley, 'Patients' Attitudes to Neurosis', *BJP*, 109 (1963), pp. 782–4.
90. Ibid., p. 784.
91. A. H. Roberts, 'Housebound Housewives – a Follow-up Study of a Phobic Anxiety State', *BJP*, 110 (1964), pp. 191–7.
92. Ibid., p. 191.
93. Ibid., p. 192.
94. Ibid., 194.
95. J. R. Morrison, R. W. Hudgens and R. G. Barchha, 'Life Events and Psychiatric Illness: A Study of 100 Patients and Controls', *BJP*, 114 (1968), pp. 423–32.
96. Ibid., p. 428.
97. A. D. Forrest, R. H. Fraser and R. G. Priest, 'Environmental Factors in Depressive Illness', *BJP*, 111 (1965), pp. 243–53, on p.244.
98. Ibid., p. 251.
99. N. Kreitman, 'Married Couples Admitted to Mental Hospital', *BJP*, 114 (1968), pp. 699–718. Norman Kreitman was a psychiatrist at the Unit for Research on the Epidemiology of Psychiatric Illness, University of Edinburgh Department of Psychiatry.

200 *Notes to pages 93–6*

100. Ibid., p. 706.
101. Ibid., p. 714. See also C. W. Buck and K. L. Ladd, 'Psychoneurosis in Marital Partners', *BJP*, 111 (1965), pp. 587–90. The argument had been mooted previously by these Canadian clinicians from the University of Western Ontario. They found in their research that neurotic illness in married couples developed over a period of marriage and was not usually present before, or during the early stages of the partnership. Thus, their findings support the contagion theory.
102. N. Parker, 'Close Identification in Twins Discordant for Obsessional Behaviour', *BJP*, 110 (1964), pp. 496–504.
103. Ibid., p. 503.
104. E. Slater and M. Woodside, *Patterns of Marriage: a Study of Marriage Relationships in the Urban Working Classes* (London: Cassell and Company Ltd, 1951).
105. Ibid., p. 240.
106. See E. Slater, *Psychotic and Neurotic Illness in Twins* (London, HMSO, 1953).
107. Slater and Woodside, *Patterns of Marriage*, p. 125.
108. Ibid., p. 274.
109. A. Munro, 'Some Familial and Social Factors in Depressive Illness', *BJP*, 112 (1966), pp. 429–41, on p. 437.
110. J. D. Pollit, 'Suggestions for a Physiological Classification of Depression', *BJP*, 111 (1965), pp. 489–95, on p. 489.
111. Ibid., 490.
112. Ibid., 493. See also J. Pollitt, *Depression and Its Treatment* (London, William Heinemann Medical Books, 1965). Endocrinology had become central to studies of stress and disease from the 1930s. Walter Cannon coined the term 'homeostasis' to describe the human body's ability to regulate hormones and maintain stability under 'stress' – the 'fight or flight' phenomenon. See Porter, *Greatest Benefit to Mankind*, p. 562; and Cooper and Dewe, *Stress*, p. 14.
113. Catecholmines produce physiological changes to prepare the body for the fight or flight response. Typically, this effect produces a raise in blood-pressure and heart rate. Serotonin is thought to influence the regulation of, among other things, temperature, sleep, mood, libido and appetite. Low levels of serotonin are associated with depression.
114. MAOIs prevent the breakdown of monoamine transmitters (including serotonin), and thus, increase the concentrations in the brain. The tricyclics inhibit the 'reuptake' of serotonin and noradrenalin by nerve cells.
115. A. Coppen, 'The Biochemistry of Affective Disorders', *BJP*, 113 (1967), pp. 1237–64. For further agreement relating to the biochemical factors in depressive illness, see also: 'Conference Report: Depression in General Practice', *BMJ*, 30 October 1965, pp. 1052–3.
116. D. Kelly and C. J. S. Walter, 'A Clinical and Physiological Relationship between Anxiety and Depression', *BJP*, 115 (1969), pp. 401–6.
117. H. Miller, 'Depression', *BMJ*, 4 February 1967, pp. 257–62, on p. 257.
118. Ibid., pp. 258, 259.
119. Ibid., p. 262.
120. See F. N. Pitts and G. Winokur, 'Affective Disorder: VII. Alcoholism and Affective Disorder', *Journal of Psychiatric Research*, 4 (1966), pp. 37–50.
121. See for example, C. McCance and P. T. McCance, 'Alcoholism in North East Scotland: Its Treatment and Outcome', *BJP*, 115 (1969), pp. 189–98.

122. G. A. Foulds and C. Hassall, 'The Significance of Age of Onset of Excessive Drinking in Male Alcoholics', *BJP*, 115 (1969), pp. 1027–32, on p. 1027.
123. Ibid., p. 1029.
124. C. G. Smith, 'Alcoholics, Their Treatment and Their Wives', *BJP* 115 (1969), 1039–42, on p. 1039.
125. G. Winokur and P. Clayton, 'Sex Differences and Alcoholism in Primary Affective illness', *BJP*, 113 (1967), pp. 973–89.
126. Usually only in cases of severe endogenous depression.
127. 'Tranquilizers in Psychiatry', *Lancet*, 15 October 1960, pp. 855–6, on p. 855.
128. Ibid., p. 855.
129. Sargant, 'Drugs in the Treatment of Depression', p. 225.
130. See for example: Ibid.; and also: 'Drugs for Anxiety', *BMJ*, 6 January 1962, pp. 38–9; Hare and Sharpe, 'Phenelzine and dexamphetamine', pp. 9–12; and Sargant and Dally, 'Treatment of Anxiety States by Antidepressant Drugs', pp. 6–9.
131. Sargant and Dally, 'Treatment of Anxiety States by Antidepressant Drugs', p. 8.
132. See: Healy, *The Antidepressant Era*, pp. 186–7; 'Clinical Trial of the Treatment of depressive illness', *BMJ*, 3 April 1965, pp. 881–6; and 'Treatment of Depression', *BMJ*, 3 April 1965, pp. 878–9. These articles reported on the Medical Research Council's Clinical Psychiatry Committee's six-month trial which compared the results of imipramine (a tricyclic) and phenelzine (Nardil, a MAOI), with ECT and a placebo. Phenelzine proved to be no more effective than a placebo.
133. 'Today's Drugs: Hypnotics – Barbiturates', *BMJ*, 5 January 1963, pp. 39–40.
134. 'Shadow over the Barbiturates', *The Lancet*, 10 July 1954, p. 75.
135. See for example, correspondence sections of *The Lancet*: 17 July 1954 and 24 July 1954.
136. 'Abuse of Barbiturates', *BMJ*, 25 December 1954, p. 1534.
137. Notes in parliament, *BMJ*, 15 December 1962, p. 1624.
138. In parliament, *The Lancet*, 1 December 1962, p. 1176.
139. See debate in the *BMJ* initiated by William Sargant, 23 January 1965, p. 251 and subsequent correspondence: 6 February 1965, p. 383; 20 February 1965, p. 521.
140. Correspondence, *BMJ*, 27 February 1965, p. 589.
141. 'Today's Drugs: Benzodiazepines', *BMJ*, 1 April 1967, p. 36.
142. Ibid.
143. M. Lader, 'History of Benzodiazepine Dependence', *Journal of Substance Abuse*, 8 (1991), pp. 53–9, on p. 56.
144. 'Today's Drugs: Benzodiazepines' *BMJ*, 1 April 1967, p. 37.
145. Sargant and Dally, 'Treatment of Anxiety States by Antidepressant Drugs', p. 7.
146. Ibid.
147. Ibid.
148. Ibid.
149. Callahan and Berrios, *Reinventing Depression*, p. 38.
150. Ibid., p. 37.
151. J. Wolpe, 'Behaviour Therapy in Complex Neurotic States', *BJP*, 110 (1964), 28–32, on p. 28. Wolpe was born in South Africa and later became a citizen of the United States. He worked, during the Second World War, with soldiers suffering from what is now described as post-traumatic stress disorder and strove to find an alternative treatment to drugs. He is remembered for developing 'desensitization' treatment for phobias, in which the patient is exposed gradually to the object or situation that is feared, while at the same time being taught coping techniques in order to control fear.

202 *Notes to pages 101–7*

152. H. J. Eysenck, 'Behaviour Therapy, Extinction and Relapse in Neurosis', *BJP*, 109 (1963), pp. 12–18, on p. 12.
153. Wolpe, cited in V. Meyer and M. G. Gelder, 'Behaviour Therapy and Phobic Disorder', *BJP*, 109 (1963), pp. 19–28, on p. 19.
154. Eysenck, 'Behaviour Therapy, Extinction and Relapse in Neurosis', p. 12.
155. Ibid.
156. Wolpe, 'Behaviour Therapy in Complex Neurotic States', p. 29.
157. Ibid.
158. Meyer and Gelder, 'Behaviour Therapy and Phobic Disorder', p. 28.
159. See M. Balint, *The Doctor, His Patient and the Illness* (London: Pitman Medical, 1957).
160. B. Cooper and A. C Brown, 'Psychiatric Practice in Great Britain and America: A Comparative Study', *BJP*, 113 (1967), pp. 625–36.
161. Modified electroplexy requires that an anaesthetic drug is administered prior to treatment to minimize injury from convulsions. Unmodified elextroplexy had 'fallen from favour' in both countries by the mid-1960s.
162. Cooper and Brown, 'Psychiatric Practice in Great Britain and America', p. 633.
163. Ibid.
164. See W. S. Appleton and C. Chien, 'American Psychopharmacology: Second Class Status?', *BJP*, 113 (1967), pp. 637–41.

5 Not Something You Talk About

1. J. Ussher, *Women's Madness: Misogyny or Mental Illness?* (Hertfordshire: Harvester Wheatsheaf, 1991), p. 98.
2. A. Miles, *Women and Mental Illness* (Brighton: Wheatsheaf, 1988), p. 7.
3. Ibid.
4. I. K. Zola, cited in: K. Koumjian, 'The Use of Valium as a Form of Social Control', *Social Science and Medicine*, 15E (1981), pp. 245–9, on p. 246.
5. T. Scheff, *Being Mentally Ill: A Sociological Theory*, 3rd edn (London: Weidenfeld and Nicolson, 1999 [1966]).
6. Miles, *Women and Mental Illness*, pp. 17–19.
7. W. R Gove, 'Societal Reaction as an Explanation of Mental Illness: An Evaluation', *American Sociological Review*, 35 (1970), pp. 873–84, on p. 882. See also: W. Gove (ed.), *The Labelling of Deviance: Evaluating a Perspective* (Beverly Hills, CA and London: Sage, 1980) and W. Gove (ed.), *Deviance and Mental Illness* (Beverly Hills, CA and London: Sage, 1982).
8. Scheff, *Being Mentally Ill*, p. ix.
9. M. Foucault, *Madness and Civilization* (London: Tavistock Publications, 1967).
10. T. Szasz, *The Myth of Mental Illness* (Hertfordshire: Paladin, 1975 [1962]), pp. 37–8.
11. Laing, *The Politics of the Family*. See also D. Cooper, *The Death of the Family* (London: Allen Lane, 1971).
12. Rose, *Inventing Our Selves*, p. 112.
13. Ibid.
14. Miles, *Women and Mental Illness*, p. 47.
15. Ibid. p. 12.
16. Showalter, *The Female Malady*, p. 3.
17. This debate is addressed in detail in Showalter, *The Female Malady;* Miles, *Women and Mental Illness;* Ussher, *Women's Madness;* H. Graham, *Hardship and Health in Women's*

Notes to pages 107–12

Lives (Hertfordshire: Harvester Wheatsheaf, 1993) and C. Niven and D. Carroll, *The Health Psychology of Women* (Switzerland: Harwood, 1993); Busfield, *Men, Women and Madness*; and L. Appignanesi, *Mad, Bad and Sad; A History of Women and the Mind Doctors from 1800 to the Present* (London: Virago, 2008).

18. Chesler, *Women and Madness*, p. 53.

19. W. R. Gove, 'Mental Illness and Psychiatric Treatment among Women', in M. R. Walsh, *The Psychology of Women – Ongoing Debates* (New Haven, CT: Yale University Press, 1987), pp. 102–18, on p. 104.

20. W. R Gove, 'The Relationship between Sex Roles, Marital Status and Mental Illness', *Social Forces*, 51 (1972), pp. 34–44, on p. 42.

21. W. R. Gove and J. F. Tudor, 'Adult Sex Roles and Mental Illness', *The American Journal of Sociology*, 78 (1973), pp. 812–35, on p. 814.

22. Ibid.

23. Ibid., p. 815.

24. Ibid., p. 814.

25. Ibid.

26. Gove, 'The Relationship between Sex Roles', p. 35.

27. Ibid.

28. R. Cooperstock, *The Effects of Tranquilization: Benzodiazepine Use in Canada* (Minister of National Health and Welfare, 1982).

29. R. Cooperstock, 'Sex Differences in Psychotropic Drug Use', *Social Science and Medicine*, 12B (1978), pp. 179–86.

30. R. Cooperstock and H. L. Lennard, 'Some Social Meanings of Tranquilizer Use', *Sociology of Health and Illness*, 1 (1979), pp. 331–47, on p. 335.

31. Ibid.

32. Ibid., pp. 337–8.

33. Ibid., p. 340.

34. Ibid., p. 345.

35. Cooperstock, 'Sex Differences in Psychotropic Drug Use', p. 182.

36. *BMJ*, 4 December 1965.

37. G. W. Brown and T. Harris, *Social Origins of Depression: A Study of Psychiatric Disorder in Women*, paperback edition (London: Tavistock Publications, 1979), p. 279.

38. Ibid., p. 22.

39. Busfield, *Men, Women and Madness*, pp. 95–6.

40. Ibid., p. 97.

41. M. Johnson, 'Mental Illness and Psychiatric Treatment among Women: A Response', in Walsh, *The Psychology of Women*, pp. 119–27, on p. 119.

42. Ibid., p. 120.

43. L. Jordanova, 'Mental Illness, Mental Health: Changing Norms and Expectations', in Cambridge Women's Study Group, *Women in Society: Interdisciplinary Essays* (London: Virago, 1981), pp. 95–114.

44. Ibid., p. 112.

45. Eileen Bailey. Interviewed on 30 November 2004.

46. Ibid.

47. Ibid.

48. Ibid.

49. Ibid.

50. Ibid.

204 *Notes to pages 112–19*

51. Jean Hill.
52. Ibid.
53. Ibid.
54. Anne Shepherd.
55. Jean Bills.
56. Nora Kelly. Interviewed 25 September 2004. For current theories about postpartum psychiatric illness set in historical context, see I. Brockington, *Motherhood and Mental Health* (New York: Oxford University Press, 1998). See also I. Brockington, 'Postpartum Psychiatric Disorders', *The Lancet*, 363 (2004), pp. 303–10.
57. Ibid.
58. Ibid.
59. Ibid.
60. Ibid.
61. Ibid.
62. Ibid.
63. Mary Grant's problem page, *Woman's Own*, 17 February 1962, p. 77.
64. Evelyn Home, *Woman*, 20 June 1959, p. 65.
65. Ibid.
66. Doctor's diary, *Woman's Own*, 15 September 1955, p. 4.
67. Doctor's diary, *Woman's Own*, 12 May 1962, p. 4.
68. Doctor's diary, *Woman's Own*, 9 March 1968, p. 4.
69. See: D. Grant, *Feeding the Family in Wartime* (London: G. G. Harrap, 1942) and D. Grant, *Your Daily Bread* (London: Faber and Faber, 1944). Doris Grant criticized the use of refined carbohydrates in food, particularly in bread, and became a supporter of the food-combining principals of Dr William Hay.
70. 'You and Your Nerves', *Woman's Own*, 11 May 1968, pp. 14–15.
71. Ibid.
72. C. Weeks, *Self Help for Your Nerves* (London: Angus Robertson, 1963), p. 6.
73. Ibid., p. 7.
74. Ibid.
75. Ibid., p. 110.
76. Ibid., p. 16.
77. Ibid., p. 15.
78. R. Martin, 'Emotional Distress, Signs and Symptoms', *Woman's Own*, 6 April 1968, pp. 70–71. Ruth Martin was Health Editor for the magazine.
79. Ibid.
80. J. Metzl, *Prozac on the Couch* (Durham, NC: Duke University Press, 2003) p. 74.
81. Ibid., p. 81.
82. Ann Coles.
83. Ibid.
84. Ibid.
85. Ibid.
86. Seasonal affective disorder was first 'coined' during the 1980s in the United States by the psychiatrist and scientist Norman Rosenthal. Commonly known as 'winter blues', it is the short daylight hours during the winter that are said to affect the mood of sufferers. It is measurably present in Scandinavian countries where daylight hours are particularly short in winter.
87. Ann Coles.

Notes to pages 119–29

88. Written testimony of Barbara Rogers.
89. Barbara Vicary.
90. Ibid.
91. Ibid.
92. Betty Sanderson.
93. Margaret Windsor.
94. Doris Carter.
95. Eileen Roberts.
96. Rose Courtenay.
97. Ibid.
98. Ibid.
99. Written testimony of Rebecca Heane.
100. *Matrimonial Proceedings and Property Act*, 1970 (c. 45); and *Matrimonial Causes Act* 1973 (c. 18).
101. Frances Wilson.
102. Ibid.
103. Ibid.
104. Ibid.
105. Ibid.
106. Ibid.
107. Judith Morgan.
108. Ibid.
109. Ibid.
110. Ibid. Judith trained as an art teacher but gave up work when she had her first child. She worked part-time as an illustrator until her children were older.
111. Ibid.
112. Eve Raddon.
113. Eileen Roberts. For an exploration of 'fear' during wartime, especially the fear of anticipation and delayed shock, see Bourke, *Fear: A Cultural History*, chapter 8, 'Civilians under Attack', pp. 222–54.
114. Eileen Roberts.
115. Ibid.
116. Ibid.
117. Ibid.
118. Brown and Harris, *Social Origins of Depression*, p. 271.
119. Ibid., p. 270.
120. P. Thompson, *Voice of the Past*, 3rd edn (Oxford: Oxford University Press, 2000), p. 173.
121. Ibid., p. 126.
122. Ibid., p. 137.
123. Katheine Stead.
124. R. Martin, 'Not Something You Talk About', *Woman's Own*, 24 January 1970, pp. 12–13.
125. 'Coming through a Crisis', *Times*, 23 November 1970, p 5.
126. See especially, Metzl, *Prozac on the Couch*.

6 For Ladies in Distress

1. G. Stimson, 'Women in a Doctored World', *New Society*, 1 May 1975, pp. 265–7.
2. Ibid., p. 267.

206 *Notes to pages 129–34*

3. Cooperstock, 'Sex Differences in Psychotropic Drug Use', p. 181.
4. Jordanova, 'Mental Illness, Mental Health', p. 107.
5. Metzl, *Prozac on the Couch*.
6. Ibid., pp. 81, 17.
7. Stimson, 'Women in a Doctored World', p. 267.
8. Metzl, *Prozac on the Couch*, p. 21.
9. J. Metzl, "Mother's Little Helper': The Crisis of Psychoanalysis and the Miltown Resolution', *Gender and History* 15 (2003), pp. 240–67, on p. 241.
10. A. Melville and C. Johnson, *Cured to Death: the Effects of Prescription Drugs* (Seven Oaks: New English Library, 1983), p. 61.
11. S. Anderson, 'From Bespoke to off-the-Peg: Community Pharmacists and the Retailing of Medicines in Great Britain 1900 to 1970', in L. Curth (ed.), *Physick to Pharmacology: Consumption and Retailing of Medicinal Drugs in England* (London: Ashgate, 2006), pp. 105–42. See also S. Anderson (ed.), *Making Medicines: A Brief History of Pharmacy and Pharmaceuticals* (London: The Pharmaceutical Press, 2005).
12. J. Liebenau, 'The Rise of the British Pharmaceutical Industry', *BMJ*, 3 October 1990, pp. 742–8, on p. 725.
13. William Osler, cited in Healy, *Psychiatric Drugs Explained*, p. xii.
14. Anderson, 'From Bespoke to off-the-Peg', p. 5.
15. Ibid., p. 6.
16. Ibid., p. 7.
17. Ibid.
18. Ibid.
19. Ibid., p. 9.
20. The Penicillin Act 1947, The Therapeutic Substances Act 1953 and The Therapeutic Substances Act 1956.
21. Anderson, 'From Bespoke to off-the-Peg', p. 9.
22. Healy, *Psychiatric Drugs Explained*, p. xii.
23. Healy, *The Anti-Depressant Era*, p. 264.
24. Healy, *Psychiatric Drugs Explained*, p. xii.
25. Anderson, 'From Bespoke to off-the-Peg', p. 8.
26. Ibid.
27. *BMJ*, 5 December 1959, p. 1240.
28. See *BMJ*, 17 March 1962, p. 803.
29. Ibid., pp. 780, 781.
30. *BMJ*, 24 November 1962, p. 1366.
31. Ibid., p. 1480.
32. Ibid., p. 1618.
33. Ibid., p. 1326.
34. *BMJ*, 27 March 1965, p. 857.
35. *BMJ*, 29 January 1966, p. 297.
36. Ibid.
37. 'Some Influences on Drug Prescribing', Section III, 'The Prescribing of Psychotropic Drugs in General Practice', *The Journal of the Royal College of General Practitioners*, 21, Supplement 4 (1971), pp. 54–67, on p.63.
38. Metzl, *Prozac on the Couch*, p. 127.
39. Ibid., p. 131.
40. Ibid., p. 10.

41. Ibid., p. 16.
42. Ibid., p. 151.
43. Ibid., p. 121.
44. Healy, *Psychiatric Drugs Explained*, p. 10.
45. Ibid.
46. *BMJ*, 27 July 1963.
47. *BMJ*, 5 September 1964.
48. *BMJ*, 11 December 1965.
49. *BMJ*, 5 April 1965.
50. *BMJ*, 4 July 1964.
51. *BMJ*, 26 September 1964.
52. *BMJ*, 1 May 1965 and 22 May 1965.
53. *BMJ*, 18 November 1961.
54. Melville and Johnson, *Cured to Death*, p. 76.
55. Ibid., p. 77.
56. *BMJ*, 11 September 1965.
57. Healy, *Psychiatric Drugs Explained*, p. 52.
58. See Healy, *The Antidepressant Era*, pp. 186–7 and *BMJ*, 3 April 1965, pp. 878–9.
59. Healy, *The Antidepressant Era*, pp. 186–7.
60. Ibid., p. 187.
61. Ibid., p. 186.
62. Ibid.
63. *BMJ*, 2 September 1961. The copyright holders of the brand 'Nardil' have asked that the name of the drug is removed from the illustration in this book.
64. *BMJ*, 12 March 1966.
65. Sargant and Dally, 'Treatment of Anxiety States by Antidepressant Drugs'.
66. Healy, *Psychiatric Drugs Explained*, p. 294.
67. Sargant and Dally, 'Treatment of Anxiety States by Antidepressant Drugs', p. 8.
68. Tone, 'Tranquilizers on Trial', p. 165.
69. Healy, *Psychiatric Drugs Explained*, p. 284.
70. *BMJ*, 2 March 1963.
71. Healy, *Psychiatric Drugs Explained*, p. 136.
72. *BMJ*, 15 August 1963.
73. *BMJ*, 5 January 1963.
74. *BMJ*, 13 May 1961.
75. *BMJ*, 18 September 1965.
76. See for example *BMJ*, 7 September 1963.
77. The most commonly prescribed compounds were marketed under trade names Librium, Valium and later Nobrium.
78. Healy, *Psychiatric Drugs Explained*, p. 139.
79. Lader, 'History of Benzodiazepine Dependence', p. 54.
80. *BMJ*, 14 August 1965.
81. *BMJ*, 2 February 1963.
82. *BMJ*, 24 April 1965.
83. Cooperstock, 'Sex Differences in Psychotropic Drug Use', p. 182.
84. *BMJ*, 25 April 1961.
85. *BMJ*, 4 December 1965.
86. *BMJ*, 16 April 1966.

87. Cooper and Dewe, *Stress*, p. 42.
88. *BMJ*, 4 May 1963 and 8 July 1963.
89. *BMJ*, 27 August 1963.
90. Healy, *Psychiatric Drugs Explained*, p. 140.
91. *BMJ*, 19 March 1966.
92. *BMJ*, 23 October 1965.
93. Both advertisements featured in *The Chemist and Druggist*, 19 March 1955.
94. *BMJ*, 15 December 1952, p. 1624.
95. *Lancet*, 1 December 1962, p. 1176.
96. I. Atkin, 'The Lotus Eaters, or Stress, Neurosis and Tranquillizers?' *BMJ* (1959), p. 1477.
97. Ibid., p. 1478.
98. I. Atkin, 'Mental Disorders and External Stress', *Lancet*, 17 March 1962, p. 581.
99. Cited in ibid. Max Nordau (1849–1923) was a Hungarian physician whose views reflected concerns about a degenerating society that was undergoing huge social upheaval and industrial advancement. He associated degeneration with mental disorder. See R. Porter, 'Diseases of Civilization', in W. F. Bynum and R. Porter (eds), *Companion Encyclopaedia of the History of Medicine* (London: Routledge, 1992); and C. E. Rosenberg, 'Pathologies of Progress: The Idea of Civilization as Risk', *Bulletin of the History of Medicine*, 72 (1998), pp. 714–30.
100. Atkin, 'Mental Disorders and External Stress', p. 582.
101. Metzl, *Prozac on the Couch*, p. 75.
102. Ibid., p. 74.
103. Ibid.
104. Porter, *The Greatest Benefit to Mankind*, p. 518.
105. Healy, *The Creation of Psychopharmacology*, p. 140.
106. Metzl, *Prozac on the Couch*, p. 74.
107. Ibid, see pp. 36, 75.
108. For the US perspective on women as consumers of health products, see N. Tomes, 'Skeletons in the Medicine Closet: Women and "Rational Consumption" in the Inter-War American Home', in Jackson (ed.), *Health and the Modern Home*, pp. 177–95.
109. White, *Women's Magazines 1693–1968*, p. 157.
110. P. Howlett, 'The "Golden Age", 1955–1973', in Johnson (ed.), *Twentieth Century Britain: Economic, Social and Cultural Change*, pp. 320–39.
111. Ibid., p. 321.
112. White, *Women's Magazines*, p. 156.
113. Ibid., p. 97.
114. Ibid., p. 63.
115. Ibid., p. 115.
116. Ibid., p. 179.
117. Ibid, p. 181.
118. Ibid., p. 158.
119. V. Packard, *The Hidden Persuaders* (Middlesex: Pelican, 1981 [1957]).
120. Ibid., p. 14.
121. Ibid., p. 33.
122. Ibid., p. 37.
123. Ibid., p. 56.
124. Ibid,. p. 92.
125. Ibid., pp. 24, 140.

Notes to pages 156–69 209

126. White, *Women's Magazines*, p. 219.
127. Ibid., p. 222.
128. Packard, *The Hidden Persuaders*, p. 63.
129. *Woman's Own*, 3 March 1955.
130. *Woman*, 5 September 1959.
131. *Woman's Own*, 24 February 1955.
132. *Woman's Own*, 8 September 1955.
133. *Times*, 26 March 1956.
134. *Times*, 19 February 1954.
135. *Times*, 2 April 1952.
136. *Times*, 19 February 1954.
137. *Woman's Own*, 25 June 1960.
138. *Woman's Own*, 20 August 1960.
139. *Woman's Own*, 11 June 1960.
140. *Woman's Own*, 28 April 1955.
141. *Woman's Weekly*, 30 September 1961.
142. *Woman's Weekly*, 11 November 1961.
143. *Woman's Own*, 3 February 1962.
144. *Woman's Weekly*, 16 September 1961.
145. *Woman*, 28 January 1967.
146. Millum, *Images of Women*, p. 175.
147. *Woman's Own*, 7 April 1962. These adverts featured throughout 1962.
148. For an historical overview of tonic wines, see P. Homan, 'Medicated Cheer', *Pharmaceutical Journal*, 271 (2003), pp. 867–8.
149. Friedan, *The Feminine Mystique*, p. 13.
150. *Woman's Realm*, 24 September 1966.
151. *Woman*, 18 February 1967.
152. Advertisement for Wincarnis Wine, *Woman's Own*, 10 January 1970.
153. *Woman*, 11 February 1967.
154. *Woman's Realm*, 20 August 1966.
155. Mass Observation Archive, File Report 1889, 'What the Consumer Thinks of Self-Medication', August 1943, also published in *Manufacturing Chemist and Manufacturing Perfumer*, August 1943, pp. 236–8.
156. Ibid.
157. Ibid.
158. Mass Observation Archive, Bulletin New Series 48, 'National Health', February 1943.
159. Ibid.
160. Ibid.
161. Packard, *The Hidden Persuaders*, p. 69.
162. 'Psychotropic Agents', in *Today's Drugs* (London: British Medical Association, 1970), pp. 159–82.
163. 'Central-Nervous System', in *Today's Drugs* (London: British Medical Association, 1964), pp. 70–82.
164. 'Psychotropic Agents', pp. 159–82.
165. J. O'Shaughnessy and N. J. O'Shaughnessy, *Persuasion in Advertising* (London: Routledge, 1994), p. 32.
166. *Woman*, 10 May 1969.
167. Ott, *Fevered Lives*, p. 1.

Conclusion

1. K. Roiphe, *The Morning After: Sex, Fear and Feminism* (London: Penguin, 1993), p. 5.
2. These concerns are discussed in Jackson 'Home Sweet Home'.
3. Kate Millett, speaking with Sue MacGregor on BBC Radio Four, 22 March 1971.
4. A. Tone, *The Age of Anxiety: A History of America's Turbulent Affair with Tranquilizers* (New York: Basic Books, 2009), p.183.
5. Ibid., p.184.
6. For example thalidomide and the oral contraceptive pill. Ibid., p.189.
7. Ibid., p.196.
8. Ibid., p.197.
9. 'A Retrospective Study of Psychotropic Drug Prescribing by a Group of Midland General Practitioners', *Journal of the Royal College of General Practitioners*, 21, Supplement 4 (1971), pp. 11–53, on p.37. See also: J. Woodcock, 'Long-Term Consumers of Psychotropic Drugs', in M. Balint, J. Hunt, D. Joyce, M. Marinker and J. Woodcock, *Treatment or Diagnosis: a Study of Repeat Prescriptions in General Practice* (London: Tavistock Publications [1970], 1984), pp. 147–76.
10. Ibid., p. 38.
11. This topic is the subject of my current three-year research project, entitled *Masculinity and Health since the Second World War*, generously funded by the Wellcome Trust. See also D. Wilkins, *Untold Problems: a Review of the Essential Issues in the Mental Health of Men and Boys* (Men's Health Forum, 2010) and D. Wilkins and M. Kemple, *Delivering Male: Effective Practice in Male Mental Health* (Men's Health Forum, 2011).
12. Elizabeth Ettorre and Elianne Riska have suggested a 'multilayered' approach to the analysis of gender and psychotropic drug use. In order to explain the gendered social construction of psychotropic drug use, they propose a feminist analysis at each 'level' of the process: from the individual to the health care system. See E. Ettorre and E. Riska, *Gendered Moods: Psychotropics and Society* (London: Routledge, 1995).
13. Dunnell and A. Cartwright, *Medicine Takers, Prescribers and Hoarders* (London: Routledge and Kegan Paul, 1972), p. 1. Over 1,400 adults were interviewed from a sample taken from fourteen parliamentary constituencies across England, Wales and Scotland.
14. Ibid. The term 'ethical' is used to describe preparations which are advertised only to the medical, dental and pharmaceutical professions, and not directly to the consumer.
15. Ibid., p. 2.
16. Ibid., p. 21.
17. Ibid., p. 22.
18. Tomes, 'Skeletons in the Medicine Closet'.
19. Dunnell and Cartwright, *Medicine Takers*, p. 117.
20. Ibid., p. 118.
21. Jerman, *The Lively-Minded Women*, p. 19.
22. Ibid., p. 18.
23. Ibid., p. 19.
24. White, *Women's Magazines 1693–1968*, p. 279.
25. Ibid., p. 112.
26. Ibid., p. 129.
27. Ibid., p. 285–6.
28. Coontz, *A Strange Stirring*, p. 68.

Notes to pages 176–80 211

29. D. McCloskey, 'Paid Work', in Zweiniger-Bargielowska (ed.), *Women in Twentieth Century Britain*, pp. 165–79, on pp.168–9.
30. *Woman's Own*, 10 October 1970, pp. 59–65.
31. Ibid., p. 59.
32. Ibid., p. 70.
33. *Woman's Own*, 8 April 1969.
34. See for example, *Woman*, 22 March 1969.
35. Statistics taken from the Office for National Statistics, 'Employment Rates by Sex', Social trends 34, Data set ST340409.
36. *Daily Mail*, Wednesday 2 November 2005.
37. Ibid.
38. See 'The stay-at-home mum debate', *Daily Mail*, 4 November 2005.
39. *Daily Mail*, Friday 1 December 2005.
40. J. Tooley, *The Miseducation of Women* (Chicago, IL: Ivan R Dee, 2002).
41. Daphne De Marneffe, *Maternal Desire: On Children, Love and the Inner Life* (New York: Little, Brown and Co, 2004).
42. Definitions of the term 'postfeminism' vary considerably; however, it is associated with a group of theorists in Britain and the United States that include: Naomi Wolf, Katie Roiphe, Rene Denfela and Natasha Walter. These women argue that feminism in its present form is inadequate for addressing the concerns of modern women.
43. *The Observer*, 26 March 2006.
44. 'Selfish or Selfless?' *Daily Mail*, 30 March 2006.
45. Ibid.
46. O. James, *Affluenza* (London: Vermilion, 2007).
47. A. Clare, *On Men: Masculinity in Crisis* (London: Arrow, paperback edition 2001), p. 3.
48. James, *Affluenza*, p. xiii.

WORKS CITED

Primary Sources

Oral Histories

Oral and written testimonies of the thirty-five women who were recruited from the National Women's Register. Interviews took place between September 2003 and May 2005. For the biographical details of all respondents, see Appendix.

Archival Sources

National Housewives' Register Archive (Women's Library)

Letters, file reference: 5/NHR/5/3.

Magazine articles, file reference: 5/NWR/4/3.

Members contacts, file reference: 5/NWR/4/1/12.

Press cuttings, file reference: 5/NWR/4/2/2.

Survey reports, file reference: 5/NHR/1/16.

Mass Observation Archive (University of Sussex)

File Report 1151, 'The Demand for Day Nurseries', March 1942.

File Report 1453, 'Women's Opinions', October 1942.

File Report 1592, Women's Opinions', February 1943.

File Report 1616, 'Some Psychological Factors in Home-Building: What Does Home Mean to You?', March 1943.

File Report 1889, 'What the Consumer Thinks of Self-Medication', August 1943.

File Report 2019, 'Public Attitudes to Advertising', February 1944.

File Report 2015, 'Why People Marry', February 1944.

File Report 2059, 'Do the Factory Girls Want to Stay Put or Go Home?', March 1944.

File Report 2117, 'Women at Work: Attitudes to Post-War Employment', June 1944.

File Report 2495, 'State of Matrimony', June 1947.

Bulletin New Series 18, 'Domestic Male', June 1948.

– 213 –

File Report 3017, 'Employment of Women: Women's Views on Employment', July 1948.

File Report 3108, 'Chemist Shops', April 1949.

File Report 3151, 'Meet Yourself at the Doctors', August 1949.

File Report 3150, 'Teenage Girls', August 1949.

File Report 3161, 'The London middle-class housewife and Her Housekeeping Expenditure', September 1949.

Bulletin New Series 38, 'Friends and Families', October 1950.

Bulletin New Series 42, 'The Housewife's Day', June 1951.

Bulletin New Series 44, 'Babies and Children', March 1952.

New Series 48, 'National Health', February 1953.

Bulletin New Series 54, 'The Housewife's Day', June 1957.

Women's magazines

Woman

Woman's Own

Woman's Realm

Woman's Weekly

Printed Primary Sources and Film

'A Retrospective Study of Psychotropic Drug Prescribing by a Group of Midland general Practitioners', *Journal of the College of General Practitioners*, 21, Supplement 4 (1971), pp. 11–53.

Abrahams, M. J., and F. A. Whitlock, 'Childhood Experience and Depression', *BJP*, 115 (1969), pp. 883–8.

Abrams, M., 'The Home-Centred Society', *Listener*, 26 November 1959.

Abramson, J. H., 'The Cornell Medical Index as an Epidemiological Tool', *American Journal of Public Health, Nation's Health*, 56 (1966), pp. 287–98.

'Abuse of Barbiturates', *BMJ*, 25 December 1954, p.1534.

Alexander, F., *Psychosomatic Medicine: Its Principles and Applications* (New York: W.W. Norton and Co., 1950).

American Beauty, Sam Mendes, Dreamworks (1999).

Appleton, W. S., and C. Chien, 'American Psychopharmacology: Second Class Status?', *BJP*, 113 (1967), pp. 637–41.

Balint, M., *The Doctor, His Patient and the Illness* (London: Pitman Medical, 1957).

Beveridge, W., *Social Insurance and Allied Services* (London: HMSO, 1942).

Beyfus, D., *The English Marriage* (Harmondsworth: Penguin, 1971 [1968]).

Bowlby, J., *Maternal Care and Mental Health* (Geneva: World Health Organization, 1952 [1951]).

—, *Child Care and the Growth of Love* (Middlesex: Pelican, 1963 [1953]).

—, *Attachment and Loss; Volume 1, Attachment* (London: Hogarth, 1969).

—, *Attachment and Loss; Volume 2, Separation Anxiety and Anger* (London: Hogarth, 1973).

Bovet, T., *A Handbook to Marriage and Marriage Guidance* (London: Longmans Green and Co., Ltd, 1958).

Brayshaw, A. J., *The Stability of Marriage* (London: The National Marriage Guidance Council, 1952).

Brown, G. W., and T. Harris, *Social Origins of Depression: A Study of Psychiatric Disorder in Women*, paperback edn (London: Tavistock Publications, 1979).

Buck, C. W., and K. L. Ladd, 'Psychoneurosis in Marital Partners', *BJP*, 111 (1965), pp. 587–90.

Caplow, T. H., M. Bahr, B. A. Chadwick, R. Hill, and M. Holmes Williamson, *Middletown Families: Fifty Years of Change and Continuity* (Minneapolis, MN: University of Minnesota Press, 1982).

Cannon, W., *Bodily Changes in Pain, Hunger, Fear and Rage* (New York: D Appleton and Co., 1920).

—, *The Wisdom of the Body* (New York: WW Norton and Co., 1939).

Carstairs, G. M., *This Island Now: The 1962 Reith Lectures* (Middlesex: Penguin, 1963).

Chacon, C., and E. T. Downham, 'Amitriptyline and Amitriptyline-with-Perphenazine in Depression – a Retrospective Study', *BJP*, 113 (1967), pp. 201–7.

Chesler, P., *Women and Madness* (London: Allen Lane, 1974).

Chodorow, N., *The Reproduction of Mothering* (London: The University of California Press, 1999 [1978]).

Conference report, 'Depression in General Practice', *BMJ*, 30 October 1965, pp. 1052–3.

Cooper, B., and A. C. Brown, 'Psychiatric Practice in Great Britain and America: A Comparative Study', *BJP*, 113 (1967), pp. 625–36.

Cooper, D., *The Death of the Family* (London: Allen Lane, 1971).

Cooperstock, R., 'Sex Differences in Psychotropic Drug Use', *Social Science and Medicine*, 12B (1978), pp. 179–86.

—, *The Effects of Tranquilization: Benzodiazepine Use in Canada* (Minister of National Health and Welfare, 1982).

Cooperstock, R., and H. L. Lennard, 'Some Social Meanings of Tranquilizer Use', *Sociology of Health and Illness*, 1 (1979), pp. 331–47.

Coppen, A., 'The Biochemistry of Affective Disorders', *BJP*, 113 (1967), pp. 1237–64.

Costello, C. G., and M. M. Selby 'The Relationship between Sleep Patterns and Reactive and Endogenous Depressions', *BJP*, 111 (1965), pp. 497–501.

Dally, P. J., and P. Rohde, 'Comparison of Antidepressant Drugs in Depressive Illness', *Lancet*, 7 January 1961, pp. 18–20.

Dally, A., *Mothers: Their Power and Their Influence* (London: Weidenfeld and Nicolson, 1975).

Denning, A., *The Equality of Women* (Liverpool: Liverpool University Press, 1960).

'Drugs for Anxiety', *BMJ*, 6 January 1962, pp. 38–9.

Dunnell, K., and A. Cartwright, *The Medicine Takers: Prescribers and Hoarders* (London: Routledge and Kegan Paul, 1972).

Eysenck, H. J,. 'Behaviour Therapy, Extinction and Relapse in Neurosis', *BJP*, 109 (1963), pp. 12–18.

Eysenck, H. J,. and S. B. G. Eysenck, *The Personality Questionnaire* (London: Hodder and Stoughton 1975).

Far From Heaven, Todd Haines, Focus Features (2002).

Firestone, S., *The Dialectic of Sex: The Case for Feminist Revolution* (London: Jonathan Cape, 1971).

Flanders Dunbar, H., *Synopsis of Psychosomatic Diagnosis and Treatment* (St Louis, MO: C.V. Mosby Co., 1948).

Fletcher, R., *The Family and Marriage in Britain* (London: Penguin, 1962).

Forrest, A. D., R. H. Fraser and R. G. Priest, 'Environmental Factors in Depressive Illness', *BJP*, 111 (1965), pp. 243–53.

French, M., *The Women's Room* (London: Virago, 2006 [1977]).

Foucault, M., *Madness and Civilization* (London: Routledge, 2006 [1961]).

Friedan, B., *The Feminine Mystique* (London: Penguin, [1963] 1992).

Gavron, H., *The Captive Wife* (London: Routledge and Kegan Paul, 1966).

Gilman, C. P., *The Yellow Wallpaper* (New York: The Feminist Press, [1892] 1996).

Goulds, G. A., and C. Hassall, 'The Significance of Age of Onset of Excessive Drinking in Male Alcoholics', *BJP*, 115 (1969), pp. 1027–32.

Gove, W. R., 'Societal Reaction as an Explanation of Mental Illness: An Evaluation', *American Sociological Review*, 35 (1970), pp. 873–84.

—, 'The Relationship between Sex Roles, Marital Status and Mental Illness', *Social Forces*, 51 (1972), pp. 34–44.

— (ed.), *The Labelling of Deviance: Evaluating a Perspective* (Beverly Hills, CA and London: Sage, 1980).

— (ed.), *Deviance and Mental Illness* (Beverly Hills, CA and London: Sage, 1982).

—, 'Mental Illness and Psychiatric Treatment among Women', in M. R. Walsh (ed.), *The Psychology of Women: Ongoing Debates* (New Haven, CT: Yale University Press, 1987), pp. 102–18.

Gove, W. R., and J. F. Tudor, 'Adult Sex Roles and Mental Illness', *The American Journal of Sociology*, 78 (1973), pp. 812–35.

Grant, D., *Feeding the Family in Wartime* (London: G. G. Harrap and Co., 1942).

—, *Your Daily Bread* (London: Faber and Faber, 1944).

Greer, G., *The Female Eunuch* (London: Flamingo, 1999 [1970]).

Halliday, J. L., *Psychosocial Medicine: A Study of the Sick Society* (London: William Heinemann, 1948).

Hamilton, M., 'A Rating Scale for Depression', *Journal of Neurology, Neurosurgery and Psychiatry*, 23 (1960), pp. 56–62.

Hare, E. H., J. Dominian and L. Sharpe, 'Phenelzine and Dexamphetamine in Depressive Illness', *BMJ*, 6 January 1962, pp. 9–12.

Hare, E. H., and G. K. Shaw, *Mental Health on a New Housing Estate: A Comparative Study of Health in Two Districts of Croydon* (London: Oxford University Press, 1965).

Howarth, E., 'Headache, Personality and Stress', *BJP*, 111 (1965), pp. 1193–7.

Hooper, D., and J. Roberts, *Education Today: Disordered Lives, an Interpersonal Account* (London: Longmans, 1967).

Hubback, J., *Wives Who Went to College* (London: William Heinemann, 1957).

Johnson, M., 'Mental Illness and Psychiatric Treatment among Women: A Response', in M. R. Walsh (ed.), *The Psychology of Women: Ongoing Debates* (New Haven, CT: Yale University Press, 1987), pp. 119–26.

Kelly. D., and C. J. S. Walter, 'A Clinical and Physiological Relationship between Anxiety and Depression', *BJP*, 115 (1969), pp. 401–6.

Kessel, N., and M. Shepherd, 'Neurosis in Hospital and General Practice', *Journal of Mental Science*, 108 (1962), pp. 156–66.

Kirk, K., *Marriage and Divorce* (London: Hodder and Stoughton, 1948).

Klein, V., *Britain's Married Women Workers* (London: Routledge and Kegan Paul, 1965).

Kreitman, N., 'Married Couples Admitted to Mental Hospital', *BJP*, 114 (1968), pp. 699–718.

Laing, R. D., *The Politics of the Family and Other Essays* (London: Tavistock Publications, 1971).

Langley, G., 'Patients' Attitudes to Neurosis', *BJP*, 109 (1963), pp. 782–4.

Lessing, D., *The Golden Notebook* (New York: Harper Perennial, 1999 [1962]).

Little Children, Todd Field, New Line Cinema (2006).

Lynd, R. S., and H. M. Lynd, *Middletown: A Study in American Culture* (New York: Harcourt Brace, 1956 [1929]).

—, *Middletown in Transition* (New York: Harcourt Brace, 1937).

Lyon, H., *Happy Ever After?* (London: The National Marriage Guidance Council, 1950).

Macaulay, M., *The Art of Marriage* (London: Delisle Ltd, 1956).

Marcuse, H., *One-Dimensional Man* (Abingdon: Routledge Classics, 2002 [1964]).

McCance, C., and P. T. McCance, 'Alcoholism in North east Scotland: Its Treatment and Outcome', *BJP*, 115 (1969), pp. 189–98.

McDonaghy, N., A. D. Joffe and B. Murphy, 'The Independence of Neurotic and Endogenous Depression', *BJP*, 113 (1967), pp. 479–84.

McGregor, O. R., *Divorce in England: A Centenary Study* (London: William Heinemann, 1957).

Meyer, V., and M. G. Gelder, 'Behaviour Therapy and Phobic Disorder', *BJP*, 109 (1963), pp. 19–28.

Miller, H., 'Depression', *BMJ*, 4 February 1967, pp. 257–62.

Millum, T., *Images of Woman: Advertising in Women's Magazines* (London: Chatto Windus, 1975).

Morrison, J. R., R. W. Hudgens and R. G. Barchha, 'Life Events and Psychiatric Illness: A Study of 100 Patients and Controls', *BJP*, 114 (1968), pp. 423–32.

Mortimer, P., *The Pumpkin Eater* (London: Bloomsbury, 1995 [1962]).

Munro, A., 'Some Familial and Social Factors in Depressive Illness', *BJP*, 112 (1966), pp. 429–4.

Myrdal, A., and V. Klein, *Women's Two Roles: Home and Work* (London: Routledge and Kegan Paul, 1956).

The National Marriage Guidance Council, *Sex Difficulties in the Wife* (London: 1958).

The National Marriage Guidance Council, *A Home of Your Own* (London: 1963).

Oakley, A., *Sex, Gender and Society* (Aldershot: Gower, 1989 [1972]).

—, *The Sociology of Housework* (London: Martin Robertson, 1974).

—, *Woman's Work: The Housewife Past and Present* (London: Penguin, 1974).

—, *From Here to Eternity: Becoming a Mother* (Oxford: Martin Robertson, 1979).

O'Brien, John, A., *Happy Marriage: Guidance Before and After* (London: WH Allen, 1956).

Office for National Statistics, *Psychiatric Morbidity among Adults Living in Private Households* (2000).

Orwell, G., *Coming up for Air* (1939), in *The Complete Novels* (London: Penguin, 2000).

Packard, V., *The Hidden Persuaders* (New York: David McKay, 1957).

Parker, N., 'Close Identification in Twins Discordant for Obsessional Behaviour', *BJP*, 110 (1964), pp. 496–504.

Pincus, L., (ed.), *Marriage; Studies in Emotional Conflict and Growth* (London: Methuen, 1960).

Pitts, F. N., and G. Winokur, 'Affective Disorder: VII. Alcoholism and Affective Disorder', *Journal of Psychiatric Research*, 4 (1966), pp. 37–50.

Pollitt, J., *Depression and Its Treatment* (London: William Heinemann Medical Books, 1965).

—, 'Suggestions for a Physiological Classification of Depression', *BJP*, 111 (1965), pp. 489–95.

Pond, D. A., A. Ryle and M. Hamilton, 'Marriage and Neurosis in a Working-Class Population', *BJP*, 109 (1963), pp. 592–8.

'Psychological Medicine in General Practice', *British Medical Journal*, 6 September 1958, pp. 585–90.

Reed, A., *The First Five Years of Marriage* (London: The National Marriage Guidance Council, 1963).

Revolutionary Road, Sam Mendes, Dreamworks/BBC (2008).

Reynolds, M., 'Little Boxes' (1962).

Riesman, D., N. Glazer, and R. Denney, *The Lonely Crowd: A Study of the Changing American Character* (New Haven, CT: Yale University Press, [1950], 2001).

Roberts, A. H., 'Housebound Housewives – a Follow-up Study of a Phobic Anxiety State', *BJP*, 110 (1964), pp. 191–7.

Rolling Stones, 'Mother's Little Helper' (1966).

Ryle, A., *Neurosis in the Ordinary Family: A Psychiatric Survey* (London: Tavistock, 1967).

—, 'A Marital Patterns Test for Use in Psychiatric Research', *BJP*, 112 (1966), pp. 285–93.

—, 'The Whirligig of Time', *Psychiatric Bulletin* (1998), 22, pp. 263–7.

Ryle, A., and M. Hamilton, 'Neurosis in Fifty Married Couples', *Journal of Mental Science*, 108 (1962), pp. 265–73.

Rutter, M., *Maternal Deprivation Reassessed* (Baltimore: Penguin, 1972).

—, 'Maternal Deprivation, 1972–1978, New Findings, New Concepts, New Approaches', *Child Development*, 50 (1979), pp. 283–385.

Sargant, W., 'Drugs in the Treatment of Depression', *BMJ*, 28 January 1961, pp. 225–7.

Sargant, W., and P. Dally, 'Treatment of Anxiety States by Antidepressant Drugs', *BMJ*, 6 January 1962, pp. 6–8.

Scheff, T., *Being Mentally Ill: A Sociological Theory* (London: Weidenfeld and Nicolson, 1966).

Selye, H., *The Stress of Life* (New York: McGraw-Hill, 1956).

—, *Stress in Health and Disease* (Boston, MA: Butterworths, 1976).

'Shadow over the Barbiturates', *Lancet*, 10 July 1954, p. 75.

Shepherd, M., 'Research in the Field of Psychiatry', *BMJ*, 18 October 1969, pp. 161–3.

Slater, E., and M. Woodside, *Patterns of Marriage: a Study of Marriage Relationships in the Urban Working Classes* (London: Cassell and Company Ltd, 1951).

—, *Psychotic and Neurotic Illness in Twins* (London: HMSO, 1953).

Smallshaw, K., *How to Run Your Home without Help* (London: John Lehmann, 1949).

Smith, C. G., 'Alcoholics, Their Treatment and Their Wives', *BJP*, 115 (1969), pp. 1039–42.

'Some Influences on Drug Prescribing', *Journal of the College of General Practitioners*, 21, Supplement 4 (1971), pp. 54–67.

Somerville, G., *Newnes Family Health Encyclopaedia* (London: George Newnes, 1969).

Spock, B., *Baby and Child Care* (London: Bodley Head, 1973 [1955]).

The Stepford Wives, Bryan Forbes, Palomar Pictures (1975).

Stimson, G., 'Women in a Doctored World', *New Society*, 1 May 1975, pp. 265–7.

Szasz, T., *The Myth of Mental Illness* (New York: Harper and Row, 1961).

Taylor, S., 'Suburban Neurosis', *Lancet*, 26 March 1938, pp. 759–61.

Thompson, B., and A. Finlayson, 'Married Women Who Work in Early Motherhood', *British Journal of Sociology*, 14 (1963), pp. 150–68.

'Today's Drugs: Hypnotics – Barbiturates', *BMJ*, 5 January 1963, pp. 39–40.

Today's Drugs: Drugs for Depression, Panel Discussion', *BMJ*, 28 September 1963, pp. 799–802.

'Today's Drugs: Benzodiazepines', *BMJ*, 1 April 1967, p.36.

Today's Drugs (London: British Medical Association, 1964).

Today's Drugs (London: British Medical Association, 1970).

'Tranquilizers in Psychiatry', *Lancet*, 15 October 1960, pp. 855–6.

'Treatment of Depression', *BMJ*, 3 April 1965, pp. 878–9.

Vaughn, C E., and J. P. Leff, 'The Influence of Family and Social Factors on the Course of Psychiatric Illness', *British Journal of Psychiatry*, 129 (1976), pp. 125–37.

Walis, J H., *Someone to Turn to: A Description of the Remedial Work of the National Marriage Guidance Council* (London: Routledge, 1964 [1961]).

Walker, K., *Marriage, Sex and Happiness: A Frank and Practical Guide to Harmony and Satisfaction in Conjugal Life* (London: Odhams Books, 1963).

Watts, C. A. H., *Psychiatry in General Practice* (London: J and A Churchill, 1952).

—, *Depressive Disorders in the Community* (Bristol: John Wright, 1966).

Weeks, C., *Self Help for Your Nerves* (London: Angus and Robertson Ltd, 1963).

West, E., and P. J. Dally, 'Effects of Iproniazid in Depressive Syndromes', *BMJ*, 13 June 1959, pp. 1491–4.

White, C., *Women's Magazines 1693–1968* (London: Michael Joseph, 1970).

—, *The Women's Periodical Press in Britain 1946–1976: The Royal Commission on the Press* (London: HMSO, 1977).

Whyte, W. H., *The Organization Man* (New York: Doubleday Anchor, 1956).

Willmott, P., and M. Young, *Family and Class in a London Suburb* (London: New English Library, 1976 [1960]).

Wilson, S., *The Man in the Gray Flannel Suit* (London: Penguin Classics, 2005 [1955]).

Winnicott, D. W., *The Child and the Family: First Relationships* (London: Tavistock Publications, 1957).

—, *The Family and Individual Development* (London: Tavistock Publications, 1965).

Winokur G., and P. Clayton, 'Sex Differences and Alcoholism in Primary Affective Illness', *BJP*, 113 (1967), pp. 973–89.

Wolpe, J., 'Behaviour Therapy in Complex Neurotic States', *BJP*, 110 (1964), pp. 28–32.

Woodcock, J., 'Long-Term Consumers of Psychotropic Drugs', in M. Balint, J. Hunt, D. Joyce, M. Marinker and J. Woodcock, *Treatment or Diagnosis: a Study of Repeat Prescriptions in General Practice* (London: Tavistock Publications, 1984 [1970]), pp. 147–76.

Young, M., and P. Willmott, *Family and Kinship in East London* (Harmondsworth: Penguin, 1990 [1957]).

Yudkin, S., and A. Holme, *Working Mothers and Their Children* (London: Michael Joseph, 1963).

Secondary Sources

Abbott, M., *Family Affairs: A History of the Family in 20th Century England* (London: Routledge, 2003).

Albion, M. S., and P. W. Farris, *The Advertising Controversy: Evidence on the Economic Effects of Advertising* (Boston, MA: Auburn House, 1981).

Allen, G., and G. Crow, (eds), *Home and Family: Creating the Domestic Sphere* (Basingstoke: MacMillan, 1989).

Anderson, S., (ed.), *Making Medicines: A Brief History of Pharmacy and Pharmaceuticals* (London: The Pharmaceutical Press, 2005).

— 'From Bespoke to off-the-Peg: Community Pharmacists and the Retailing of Medicines in Great Britain 1900 to 1970', in L. Curth (ed.), *Physick to Pharmacology: Consumption and Retailing of Medicinal Drugs in England* (London: Ashgate, 2006), pp. 105–42.

Angel, K., E. Jones, and M. Neve, (eds), *European Psychiatry on the Eve of War: Aubrey Lewis, the Maudsley Hospital and the Rockefeller Foundation in the 1930s* (London: The Wellcome Trust Centre for the History of Medicine at UCL, 2003).

Angell, M., *The Truth about Drug Companies* (New York: Random House, 2004).

Appignanesi, L., *Mad, Bad and Sad; A History of Women and the Mind Doctors from 1800 to the Present* (London: Virago, 2008).

Armstrong, D., 'Madness and Coping', *Sociology of Health and Illness*, 2 (1980), pp. 293–316.

Bartrip, P., *Mirror of Medicine: A History of the British Medical Journal* (Oxford: BMJ and Clarendon Press, 1990).

Beaumont, C., 'The Women's Movement, Politics and Citizenship, 1918–1950s', in I. Zweiniger-Bargielowska (ed.), *Women in Twentieth Century Britain* (Harlow: Pearson, 2001), pp. 262–7.

Benison, S., 'Oral History – a Personal View', in E. Clarke (ed.), *Modern Methods in the History of Medicine* (London: Athlone Press, 1971), pp. 286–305.

Berrios, G. E., and H. Freeman, *150 Years of British Psychiatry: Volume 2, The Atermath* (London: Athlone, 1996).

222   *Desperate Housewives, Neuroses and the Domestic Environment, 1945–1970*

—, *The History of Mental Symptoms: Descriptive Psychopathology since the Nineteenth Century* (Cambridge: Cambridge University Press, 1997).

Borland, K., "'That's Not What I Said": Interpretive Conflict in Oral History Narratives', in S. Hesse-Biber and P. Leavy (eds), *Approaches to Qualitative Research: A Reader on Theory and Practice* (Oxford: Oxford University Press, 2003), pp. 522–34.

Bourke, J., *Fear: A Cultural History* (London: Virago, 2005).

Braybon, G., and P. Summerfield, *Out of the Cage: Women's Experience of the Two World Wars* (London: Pandora, 1987).

Brockington, I., *Motherhood and Mental Health* (New York: Oxford University Press, 1998).

—, 'Postpartum Psychiatric Disorders', *Lancet*, 363 (2004), pp. 303–10.

Busfield, J., *Managing Madness: Changing Ideas and Practice* (London: Hutchinson, 1986).

—, *Men Women and Madness: Understanding Gender and Mental Disorder* (Basingstoke: Palgrave MacMillan, 1996).

Bynum, W F., R. Porter, and M. Shepherd (eds), *The Anatomy of Madness; Essays in the History of Psychiatry Volume 1: People and Ideas* (London: Tavistock Publications, 1985).

Callahan, C., and G. E. Berrios, *Reinventing Depression: A History of the Treatment of Depression in Primary Care 1940–2004* (Oxford: Oxford University Press, 2005).

Callard, D., *The Case of Anna Kavan: A Biography* (London: Peter Owen, 1992).

Card, R., 'Aspects of British Drug Legislation', *University of Toronto Law Journal*, 20 (1970), pp. 88–104.

Chodorow, N., *The Reproduction of Mothering* (London: University of California Press, 1999 [1978]).

Clark, P., *Hope and Glory: Britain 1900–1990* (London: Penguin, 1997).

Coontz, S., *The Way We Never Were* (New York: Basic Books, 1992).

—, *Marriage, a History: From Obedience to Intimacy, or How Love Conquered Marriage* (New York: Viking, 2005).

—, *A Strange Stirring: The Feminine Mystique and American Women at the Dawn of the 1960s* (New York: Basic Books 2011).

Cooper, C. L., and P. Dewe, *Stress: A Brief History* (Oxford: Blackwell, 2004).

Crossley, N., *Contesting Psychiatry: Social Movements in Mental Health* (London: Routledge, 2005).

Curtis, H., and M. Sanderson, *The Unsung Sixties: Memoirs of Social Innovation* (London: Whiting and Birch, 2004).

Dain, N., 'Critics and Dissenters: Reflections on Anti-Psychiatry in the US', *Journal of the History of the Behavioural Sciences*, 25 (1989), pp. 2–25.

Dally, A., *Understanding: Coming to Terms with Moments of Inadequacy – Neurosis, Isolation, Depression, Masochism, Frustration* (New York: Stein and Day, 1979).

—, *Inventing Motherhood* (London: Burnett Books, 1982).

Darke, J., 'Women and the Meaning of Home', in R. Gilroy and R. Woods (eds), *Housing Women* (London: Routledge,1994), pp. 11–30.

Davidson, C., *A Woman's Work Is Never Done: A History of Housework in the British Isles, 1650–1950* (London: Chatto and Windus, 1982).

De Marneffe, D., *Maternal Desire: on Children, Love and the Inner Life* (New York: Little, Brown and Co, 2004).

Dicks, H. V., *Fifty Years of the Tavistock Clinic* (London: Routledge and Kegan Paul, 1970).

Easterlin, R., *Birth and Fortune: The Impact of Numbers on Personal Welfare* (London: Grant Mcintyre, 1980).

Ehrenreich, B., and D. English, *For Her Own Good: 150 Years of Experts Advice to Women* (London: Pluto, 1979).

Ettorre, E., and E. Riska, *Gendered Moods: Psychotropics and Society* (London: Routledge, 1995).

Francis, M., 'Leisure and Popular Culture', in I. Zweiniger-Bargielowska, *Women in Twentieth-Century Britain* (Harlow: Pearson, 2001), pp. 229–43.

Freeman, Hugh L., *Mental Health and the Environment* (London: Churchill Livingstone, 1984).

Garfield, S., *Our Hidden Lives: The Everyday Diaries of Forgotten Britain 1945–1948* (London: Ebury Press, 2004).

Gijswijt-Hofstra, M., and R. Porter (eds), *Cultures of Psychiatry and Mental Health Care in Britain and the Netherlands* (Amsterdam: Editions Rodopi B.V, 1998).

—, H. Oosterhuis, J. Vijselaar, and H. Freeman (eds), *Psychiatric Cultures Compared: Psychiatry and Mental Health Care in the Twentieth Century: Comparisons and Approaches* (Amsterdam: Amsterdam University Press, 2005).

Giles, J., *Women, Identity and Private Life in Britain 1900–50* (Basingstoke: Macmillan, 1995).

—, *The Parlour and the Suburb: Domestic Identities, Class, Femininity and Modernity* (Oxford: Berg, 2004).

Gill, J., *Anne Sexton's Confessional Poetics* (Gainesville, FL: University Press of Florida, 2007).

—, 'Anne Sexton's Poetics of the Suburbs', in M. Jackson (ed.), *Health and the Modern Home* (New York: Routledge, 2007), pp. 63–83.

Gillis, J. R., *For Better for Worse: British Marriages 1600 to the Present* (Oxford: Oxford University Press, 1985).

—, *A World of Their Own Making: Myth, Ritual and the Quest for Family Values* (New York: Basic Books, 1996).

Gittins, D., *Madness in Its Place* (London: Routledge, 1998).

Glendinning, V., *Elizabeth Bowen* (New York: Avon, 1977).

Gluck, S. B., and D. Patai (eds), *Women's Words: The Feminist Practice of Oral History* (London: Routledge, 1991).

Gordon, P., and D. Doughan, *Dictionary of British Organisations 1825–1969* (London: Woburn Press, 2001).

Graham, H., *Hardship and Health in Women's Lives* (New York and London: Harvester Wheatsheaf, 1993).

Hardyment, C., *Dream Babies, Childcare from Locke to Spock* (London: Jonathan Cape, 1983).

Hays, S., *The Cultural Contradictions of Motherhood* (London and New Haven, CT: Yale University Press, 1996).

Hayward, R., 'Desperate Housewives and Model Amoebae: The Invention of Suburban Neurosis in Inter-War Britain', in M. Jackson (ed.), *Health and the Modern Home* (New York: Routledge, 2007), pp. 42–62.

Healy, D., *Psychiatric Drugs Explained* (London: Churchill Livingstone, 1997).

—, *The Anti-Depressant Era* (Cambridge, MA: Harvard University Press, 1999).

—, *The Creation of Psychopharmacology* (Cambridge, MA: Harvard University Press, 2002).

Hermes, J., *Reading Women's Magazines* (Cambridge: Polity, 1997).

Holdsworth, A., *Out of the Doll's House: The Story of Women in the Twentieth Century* (London: BBC, 1988).

Holmes, J., *John Bowlby and Attachment Theory* (London: Routledge, 1993).

Homan, P., 'Medicated Cheer', *Pharmaceutical Journal*, 271 (2003), pp. 867–8.

Horowitz, D., *Betty Friedan and the Making of the Feminine Mystique: The American Left, the Cold War and Modern Feminism* (Amherst, MA: University of Massachusetts Press, 2000).

Howlett, P., '"The Golden Age", 1955–1973', in P. Johnson (ed.), *Twentieth Century Britain: Economic, Social and Cultural Change* (London: Longman, 1994), pp. 320–39.

Jackson, M., 'In Search of Stability: Hans Selye and the Biology of Stress', *Wellcome History*, 3 (2006), pp. 1–4.

—, '"Home Sweet Home": Historical Perspectives on Health and Home', in Mark Jackson (ed.), *Health and the Modern Home* (New York: Routledge, 2007), pp. 1–17.

James, O., *Affluenza* (London: Vermilion, 2007).

Jerman, B., *The Lively-Minded Women: The First Twenty Years of the National Housewives' Register* (London: Heinemann, 1981).

Johnson, L., and J. J. Lloyd, *Sentenced to Everyday Life: Feminism and the Housewife* (Oxford: Berg, 2004).

Jones, H., *Health and Society in Twentieth Century Britain* (London: Longman 1994).

Jones K., *A History of Mental Health Services* (London: Routledge and Kegan Paul, 1972).

Jordanova, L., 'Mental Illness, mental Health: Changing Norms and Expectations', in Cambridge Women's Study Group, *Women in Society: Interdisciplinary Essays* (London: Virago, 1981), pp. 95–114.

—, *Sexual Visions: Images of Gender in Science and Medicine between the Eighteenth and Twentieth Centuries* (Hemel Hempstead: Harvester Wheatsheaf, 1989).

Works Cited

Karpf, A., *Doctoring the Media* (London: Routledge, 1988).

Koumjian, K., 'The Use of Valium as a Form of Social Control', *Social Science and Medicine*, 15E (1981), pp. 245–49.

Lader, M., 'History of Benzodiazepine Dependence', *Journal of Substance Abuse Treatment*, 8 (1991), pp. 53–9.

Leese, P., *Shell Shock: Traumatic Neurosis and the British Soldiers of the First World War* (Basingstoke: Palgrave Macmillan, 2002).

Lewis, J., *Women in Britain since 1945* (Oxford: Blackwell, 1992).

—, 'Gender and Welfare in the Late Nineteenth and Early Twentieth Centuries', in A. Digby, and J. Stewart (eds), *Gender Health and Welfare* (London and New York: Routledge, 1996), pp. 208–28.

—, *The End of Marriage? Individualism and Intimate Relations* (Cheltenham, Edward Elgar, 2001).

Lewis, J., D. Clark and D. Morgan, *Whom God Hath Joined Together: The Work of Marriage Guidance* (London: Routledge, 1992).

Lickey, M. E, and B. Gordon, *Medicine and Mental Illness: The Use of Drugs in Psychiatry* (New York: WH Freeman, 1991).

Liebenau, J., *Medical Science and Medical Industry: The Formation of the American Pharmaceutical Industry* (London: MacMillan Press, 1987).

—, 'The Rise of the British Pharmaceutical Industry', *British Medical Journal*, 3 October 1990, pp. 724–8.

Loudermilk, K. A., *Fictional Feminism: How American Bestsellers Affect the Movement for Women's Equality* (New York: Routledge, 2004).

Ludwig, A. M., *The Price of Greatness* (New York: The Guilford Press, 1995).

MacLaren, A., *Twentieth Century Sexuality* (Oxford: Blackwell, 1999).

Madigan, R., M. Munro, and S. J. Smith, 'Gender and the Meaning of Home', *Journal of Urban and Regional Research*, 14 (1990), pp. 625–47.

Maier, T., *Dr Spock, an American Life* (New York: London, Harcourt Brace, 1998).

Marinoff, L., *Plato Not Prozac* (New York: Harper Collins, 1999).

Martin, L. W., *Silvia Plath: A Literary Life* (Basingstoke: Palgrave MacMillan, 2003).

McCloskey, D., 'Paid Work', in I. Zweiniger-Bargielowska (ed.), *Women in Twentieth-Century Britain* (Harlo: Essex, Pearson, 2001), pp. 59–65.

Melville, A., and C. Johnson, *Cured to Death: The Effects of Prescription Drugs* (Seven Oaks: New English Library, 1983).

Metzl, J., *Prozac on the Couch: Prescribing Gender in the Era of Wonder Drugs* (Durham, NC: Duke University Press, 2003).

—, '"Mother's Little Helper': The Crisis of Psychoanalysis and the Miltown Resolution', *Gender and History* 15 (2003), pp. 240–67.

Meyerowitz, J., 'Beyond the feminine mystique: a reassessment of post-war mass culture', in J. Meyerowitz (ed.), *Not June Cleaver: Women and Gender in Post-War America, 1945–1960* (Philadelphia, PA: Temple University Press, 1994).

Micale, M. S., *Approaching Hysteria: Disease and Its Interpretations* (Princeton, NJ: Princeton University Press, 1995).

—, *Hysterical Men: The Hidden History of Male Nervous Illness* (Cambridge, MA: Harvard University Press, 2008).

Micale, M. S., and R. Porter (eds), *Discovering the History of Psychiatry* (Oxford: Oxford University Press, 1994).

Middlebrook, D. W., *Anne Sexton: A Biography* (Boston, MA: Houghton Mifflin, 1991).

Miles, A., *Women and Mental Illness* (Brighton: Wheatsheaf, 1988).

Millar, E., 'Twentieth Century British Clinical Psychology and Psychiatry', in H. Freeman and G. E. Berrios, *150 Years of British Psychiatry, Vol. II: The Aftermath* (London: Athlone, 1996), pp. 156–68.

Millum, T., *Images of Woman: Advertising in Women's Magazines* (London: Chatto and Windus, 1975).

Mortimer, P., *About Time* (Harmondsworth: Penguin, reprint 1981).

—, *About Time Too*, paperback edn (London: Phoenix, 1994).

Mullen, B., *R D Laing: A Personal View* (London: Gerald Duckworth 1999).

Niven, C., and D. Carroll, *The Health Psychology of Women* (Switzerland: Harwood, 1993).

Oakley, Ann, *Man and Wife: Richard and Kay Titmuss: My Parents' Early Years* (London: Harper Collins, 1996).

—, *Gender on Planet Earth* (Cambridge: Polity Press, 2002).

Oppenheim, J., *Shattered Nerves: Doctors, Patients and Depression in Victorian England* (Oxford: Oxford University Press, 1991).

Orbach, S., *Fat Is a Feminist Issue* (New York and London: Paddington Press, 1978).

O'Shaughnessy, J., and N. J. O'Shaughnessy, *Persuasion in Advertising* (London: Routeledge, 2004).

Ott, K., *Fevered Lives: Tuberculosis in American Culture since 1870* (Cambridge, MA: Harvard University Press, 1996).

Parfrey, A., *It's a Man's World: Men's Adventure Magazines – the Post-War Pulps* (Los Angeles, CA: Feral House, 2003).

Parry-Jones, B., 'Historical Terminology of Eating Disorders', *Psychological Medicine*, 21 (1991), pp. 21–8.

—, 'History of Bulimia and Bulimia Nervosa', in K. D. Brownell and C. G. Fairburn, *Eating Disorders and Obesity* (New York: Guildford, 1995), pp. 145–50.

Phillips, R., *Putting Asunder* (Cambridge: Cambridge University Press, 1988).

Works Cited

Popay, J., '"My Health Is Alright but I'm Just Tired All the Time": Women's Experience of Ill-Health', in H. Roberts (ed.), *Women's Health Matters* (London: Routledge, 1991), pp. 98–120.

Pope, D., *The Making of Modern Advertising* (New York: Basic Books, 1983).

Porter, R., *A Social History of Madness* (London: Weidenfeld and Nicholson, 1987).

—, *Mind-Forg'd Manacles: A History of Madness in England from the Restoration to the Regency* (London: Athlone, 1987).

—, 'Diseases of Civilization', in W. F. Bynum and R. Porter (eds), *Companion Encyclopaedia of the History of Medicine* (London: Routledge, 1992), pp. 585–600.

—, *The Greatest Benefit to Mankind: A Medical History of Humanity From Antiquity to the Present* (London: Fontana, 1999).

—, *Madness: A Brief History* (Oxford: Oxford University Press, 2002).

—, *Madmen: A Social History of Madhouses, Mad Doctors and Lunatics*, 3rd edn (Stroud: Tempus, 2006).

Porter, R., and D. Wright (eds), *The Confinement of the Insane: International Perspectives* (Cambridge: Cambridge University Press, 2003).

Pratkanis, A., and E. Elliot, *Age of Propaganda: the Everyday Use and Abuse of Persuasion* (New York: WH Freeman, 1992).

Pugh, M., *State and Society: A Social and Political History of Britain 1870–1997* (London: Arnold, 1999).

—, *Women and the Women's Movement in Britain 1914–1999*, 2nd edn (Basingstoke: Macmillan, 2000).

Rasmussen, N., *On Speed: the Many Lives of Amphetamine* (New York: New York University Press, 2008).

Reed, J., *A Stranger on Earth: The Life and Work of Anna Kavan* (London: Peter Owen, 2006).

Riley, D., '"The Free Mothers": Pronatalism and Working Women in Industry at the End of the Last War', *History Workshop Journal*, 11 (1981), pp. 59–118.

—, *War in the Nursery: Theories of the Child and the Mother* (London: Virago, 1983).

Rivet, G., *From Cradle to Grave: Fifty Years of the NHS* (London: King's Fund, 1997).

Roberts, E., *Women and Families: An Oral History 1940–1970* (Oxford; Blackwell, 1995).

Rose, N., *Governing the Soul: The Shaping of the Private Self* (London: Routledge, 1990).

—, *Inventing Our Selves: Psychology, Power and Personhood* (Cambridge: Cambridge University Press, 1998).

Rosenberg, C. E., 'Pathologies of Progress: The Idea of Civilization as Risk', *Bulletin of the History of Medicine*, 72 (1998), pp. 714–30.

Rowbotham, S., *A Century of Women: The History of Women in Britain and the United States* (London: Penguin, 1999).

Russell, D., *Women Madness and Medicine* (Cambridge: Polity, 1995).

Scales, A., *Legal Feminism: Activism, Lawyering and Legal Theory* (New York and London: New York University Press, 2006).

Scott, J., 'Gender: A Useful Category of Historical Analysis', in J. Scott (ed.), *Feminism and History* (Oxford: Oxford University Press, 1996), pp. 152–80.

Scull, A., *Museums of Madness: The Social Organization of Insanity in Nineteenth-Century England* (London: Allen Lane, 1979).

—, *Decarceration: Community Treatment and the Deviant – A Radical View* (Cambridge, Polity Press, 1984).

—, *Social Order/Mental Disorder: Anglo-American Psychiatry in Historical Perspective* (London: Routledge, 1989).

Sheridan, D., (ed.), *The Mass Observation Diaries: An Introduction* (Sussex: The Mass Observation Archive and University of Sussex, 1991).

— (ed.), *Wartime Women: A Mass-Observation Anthology* (London: Mandarin, 1991).

Shorter, E., *The Making of the Modern Family* (New York: Basic Books, 1975).

—, *A History of Psychiatry: From the Era of the Asylum to the Age of Prozac* (New York Chichester; John Wiley, 1997).

—, *Before Prozac: The Troubled History of Mood Disorders in Psychiatry* (Oxford: Oxford University Press, 2009).

Showalter, E., *Hystories* (London: Picador, 1997).

—, *The Female Malady: Women, Madness and English Culture 1830–1980* (London: Virago, 2001).

Slinn, J., 'Research and Development in the UK Pharmaceutical Industry from the Nineteenth Century to the 1960s', in R. Porter and M. Teich (eds), *Drugs and Narcotics in History* (Cambridge: Cambridge University Press, 1995), pp. 169–86.

Smart, C., *The Ties That Bind: Law, Marriage and the Reproduction of Patriarchal Relations* (London: Routledge, 1984).

— (ed.), *Regulating Womanhood: Historical Essays on Marriage, Motherhood and Sexuality* (London: Routledge, 1992).

Smith, H. L., *War and Social Change: British Society in the Second World War* (Manchester: Manchester University Press, 1986).

Smith, M. C., *A Social History of the Minor Tranquillizers: The Quest for Small Comfort in the Age of Anxiety* (New York: Pharmaceutical Products Press, 1991).

Spock, B., and M. Morgan, *Spock on Spock: A Memoir of Growing up with the Century* (New York: Pantheon, 1989).

Stearns, P. N., *Fat History: Bodies and Beauty in the Modern West* (New York: New York University Press, 1997).

Stone, L., *The Family, Sex and Marriage in England 1500–1800* (London: Weidenfield and Nicolson, 1977).

—, *Road to Divorce* (Oxford: Oxford University Press, 1990).

Works Cited

Stoppard, J., 'Women's Bodies, Women's Lives: Towards a Reconciliation of Material and Discursive Accounts', in J. Ussher (ed.), *Body Talk: The Material and Discursive Regulation of Sexuality, Madness and Reproduction* (London: Routledge, 1997), pp. 10–32.

Summerfield, P., *Women Workers in the Second World War: Production and Patriarchy in Conflict* (London: Croom Helm, 1984).

—, 'Mass-Observation: Social Research or Social Movement?', *Journal of Contemporary History*, 20 (1985), pp. 435–52.

—, 'Women in Britain since 1945: Companionate Marriage and the Double Burden', in P. Catterall, and J. Obelkevich (eds), *Understanding Post War British Society* (London: Routledge, 1994), pp. 58–72.

—, 'Women and War in the Twentieth Century', in J. Purvis (ed.), *Women's History: Britain 1850–1945* (London: UCL Press, 1995), pp. 307–32.

—, 'Approaches to Women and Social Change in the Second World War', in B. Brivati and H. Jones (eds), *What Difference Did the War Make?* (London: Leicester University Press, 1995 edition), pp. 64–79.

—, *Reconstructing Women's Wartime Lives: Discourse and Subjectivity in Oral Histories of the Second World War* (Manchester: Manchester University Press, 1998).

—, 'Intersubjectivities in Oral History', in T. Cosslett, C. Lury and P. Summerfield (eds), *Feminism and Autobiography: Text, Theories, Methods* (London: Routledge, 2000), pp. 91–106.

Sutherland, J., *Reading the Decades: Fifty Years of the Nation's Bestselling Books* (London: BBC, 2002).

Thomson, M., 'Before Anti-Psychiatry: "Mental Health" in Wartime Britain', in M. Gijswijt-Hofstra and R. Porter (eds), *Cultures of Psychiatry* (Amsterdam: Editions Rodopi B.V, 1998), pp. 43–59.

—, *Psychological Subjects: Identity, Culture and Health in Twentieth-Century Britain* (Oxford: Oxford University Press, 2006).

Thompson, P., *The Voice of the Past* (Oxford: Oxford University Press, 1988).

Thompson, P., with R. Perks, *An Introduction to the Use of Oral History in the History of Medicine* (London: The National Life Story Collection, 1993).

Thornton, S., 'Second-Wave Feminism', in S. Gamble (ed.), *The Routledge Companion to Feminism and Postfeminism*, 2nd edn (London: Routledge, 2004), pp. 29–42.

Tomes, N., 'Feminist Histories of Psychiatry', in M. Micale and R. Porter (eds), *Discovering the History of Psychiatry* (Oxford: Oxford University Press, 1994), pp. 348–83.

—, 'Skeletons in the Medicine Closet: Women and "Rational Consumption" in the Inter-War American Home', in M. Jackson (ed.), *Health and the Modern Home* (New York: Routledge, 2007), pp. 177–95.

Tone, A., 'Tranquilizers on Trial: Psychopharmacology in the Age of Anxiety', in A. Tone and E. Siegel Watkins (eds), *Medicating Modern America* (New York: New York University Press, 2007), pp. 156–79.

—, *The Age of Anxiety: A History of America's Turbulent Affair with Tranquilizers* (New York: Basic Books, 2009).

Tooley, J., *The Miseducation of Women* (Chicago, IL: Ivan R Dee, 2002).

Turner, T., 'James Crichton-Brown and the Anti-Psychoanalysts', in H. Freeman and G. E., Berrios, '*150 Years of Psychiatry: Volume Two, the Aftermath* (London: Athlone, 1996), pp. 144–55.

Tyrrell, M., 'The Politics of George Orwell (1903–1950): From Tory Anarchism to National Socialism and More Than Half Way Back', *Cultural Notes*, 36 (London: Libertarian Alliance 1997).

Ussher, J., *Women's Madness, Misogyny or Mental Illness?* (Hertfordshire: Harvester Wheatsheaf, 1991).

—, (ed.), *Body Talk: the Material and Discursive Regulation of Sexuality, Madness and Reproduction* (London: Routledge, 1997).

Valenstein, E., *Blaming the Brain: The Truth about Drugs and Mental Health* (New York: Free Press, 1998).

Vicedo, M., 'The Social Nature of Mother's Tie to Her Child: John Bowlby's Theory of Attachment in Post-War America', *British Journal for the History of Science*, 44 (2011), pp. 401–26.

Ward, G., 'The Wibberlee Wobberlee Walk: Lowry, Hamilton, Kavan and the Addictions of 1940s Fiction', in Rod Mengham and N. H., Reeve (eds), *The Fiction of the 1940s: Stories of Survival* (Basingstoke: Palgrave, 2001), pp. 26–45.

Weeks, J., *Sex, Politics and Society: The Regulation of Sexuality since 1800* (Harlow: Longman, 1989).

Weiner, H., 'The Concept of Psychosomatic Medicine', in E. R. Wallace IV and J. Gach (eds), *History of Psychiatry and Medical Psychology* (New York: Springer, 2008), pp. 485–516.

—, 'Psychosomatic Medicine and the Mind-Body Relation', in E. R. Wallace IV and J. Gach (eds), *History of Psychiatry and Medical Psychology* (New York: Springer, 2008), pp. 781–834.

Wilkins, D., *Untold Problems: A Review of the Essential Issues in the Mental Health of Men and Boys* (Men's Health Forum, 2010).

Wilkins, D., and M. Kemple, *Delivering Male: Effective Practice in Male Mental Health* (Men's Health Forum, 2011).

Williamson, J., *Decoding Advertisements: Ideology and Meaning in Advertising* (London: Marion Boyars, 2002).

Wilson, E., *Only Half Way to Paradise* (London: Tavistock Publications, 1980).

Winship, J., *Inside Women's Magazines* (London: Pandora, 1987).

INDEX

Page numbers printed in italics refer to figures and those including 'n' e.g. 204n7 refer to notes.

Abbott Laboratories (drug company), 147
advertising
    fears and anxieties, manipulation of, 156, 158
    impulse buying, 156
    motivational analysis, 155–6, 167
    see also drug advertising
aetiology, 86–97
affective disorders *see* mental illness
Affluenza (Oliver), 178–9
agony aunts, 114–15
alcohol abuse, 77, 96–7, 101
Alexander, Franz (psychoanalyst), 81
Allegron (drug), 139
Allen and Hanburys (drug company), 151
American Beauty (film), 22, 179
amphetamines, 77–8
Anadin (painkillers), 161
Angier Chemical Company, 157–8
anti-psychiatry movement, 79–80
Antidepressant Era, The (Healy), 141
antidepressants, 78, 85, 95, 98, 99
anxiety, 33, 77, 79, 84, 85, 90–1, 99–100, 105, 116–17, 143, 148
appetite disorders, *145*, 148
Ariel (Plath), 11
Art of Marriage, The (Macaulay), 36
Atarax (drug), 146
Atkin, I. (psychiatrist), 151–2
atomic warfare, fear of, 1, 44, 44–5, 68–9
atypical depression, 84, 85, 99, 141, 143
Aventyl (drug), 139, *140*
aversion therapy, 101–2

Bailey, Eileen (interviewee), 65–6, 69–70, 111–12
Bakewell, Joan (journalist), 73–4
Balint, Michael (psychoanalyst), 102
barbiturates, 98–9, 147, 168
behaviour therapy, 8, 43, 101–2, 171
Bell Jar, The (Plath), 11, 23
Bengers (digestive aid), 161
Benzedrine (drug), 77
benzodiazepine compounds, 79, 99, 118, 139, 147–8, 151, 168
Beplete (drug), 148
Berryman, John (poet), 26–7
Beveridge, William (social reformer), 31, 59
Beyfus, Drusilla (journalist), 63
Bile Beans (laxative), 158
Bills, Jean (interviewee), 58–9
birth control, 1, 33
Bournvita (malted drink), 162
Bovet, Theodore (psychoanalyst), 35, 45
Bowen, Elizabeth (novelist), 26
Bowlby, John (psychologist), 31, 39–42
Braithwaite, Diane (interviewee), 55, 67, 71
Brayshaw, Alfred (General Secretary, NMGC), 34
Britain
    average earnings, 154
    economic growth, 154
    new towns, 15
    nuclear weapons, development of, 44
    social insurance measures, 31, 59
    suburban society, 13

Britain's Married Women Workers (Klein), 16

British Code of Advertising, 155

British Journal of Psychiatry, 90, 91, 101

British Medical Journal, 75, 98, 132, 133, 134, *135*, 136, *137–8*, *142*, *144–5*

Brown, George (sociologist), 109

Buckfast Tonic Wine, 162

Burnham, Lester (film character), 179

Busfield Joan (sociologist), 2, 109–10

butabarbitol (drug), 148

caffeine, 165

Calderwood, Christine (interviewee), 53, 63, 64–5, 71, 72, 194n85

Cannon, Walter (stress researcher), 81

Carter, Doris (interviewee), 60–1

Cavendish, Lucy (writer), 177

charity work, 178

Chateleine (magazine), 156

Chave, Sidney, 14–15

Chemist and Druggist, The, 151

Chesler, Phyllis (psychologist), 107

childbirth, 63

childcare, 15, 30, 35, 65, 68–71
  attitudes to, 16–17, 37–46
  fathers, 71
  manuals, 70

childhood, adverse experiences, 12, 111, 122–5, 171
  correlation with marital adjustment, 87–8

chlordiazepoxide (drug), 79, 100, 147, 148

chlorpromazine (drug), 8, 77, 78, 79, 97, 99, 134–6, *135*, *137*, *138*

cleaning *see* housework

Cold War *see* atomic warfare, fear of

Coles, Ann (interviewee), 62, 118–19

Collins, Gwen (interviewee), 53–4, 61, 66, 69, 72

Coming up for Air (novel, Orwell), 20

Common Sense Book of Baby and Child Care (Spock), 43

communism, 44

Complan (meal replacement), 165, *166*

constructionist theories, 30

cooking, 60, 61

Coontz, Stephanie (writer), 2, 176

Cooper, David (psychiatrist), 79

Cooperstock, Ruth (sociologist), 108–9, 129, 147

Coppen, Alec (neuroscientist), 95–6

Cornell Medical Index, 83–4, 87

cosmetic products, 169

Council of the College of General Practitioners, 86

counselling, 102, 112

Courtenay, Rose (interviewee), 70, 121

Crichton-Brown, James (psychiatrist), 81

Crichton-Miller, Hugh (psychiatrist), 80

Daily Mail, 177, 178

Dally, Ann (psychiatrist), 37–8

Dally, Peter (psychiatrist), 85, 98, 99, 143

Dartalan (tranquillizing agent), 148

Davy, Jane (interviewee), 56

DCL Yeast Tablets, 158

Denning, Lord, 34–5

depression, 75, 78, 79, 83–5, 96, 98, 99, 105, 141, 143, 168
  see also mental illness

Dexedrine (drug), 77–8

Diagnostic Statistical Manual (DSM), 105

diazepam (drug), 17, 79, 119, 134, 139, 148

Dichter, Ernest (psychologist), 155, 156, 167

Distval, 133

divorce *see* marital relationships

domestic appliances, 60

domesticity
  association with mental illness, 1, 2, 10, 12, 17, 22–3, 26–7, 106, 107–8, 125–6, 171, 174–5
  descriptions of, 57–64

Dr Cassells tablets, 156–7

Dr William's Pink Pills (iron tablets), 161

drug addiction, 26, 172–3

drug advertising, 129–30, 132–53, 172
  complaints from general practitioners, 133, 134
  examples of, *135*, *137*, *138*, *140*, *142*, *144–5*, *149–50*
  extreme imagery, use of, 146–7
  lack of information about drug, 136
  men, image of, 139, *140*, *142*, 143, 153
  over-the-counter medications, 153–67

'Previous Good Personality' (PGP)
 patient, 143
techniques, 167
women, image of, 129, 134, *135*, 139–40,
 143, *150*, 152, 155, 172–3
drugs
 amphetamines, 77–8
 barbiturates, 98–9, 147, 168
 benzodiazepine compounds, 79, 99, 118,
  139, 147–8, 151, 168
 chlorpromazine, 8, 77, 78, 79, 97, 99,
  134–6, *135*, *137*, *138*
 combining, 99
 comparison studies, 141, 143
 compounds mixed with barbiturates,
  147–8
 dependence, 99, 118
 laudanum, 131
 monoamine oxidase inhibitors (MAOIs),
  78, 95, 98, 99, 141, 143, 200n114
 overprescribing, 98–9, 108, 116, 118,
  151, 174
 over-the-counter medications, 130,
  153–67, *159–60*, *163–4*, *166*, 168–9,
  172, 174
 painkillers, 156, 161
 psychotropic medications, 2, 10, 96,
  108–9, 117, 118
 recreational use, 77
 regulation, 131–4
 sedatives, 77, 117, 168
 serotonin reuptake inhibitors, 179
 thalidomide, 133
 tranquillizers, 79, 97, 98–9, 108–9, 133,
  151–2, 172–3
 tricyclic antidepressants, 78, 95, 98, 141,
  168
 women's experiences of drug treatment,
  118–19
Dunbar, Helen Flanders (psychiatrist), 81
Durophet-M (drug), *144*, 148, *150*

electroconvulsive therapy, 24, 25, 76, 80, 85,
 91, 96, 97, 98, 141
Eleven Plus exam, 1, 3, 52–3
Eli Lilly (drug company), 139, *140*
Ellis, Havelock (sex researcher), 33

endogenous depression, 84, 85, 96, 141, 143,
 168
Equanil (drug), 79, 97, 99, 146
Even Toddlers Need Fathers (parenting
 organization), 40
Eysenck, Hans (psychologist), 83, 101,
 198n57
Eysenck Personality Inventory, 83

Family and Class in a London Suburb (Willmott and Young), 51–2
Family and Kinship in East London (Willmott and Young), 51
Family Circle (magazine), 156
family life, 6, 9
 importance to children, 45–6, 69
 oral history project respondents' descriptions of, 57–64
 surveys, 51
Far From Heaven (film), 22, 179–80
fathers, 40–1, 42, 47
 childcare, 71
 housework, 62–3
Faux, Jill (interviewee), 65
fear, 117
Female Eunuch, The (Greer), 13–14, 105
Female Malady, The (Showalter), 23
Feminine Mystique, The (Friedan), 1, 11, 14,
 17, 27, 50
feminist movement, 11–13, 171
fetishism, 101
films
 feminist messages, 22
 portrayal of suburban society, 21–2,
  179–80
Forbes, Bryan, (film director), 22
Fortune (business magazine), 20
Foucault, Michel (philosopher), 79, 106,
 110
Frankfurt School theorists, 19
French, Marilyn (novelist), 17
Friedan, Betty, 1, 2, 11, 12–14, 27, 28, 162,
 165
 and women's education, 15–16

Gavron, Hanna (social researcher), 64
Geigy (drug company), 147

general practitioners
  complaints about drug advertising, 133, 134
  as informal counsellors, 102
Gilman, Charlotte Perkins (writer), 11
Glaxo (drug company), 147
Goodridge, Edna (interviewee), 60, 73
Gove, Walter (sociologist), 106, 107–8, 110
grammar schools, 52–4, 55–6
Grant, Doris (food writer), 116
Grant, Mary (agony aunt), 114
Gray, Herbert (NMGC founding member), 33–4, 36
Greenham, Kath (interviewee), 53, 62
Greer, Germaine (feminist), 13–14
Grieve, Mary (editor), 7
Guardian, The, 175

Halliday, James (physician), 81–2
Hall's Wine, 162
Hamilton, Madge (psychiatric social worker), 87–90
Hamilton Rating Scale for Depression, 83, 84
Handbook to Marriage and Marriage Guidance (Bovet), 35
Happily Ever After (Lyon), 34
Hare, E. H. (physician), 15
Harley, Denis (psychologist), 64
Harris, Tirril (sociologist), 109
Harvey Pharmaceuticals (drug company), 146
Healy, D. (psychiatrist), 141, 143, 152–3
Heane, Rebecca (interviewee), 121
Hidden Persuaders, The (Packard), 155
Hill, Jean (interviewee), 52–3, 61, 62–3, 112–13
Holmes, Thomas (psychologist), 87
Home Chat (magazine), 7
Home, Evelyn (agony aunt), 114
home life
  importance of, 1, 5–6, 51–2
  psychological aspects, 32
home-ownership, 1, 6, 32, 63
homosexuality, 101, 179–80
Hooper, Douglas (clinical psychologist), 45, 47
Hoover, J. Edgar, 44

Horlicks, *160*, 161
housewives
  creative activities, 64–7
  domestic role, benefits of, 57–60
  drug advertising, 134, *135*, 139, 141
  family networks, 66
  in fiction, 17–19
  friendships, 66–7
  health problems, 63
  'housewives blight' (medical condition), 13
  image of, 2, 17
  isolation, feelings of, 15–16, 57, 64, 67
  mental illness report 1964, 90–1
  product marketing, 162
  skills, lack of, 108
  social pressures, 62
  support networks, 64–7
Housewives Beware (Grant), 116
housework, 60, 61–2
  husbands' role, 62–3
housing shortages, 32
Hubback, Judith (social researcher), 16, 28, 64, 73
hypertension, 81

imipramine (drug), 85, 91, 141
indigestion, 158
Inner Wheel (women's organization), 65, 195n90
Institute for Motivational Research (US), 155
Institute of Psychiatry, General Practice Research Unit, 82
International Statistical Classification of Diseases and Related Health Problems (ICD), 8, 105
iproniazid (drug compound), 78
Iron Jelloids, 157

James, Oliver (writer), 178–9, 180
Jarrell, Randall (poet), 27
John Wyeth (drug company), 146, 148, 151
Journal of Mental Science, 82

Kavan, Anna (novelist), 25–6, 27–8
Kelly, Nora (interviewee), 113–14
Kessel, Neil (psychiatrist), 82

King, Frederic Truby (health reformer), 43
Kingsley Hall (therapeutic community), 80
Klein, Viola (sociologist), 16, 28, 49, 64
Kraeplin, Emil, 8
Kumin, Maxine (poet), 27

labelling theory, 105–6
Lady Chichester Hospital (Sussex), 81
Laing, Ronald (psychiatrist), 79, 80, 106
Lancet, The, 14, 98
Langley, Gordon (senior medical officer), 90
Largactil (drug), 77, 134–6, *135*, *137*, *138*
laudanum (drug), 131
Lawson, Faith (interviewee), 56
legislation
    Dangerous Drugs Act (1920), 131
    Food and Drugs Act (1938), 132
    Matrimonial Homes Act 1967, 34–5
    Pharmacy and Medicines Act (1941), 132
    Pharmacy and Poisons Act (1868), 131
Levin, Ira (novelist), 21
Librium (drug), 79, 100, 147, 148
life events, 86–7, 91–2
Lincoln, Margaret (interviewee), 68–9
Little Boxes (song), 21
Little Children (film), 179
Lowell, Robert (poet), 27
Lucozade, 158, *159*
Lyon, Percy Hugh Beverly (poet), 34, 46

Macaulay, Mary (marriage guidance counsellor), 36, 46
Mace, David (NMGC founding member), 34
Madness and Civilization (Foucault), 106
Man in the Grey Flannel Suit, The (film and novel, Wilson), 21
Marcuse, Herbert (philosopher), 19, 20
marital relationships, 12, 18–19
    as a cause of mental illness, 87–90, 92–3, 108, 111–21
    correlation with childhood experience, 87–8, 89
    divorce, 25, 29, 33, 110–11, 121
    domination, 89
    equality issues, 34–7, 47, 60
    expectations of partners, 36
    gender roles, 30, 31, 73

    infidelity, 18–19, 91, 92, 94, 96–7, 100
    male breadwinner role, 31–2, 52
    marriage guidance, 33–5
    sexual problems, 36–7
    sexual taboos, 33
    surveys, 36
    traditional image of family life, 29–30
Marxism, 19
Mass Observation (research enterprise), 5, 16, 32, 36, 50, 59, 60, 63, 70, 74, 165
Master of Deceit (Hoover), 44
Maudsley Personality Inventory, 83
Medico-psychological Clinic (London), 81
Meggeson's Bismuth Dyspepsia Tablets, 158
Melleril (drug), 146
men
    in drug advertising, 139, *140*, 141, *142*, 143, 153
    film images, 179
    likelihood of seeking medical help, 173
    over-the-counter medications, 157, 158
menstruation, 156–7
mental hygiene, 80
mental illness
    aetiology, 86–97
    asylums, 76–7
    biochemical factors, 86, 95–6, 97, 171
    certification, 76
    childhood, adverse experiences, 12, 87–8, 111, 122–5, 171
    classification of, 8, 82–6
    data analysis, problems of, 109–10
    depressive functional shift, 95
    diagnosis, difficulties of, 8
    differences between old communities and new towns, 15
    and domesticity, 1, 2, 10, 12, 17, 22–3, 26–7, 106, 107–8, 125–6, 171, 174–5
    environmental factors, influence of, 80, 81, 86, 97, 103, 171
    experiences of women writers, 22–7
    fear, 117
    gender influences, 84
    genetic influences, 94–5, 97
    labelling theory, 105–6
    levels of illness in women compared to men, 106–7

life events, influence of, 86–7, 91–2
marital dysfunction, as a cause of,
    111–21
married couples, neuroses in, 87–90,
    92–3, 200n101
medical models, 106
nervous breakdowns, 116–17, 120
panic attacks, 91, 116
personality characteristics, 81, 83, 96
phobias, 101, 105, 143
primary care, 78–9, 82–3
schizophrenia, 76, 80
self-help, 116–17
sleep patterns, 84, 98
somatic symptoms, 95, 109
statistical representation, 173–4
twins, 93–4
women's experiences of drug treatment,
    118–19
see also drugs
meprobamate (drug), 79, 97, 99, 146, 151
Metzl, Jonathan (psychiatrist), 118, 129–30,
    134, 152–3
Meyer, Adolf (psychiatrist), 86–7
Middletown: A Study in American Culture
    (Lynd), 51
Middletown in Transition (Lynd), 51
Miles, Agnes (sociologist), 105, 106
Miller, Henry (neurologist), 96
Miltown (drug), 79, 97, 99, 146, 151
modern learning theory, 101
monoamine oxidase inhibitors (MAOIs),
    78, 95, 98, 99, 141, 143, 200n114
Morgan, Judith (interviewee), 56–7, 123–4
Morrell, D. C. (GP), 75, 86
Mortimer, Penelope (novelist), 18–19,
    24–5, 27–8
Morton Commission (marriage and
    divorce), 33
mothering, 37–46, 68–71
    life after children have left, 72–3
    maternal deprivation, effect on children,
        39–40
    maternal mortality rates, 37–8
    naturalness of, 70
    parental absence, 40, 45
    social changes, influence of, 37

women's career ambitions, 55–6
    working mothers, 41–2, 43–4, 46, 63,
        69–70, 177–9
Mother's Little Helper (song), 11, 17
motivational analysis, 155, 167
MUM (deodorant), 158
Munro, Alistair (psychiatry lecturer), 94–5
Myrdal, Alva (sociologist), 28
Myth of Mental Illness, The (Szasz), 80

Nactisol (drug), 109, *144*, 148, *149*
Nacton (drug), *144*
Nardil (drug), 85, 98, 99–100, 139, 141,
    143
National Committee for a Sane Nuclear
    Policy (SANE), 44–5
National Council for Mental Hygiene, 80
National Housewives Register *see* National
    Women's Register
National Marriage Guidance Council
    (NMGC), 33–4, 45, 46, 115
National Women's Register, 3, 57, 174
Nembutal (drug), 147
nervous breakdowns, 116–17, 120
Neuro-Phosphates (drug), 151
neuroses *see* mental illness
Nimble (bread), 158
nortriptyline (drug), 139

Oakley, Ann (sociologist), 16–17, 28, 30,
    37, 50, 61
One-Dimensional Man, The (Marcuse), 20
oral history, 4, 126
Organization Man, The (Whyte), 20
Orwell, George (writer), 19–20
Osler, William (physician), 131
over-the-counter medications, 130, 153–67,
    159, 168–9, 172
    indigestion, 158
    iron treatments, 156–7, 161
    public opinion of, 165, 167
    as safe alternatives to prescribed drugs,
        162
    tiredness and lethargy, 158, *159–60*, 161
    tonic products, 157–8, 162, *163–4*, 165,
        166, 168–9
    women's purchase of, 174
oxazepam (drug), 151

Index

Packard, Vance (journalist), 155, 156, 167
painkillers, 156, 161
panic attacks, 91, 116
Parker, Neville (Maudsley Hospital), 93–4
Parker, Val (interviewee), 59, 61, 63, 73
Patterns of Marriage (Slater), 94
Peg's Paper (magazine), 7
personal hygiene, 158
pharmaceutical companies, 2, 133
    see also drug advertising
pharmacological regulation, 131–4
phenelzine (drug), 85, 98, 99–100, 139, 141
phenobarbitone (drug), 98
phenylpropanolamine (drug), 99
Phillips Tonic Yeast, 169
phobias, 101, 105, 143
Phosferine (tonic), 157
Plath, Sylvia (poet), 11, 23, 24
Politics of the Family, The (Laing), 80
Pollit, John D. (physician), 95
Powell, Enoch (UK Health Secretary),
    98–9, 151
Pre-School Playgroups Association, 65
prefrontal leucotomy, 76
'Previous Good Personality' (PGP) patient,
    143
Pro-Banthine (drug), 148
Pro-Plus tablets (caffeine), 165
Prozac (drug), 179
Prozac on the Couch (Metzl), 118, 134
psychiatric morbidity, 15
psychiatry
    anti-psychiatry movement, 79–80
    developments in, 76–82
psychoanalysis, 81, 152–3
psychopharmacology, 2, 8
psychotherapy, 100–1
    differences between the United States
        and Britain, 102–3
psychotropic medications, 2, 10, 96, 108–9,
    117, 118
Pumpkin Eater, The (novel, Mortimer),
    18–19, 25

Radcliffe Institute, 27
Raddon, Eve (interviewee), 64, 71, 124
radio, importance of, 6
Rahe, Richard (psychologist), 87

Red Star (magazine), 7
Reed, Angela (NMGC), 46
Relaxa-Tabs (drug), 151
religion, 33, 66
Report on the British Press (1938), 154–5
Reserpine (drug), 78, 79, 97
Revolutionary Road (film), 180
Reynolds, Malvina (singer), 21
Richards, Chris (interviewee), 57, 68, 73
Riesman, David (sociologist), 19, 20–1
Riker Laboratories (drug company), 148
Riley, Denise, 49, 50
Roberts, A. H. (registrar), 90
Roberts, Eileen (interviewee), 54, 61, 65, 67,
    120, 124–5, 193n30
Roberts, John, 45, 47
Roche (drug company), 139, 147, 148
Rogers, Barbara (interviewee), 55, 58, 67,
    70, 72, 119
Rolling Stones (rock band), 17
Rose, Nikolas (sociologist), 106
Rutherford, Edie (Mass Observation diarist),
    58
Ryle, Anthony (GP), 87–90

Safe (film), 22
Sanatogen (tonic), 157, 162, *163–4*
Sanderson, A. L. (psychiatrist), 86
Sanderson, Betty (interviewee), 57–8, 68,
    72, 120
Sandoz (drug company), 146
Sargant, William (psychiatrist), 85, 98, 99,
    143
Scheff, Thomas (sociologist), 105–6
schizophrenia, 76, 80
Schwartz, Delmore (poet), 27
seasonal affective disorder, 119, 204n86
Second World War, women's experiences,
    50, 54–5, 58, 69, 124–5, 176, 192n3,
    193n30
sedatives, 77, 117, 168
Self Help for Your Nerves (Weeks), 116
Selye, Hans (stress researcher), 81
Serenid (drug), 151
serotonin, 200n113
serotonin reuptake inhibitors (drug), 179
sex
    problems in marriage, 36–7
    taboos, 33

Sex and Happiness (Walker), 35
Sexton, Anne (poet), 11, 23–4, 27
Sexual Difficulties in the Wife (NMGC), 36–7
Shaw, G. K. (physician), 15
Shepherd, Ann (interviewee), 54, 113
Shepherd, Michael (psychiatrist), 82, 86
shopping, 60–1, 174
Showalter, Elaine (writer), 23
Slater, Eliot (physician), 94
Sleep Has His House (novel, Kavan), 26
sleep patterns, 84, 98
sleep therapies, 76, 85
Smith, Charles (lecturer), 96–7
Smith Kline and French (drug company), 77, *142*
Social Adjustment Scale (Holmes and Rahe), 87
Social Insurance and Allied Services (Beveridge), 31
Social Origins of Depression: A Study of Psychiatric Disorder in Women (Brown and Harris), 109
Spock, Benjamin (paediatrician), 39, 43–5, 70
Stability of Marriage, The (Brayshaw), 34
standards of living, 6, 151
Stead, Katherine (interviewee), 62, 65, 66–7, 70, 71, 72, 126
Stelazine (drug), 141, *142*
Stepford Wives, The (film and novel, Levin), 21–2
Stopes, Marie (birth-control pioneer), 33
Stott, Mary (editor), 175
stress, 172
    as a marketing tool, 148, *150*, 151–2
suburban society, 13
    as a cause of mental illness, 14
    as portrayed in novels and films, 21–2, 179–80
suicide, 24, 26, 77
Summerfield, Penny (historian), 4, 5, 49, 50
Supavite (vitamin tablets), 157–8
Szasz, Thomas (psychiatrist), 79–80, 106

Talbot, Joan (interviewee), 68
Tavistock Clinic, 80–1

Taylor, Stephen (medical officer, Royal Free Hospital), 14–15
teenagers, 59, 69
thalidomide (drug), 133
thioridazine (drug), 146
Thompson, Paul (oral historian), 126
thumb-sucking, 43
Times, The, 157
Today's Drugs (BMA publication), 167–8
Tofranil (drug), 141, 147
Townswomen's Guild, 65, 195n90
tranquillizers, 79, 97, 98–9, 108–9, 133, 151–2, 172–3
Tricloryl (drug), 147
tricyclic antidepressants, 78, 95, 98, 141, 168
Triptafen (drug), 151
Turner, Lowri (TV presenter), 177–8
twins, 93–4

ulcers, 144, 148
United States
    communism, attitudes to, 44–5
    life myths, 20
    psychotherapy, differences between the United States and Britain, 102–3
    suburban society, 13, 179–80
    women's publishing, 176
university education, 53, 55

Valium (drug), 17, 79, 119, 134, 139, 148
Vicary, Barbara (interviewee), 55, 119–20

Walker, Kenneth (urologist), 35
washing, 61
Watts, C. A. H. (GP), 83
Weeks, Claire (physician), 116–17
Whyte, William H. (urbanologist), 19, 20
William Warner (drug company), 98, 139, 143, 146
Wilson, Frances (interviewee), 58, 66, 70, 72–3, 122–3
Wilson, Sloan (novelist), 21
Wimpole, Roderick (magazine doctor), 115–16
Wincarnis Wine, 162, 165
Windsor, Margaret (interviewee), 63, 66, 120

Index

Winnicott, Donald (psychoanalyst), 39, 42–3
Wolf, Alison (economist), 178
Wolff, Harold (stress researcher), 81
Wolpe, Joseph (psychologist), 100–1, 201n151
Woman and Home (magazine), 7
Woman (magazine), 7, 114, 154, *164*, *166*, 175
Woman's Own (magazine), 7, 60, 64, 114, 115, 116, 117, 127, 156, 157, *159*, 176–7
Woman's Realm (magazine), 59–60, *163*
Woman's Weekly (magazine), 7, *160*
women
    boredom, 1, 64, 177
    caged creativity, theories of, 24
    career ambitions, 55–6
    charity work, 178
    as consumers, 5–6, 154, 174
    creative activities, 64–7
    criticism, fear of, 62
    domestic life, descriptions of, 57–64
    drug treatments, experiences of, 118–19
    education, 4, 15–16, 52–7, 72–3, 176
    employment outside the home, 16, 41–2, 43–4, 46, 58–9, 63, 64, 177–9
    empowerment, 110
    endocrine disturbances, 95
    equality in marriage, 34–7, 47, 60
    family networks, 66
    friendships, 66–7
    image in advertisements, 129–30, 134, *135*, 139, 143, *150*, 152, 155, *159–60*, *163–4*, 165, *166*, 172–3

    isolation, feelings of, 3, 15–16, 57, 64, 67
    letters to magazines, 59–60
    levels of mental illness compared to men, 106–7
    life after children have left, 72–3
    marital dysfunction, 111–21
    menstruation, 156–7
    product marketing, 162
    reluctance to discuss personal problems, 113, 126
    Second World War experiences, 50, 54–5, 58, 124–5, 176, 192n3, 193n30
    social status, 32
    study on tranquillizer use, 108–9
    support networks, 64–7, 121, 175
    tensions between employment and homemaking, 49
    voting rights, 12
    working-class, 51
    working -class, 109
Women's Hour (radio programme), 6
Women's Liberation Movement *see* feminist movement
women's publishing, 1, 6–7, 175–6
    articles on health, 7, 115, 127
    articles on working outside the home, 176–7
    drug advertising, 130, 153–4, 156
    problem pages, 114–15
Women's Room, The (novel, French), 17–18
Woodside, Moya (psychiatric social worker), 94

Yellow Wallpaper, The (Gilman), 11